THE LAKE DISTRICT
ANGLERS' GUIDE

*Fishing from the shore at **Ullswater***

THE LAKE DISTRICT ANGLERS' GUIDE

by
Laurence Tetley

ISBN-10: 1 85284 283 0
ISBN-13: 978 1 85284 283 3

Reprinted in short-run format, without colour sections, in 2009.
Printed by Cpod, Trowbridge.

A catalogue record for this book is available from the British Library.

Other Cicerone books by the same author:
      The Yorkshire Dales Anglers' Guide

Front cover: The author sampling the free fishing at **Brotherswater** on a
      fine day

CONTENTS

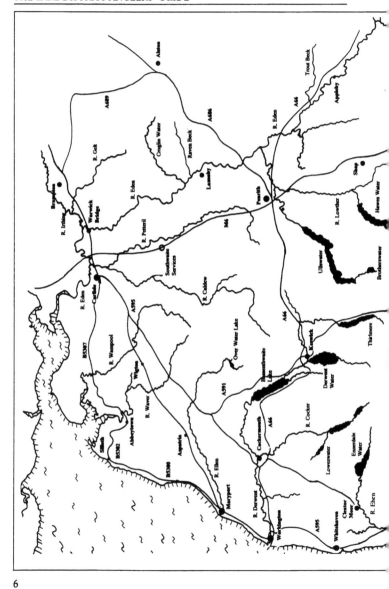

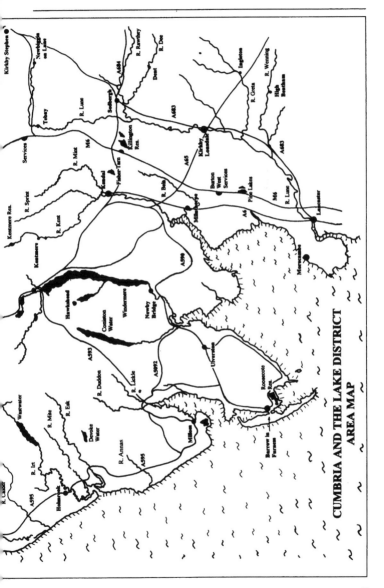

CUMBRIA AND THE LAKE DISTRICT AREA MAP

*Fishing into the sun at **Brotherswater***

Introduction

For generations, anglers have braved the weather, and the multitudes of visitors, to fish for trout amid the spectacular scenery of the Lake District National Park. This is a land of clear, clean waters, abundant lakes, torrential streams and rivers with shoals of hard fighting brown trout. But it's not just trout - salmon, char, perch, schelley, vendace and monster pike can all be found in the National Park. Outside the park, the diminutive west coast rivers provide the opportunity of connecting with a sea trout or salmon and, in the east, the legendary rivers Eden and Lune offer some of the best fishing in the country. Scattered throughout the region, numerous commercial fisheries offer well-maintained waters, heavily stocked with a vast range of coarse fish and trout.

Not surprisingly the Lake District National Park is a land with an abundance of lakes and all of them hold fish. Beautiful lakes, nestling in tight steep sided valleys and clear-water tarns set high on rugged fellsides are all home to native brown trout. Lakeland's beautifully marked red spotted trout are arguably the most perfectly formed in the country. Mostly underfed, they are trim and energetic and, especially in the hill tarns, where they hardly ever see a baited hook, are quite prepared to snap at any worm, fly or flashy spinner that's placed in front of them. The bigger fish tend to be taken from the bigger lakes. Windermere, England's largest natural lake, holds a variety of specimen fish, but they're not easy to tempt on a single visit - you'll need time to study the water to find the best fish. To guarantee a good catch, though, it's best to try one of the well-stocked fisheries like Esthwaite Water for instance. At 280 acres it is the largest rainbow trout stocked lake in the Northwest and an early stocking of some $3^{1}/_{2}$ tons of trout gets the season off to a bang!

But the National Park is not just for game anglers; many of its lakes hold monster pike. Bassenthwaite Lake, for instance, regularly delivers fish over 30lb and there are rumours of fish topping 40lb lurking in its deeps. Some of Lakeland's waters are also home to unique vendace and the schelley. Both fish are now extremely rare in Great Britain and, in order to preserve stocks, it is illegal to fish for the schelley. A colourful native of the area, the char, is also much rarer than it once was. It's a close relative of the native brown trout and just as hard a fighter when hooked. These days it's mostly caught accidentally by anglers trolling for its more prolific brother.

Until recently, Cumbria has not been home to the more traditional coarse fish found elsewhere in the British Isles. But now bream, carp, dace, roach, rudd and tench are all there to be caught in the new purpose-built fisheries that have been created throughout the region. Commercial fisheries, all stocked with quality fish, offer a good day's fishing in delightful surroundings and for a fair price. To mention every one here would be impossible, but for instance, in the north of the region Oakbank Country Park has rapidly become a great coarse fishery. In the west Ellerbeck Farm Lakes, although small, offer some fine coarse fishing in peaceful surroundings. Whins Pond in the east near Penrith is another excellent fishery brimming with specimens and further south, Bigland Tarn literally teems with coarse fish.

But Cumbria is not simply a land of lakes - excellent river and stream fishing can be found almost everywhere. In the west numerous tiny rivers, some of them beautiful and some not so pretty, drain water from the foothills of the Cumbrian mountains into the Irish Sea. They tend to be short of water in the summer and raging torrents in the winter, but each of them offers a highway for migratory fish to the spawning grounds well inland. Although the runs have decreased over the years, salmon and sea trout still find their way up river, particularly in late summer and autumn. Whilst it is possible to find good day ticket fishing, it's probably best, if you plan to spend more than a few days in the area, to join a local fishing club. The Millom and District Angling Association, for instance, has the rights to more miles of river game fishing than you can possibly cover in one holiday.

But if it is salmon that you are after, head to the east of the area where two of England's finest salmon rivers, the Eden and the Lune, form the eastern boundary of this guide. Even in the face of declining fish numbers, both rivers manage to maintain their exclusivity, a fact that is reflected in both the price and the availability of tickets. Fish of 30lb are now rare, but, in a good year, there are plenty to be had in the 10lb bracket. For reasonably priced salmon fishing on the Eden, try around Carlisle or further upstream at Lazonby. On the

Lune, the Halton Fishery is excellent, or, if this is not to your taste, try further upstream near Kirkby Lonsdale. And both rivers support a fine head of brown trout. Many local clubs and syndicates regularly stock their waters with quality brown trout to compensate fishermen for the drop in salmon numbers. The fish average about 2lb and are well worth pursuing.

Wherever and whenever you fish in The Lake District and Cumbria, enjoy!

Boats await fishermen at **Grasmere**

BAITS

Where it is appropriate, some baits have been mentioned in the text but as there is a vast variety of fishing baits currently available this section has been included to provide newcomers to the sport with an introduction to what can be purchased over the counter and what should tempt fish. Every angler has a favourite bait, one that he feels will always catch fish. In many cases this feeling is simply one of confidence in a particular food. A bait that has always caught fish will naturally be used more often than something which is new and untried. There are of course many traditional baits still in use. For instance at the right time and under the right conditions worms can't be beaten. But did you know there are many different types of worm and they can be bought over the counter in most fishing tackle shops? Another traditional bait, bread, is still very popular. As you're probably aware from supermarket shelves, bread comes in a huge range of varieties all of which seem to tempt fish. What follows is a list of the more popular baits in use today. It is not exhaustive because anglers are very inventive and constantly try new things, but it may just give you ideas.

Maggots
Probably the best known and most used bait ever. If it is permitted to use them, maggots are by far the best bait to try on a new water. They can be used as hook bait, either singly or in bunches, in a swim feeder or mixed in a proprietary ground bait. They are just about as versatile as anything you'll find and they have also undergone changes over the years. Maggots now come in bright colours each with their own devotees. Many carp anglers insist on reds, barbel men often use bronze maggots, some fishermen like them mixed and others use the simple plain white ones. Pole fishermen and match anglers like 'squats', the larvae of the house fly. They are much smaller than a standard maggot and on their day there's nothing to beat them. Short and fat 'pinkies' are popular with roach fishermen. Although they're called pinkies, they also come in different colours.

Casters

Casters are maggots undergoing metamorphosis. That is, they're changing from the maggot stage into a bluebottle. Sometimes known as 'chrysalis' they're great for tempting most species of coarse fish. Chub, perch and roach love them. Casters vary from white, through orange to a deep burgundy colour and most fishermen have their favourite. The main problem with casters is keeping them in one state. If it's hot and they're in a covered tin you'll soon hear the buzzing of bluebottles. Keep them covered with water - it slows the metamorphosis and stops them floating when you put them on the hook. Use casters singly as hook bait or throw them into a swim as feeder bait. If you do find that they are floating, take off your weights and try them on the surface. At the right time they can be deadly.

Bread

Everyone knows of bread for fishing and it's still a killer. You can use it any way you like and it will attract all kinds of fish including trout. On those warm summer days, floating bread crust is brilliant for carp. Bread paste fished in a back eddy will often bring a big barbel or chub from the depths. Float fished bread flake always attracts perch, roach and rudd in big numbers. Your local tackle dealer will carry a range of bread punches that can be used to compress or shape the bread for hook baits. There is even a range of flavours, banana and strawberry for instance, in which to soak the humble loaf to make it more attractive to fish.

Hempseed

Hempseed is a firm favourite of match anglers. It seems to attract bream, chub, roach and tench when all other baits fail. You can buy it raw and boil it yourself but it is a messy business. Buy it ready prepared from a fishing tackle shop. It's very versatile, use it as hook bait, loose feed it around a float or mix it with groundbait. It nearly always works.

Sweetcorn

Barbel, carp, chub and tench all love sweetcorn, the type you buy in cans from a supermarket. In its natural state it's yellow but fishing tackle shops will sell it flavoured. It comes in natural yellow, orange and strawberry. They're all killer baits when the fish are in the mood. Use it singly or mixed in a groundbait.

Boilies
This is one of the new baits derived from the humble potato. The exact recipes are closely guarded but 'boilies' are basically marble shaped pieces of potato plus additives. They come in various sizes, the popular ones being in the range 10 to 15mm. To entice big barbel, bream, carp, chub and tench they come in different flavours. Seafood is popular, as is chocolate. Some fishermen swear by the berries, cranberry and strawberry. Ask in your local tackle shop which flavour is best for your chosen water. Some fisheries have banned boilies because if they're left on the bank and dry out they can choke wildlife. So take them home.

Pork luncheon meat
On its day pork luncheon meat outclasses all other baits when you're after the really big fish. Barbel, carp and chub love it and of course if you've got any left you can always put it in your sandwiches!

There are lots of other possibilities most of which will catch fish at some time or another. Trout pellets (not to be used on a trout lake!), Pedigree Chum mixer, Pepperani, Maltesers, Rice Krispies or Coco Pops and corned beef to name but a few. You only need the confidence to try them and if they catch fish you'll be hooked as well.

LEGAL

In England and Wales any prospective angler, over 12 years old, who wants to fish for freshwater fish in any water, publicly or privately owned, must first obtain an Environment Agency rod licence, issued through Post Offices. Licences are valid nationally and can be used anywhere in England and Wales. Whilst the appropriate licence allows an angler to fish for salmon, trout, freshwater fish and eels, it does not provide any form of access to a fishery. Having first obtained a licence, an angler must then purchase a fishing ticket, join a fishing club or simply ask a landowner to gain access to a chosen fishing spot. In law the burden is upon the angler to be adequately licensed before starting to fish. Fishing without an Environment Agency rod licence leaves an angler open to prosecution and a hefty fine.

Apart from the legal aspect, it is important that every fisherman purchases a licence because it is income generated from sales that enables the Agency to continue its work of fishery improvement. The work of the Agency's Fisheries Department includes fishery law enforcement, restocking and monitoring fish stocks, executing fish rescue and improving fishery habitats. The Agency also keeps a continuing watch on abstraction, water levels and pollution.

If you become aware of any pollution incidents please phone the FREE Agency 24 hour hotline 0800 80 70 60 and report it. It is in your interests to keep your fishing waters clean.

Charges for rod licences are:

Salmon and migratory trout.
> Adult season £57.00. Concessionary rate £28.50.
> 8 day rate £16.50.
> Daily rate £5.50.

Non-migratory trout, grayling, coarse fish and eels.
> Adult season £18.00. Concessionary rate £9.00.
> 8 day rate £6.50.
> Daily rate £2.50.

Concessionary rates, for season tickets only, apply to retired persons receiving a state pension, registered disabled and youngsters between 12 and 16 years old (inclusive). There are no concessionary rates for short term licences.

'Virtual Licence':
Full and junior rod licences can now be purchased by telephone between 0800 and 2000, 7 days a week (not bank holidays). Tel: 0870 1662662. Pay by credit card (90p service charge). You'll be given a number that allows you to fish immediately, and the licence will be posted on.

The Environment Agency's North West Region is divided into three sub-divisions; North Area, Central Area and South Area. All the waters listed in this guide, with the exception of a few fisheries on the upper River Lune, lie within the North Area.

Fishing closed seasons (dates are inclusive):

Salmon: November 1st to January 31st, except for the River Eden system which is October 15th to January 14th.

Migratory trout: October 16th to April 30th, except the rivers Annas, Bleng, Esk, Mite, Irt, Calder, Ehen and all tributaries where it is November 1st to April 30th.

Non-migratory trout: October 1st to March 14th. These dates apply to the rivers system. Many still water fisheries, holding rainbow trout, are open throughout the year.

Coarse fish and eels: March 15th to June 15th. Again this applies to the rivers system. Many still water coarse fisheries are open throughout the year.

Size limits (measured from the tip of the snout to the fork of the tail):

    Barbel - 30cm.

    Carp - 25cm.

    Bream, chub, grayling, tench and trout - 23cm.

    Dace, perch, roach and rudd - 18cm.

Fish less than these limits must not be killed or taken away. Not more than six fish (no more than two bream or tench) may be taken away in any one day without the written consent of the owner or occupier of the fishery. In practice most fishing clubs and private waters insist that all coarse fish are carefully returned to the water unharmed.

Nets:

All landing nets and keepnets must be made of knotless material.

Bait restrictions:

Fish roe may not be used.

Undersized bream, carp, grayling, tench and trout must not be used as bait. In waters where a close season for coarse fish applies, the only baits which may be used in this period are artificial lure, fly, minnow or worms.

North West Region

Principal Fisheries, Recreation, Conservation and Biology Manager: Dr. M. Diamond.

Pollution reporting

    (Tel: 01925 53999). Emergency hot-line (Tel: 0800 807060).

North Area

Area Fisheries, Ecology and Recreation Manager: Mr N. C. Durie, Ghyll Mount, Gillan Way, Penrith 40 Business Park, Penrith CA11 9BP (Tel: 01768 866666).

Rivers controlled: Brathay, Caldew, Cocker, Crake, Derwent, Duddon, Eamont, Eden, Ehen, Ellen, Esk, Irt, Irthing, Kent, Leven, Liddel, Lyne, Petteril, Rothay, Wampool and their tributaries.

Central Area

Area Fisheries, Ecology and Recreation Manager: Jonathan Shatwell, Lostock House, Holme Road, Bamber Bridge, PR5 6RE (Tel: 01772 639882).

Rivers controlled: Alt, Calder, Crossens, Douglas, Hodder, Keer, Lune, Ribble, Wyre, Yarrow and their tributaries.

NOTES

Returning Fish to the Water

All coarse fishery, and some trout fishery, operators will at some time expect anglers to return fish to the water. In order that a fish is not damaged this should be done with extreme care. Do not remove the fish from the water - leave it in the landing net. Use forceps or pointed pliers and, without touching it, unhook the fish whilst it is still in the net and release it from there. Never take hold of a fish with your bare hands. A fish is a cold blooded animal which can be severely injured by warm human hands coming into contact with its skin. The effect is like plunging a hand into scalding water. You wouldn't like it and nor does the fish!

Put and Take

Some of Cumbria's fisheries operate a policy of "put and take" fishing. This means that the fish stock in a water can be kept at the optimum level if, when fish are removed, a record is made in the "fishing return," the paper which records how many fish have been taken. If it is a rule of the fishery, please fill in the return accurately. On those inevitable blank days, a NIL return should be made.

The Country Code

Remember that the Lake District is a fragile resource which is under great pressure from huge numbers of visitors. In your eagerness to get to the bankside make sure that you abide by the simple country code:

- Don't clamber over walls and fences. They have the habit of collapsing.
- Close all gates. Livestock should remain where the farmer has left it, not wandering about on the road.
- Park your car properly. Do not obstruct gates or other access points.
- Respect the wildlife habitat. Don't crash through nesting grounds at the edge of waters.
- Never remove birds' eggs from nests.
- Do not leave litter. Take it home.
- Never leave unused bait on the bank. It just encourages the rats which may deposit Weil's Disease.
- Never, under any circumstances, leave unattended baited hooks in or out of the water.
- Before going home make sure there are no baited hooks, or lengths of nylon line, discarded on the bank. Hooks and nylon are deadly to wildlife.

Bankside Designation
Throughout this angling guide the terms right bank and left bank relate to an angler facing downstream observing the river's flow.

Fishery Location
The location of all still water fisheries and towns have been given a map designation based on the Ordnance Survey Landranger series.

Landranger maps are over-printed with a blue grid pattern relating to latitude (horizontal) lines and longitude (vertical) lines. Figures marking the vertical lines, called 'Eastings', increment as they progress east, from left to right. Those of the horizontal lines, 'Northings,' increase as they move north, from bottom to top. On every map there are forty vertical and forty horizontal squares giving a grand total of 1,600 squares. In this guide, the map number has been quoted first followed by three figures for an easting and three more for a northing. The first two figures in each case designate a square and the third number one tenth of that square.

As an example, take the appropriately named Fisher Place, for instance. Its designation is **OS90:319184**.

OS90 refers to Ordnance Survey Landranger map number **90** (Penrith, Keswick and Ambleside area).

319 is the easting **31** and the figure **9** indicates that Fisher Place is located **9/10ths** easterly inside the square.

184 is the northing **18** with the **4** indicating that the village is **4/10ths** northerly inside the square.

Ordnance Survey Landranger maps are extremely popular and can be obtained, for a modest price, virtually anywhere. Alternatively, all local libraries carry them.

SAFETY AT THE WATER'S EDGE

Wading
Wading in the tiny streams and rivers of the Lake District can be difficult and sometimes dangerous, particularly when they are in flood. Because of the extreme water clarity the depth is often deceptive. Water which looks to be just a few inches deep can often be several feet deep. Many of the streams tumble over boulders which can easily be seen and avoided, but there are other underwater obstructions which can't, particularly when the surface is rippled by the wind. When you're concentrating on a trout rising in an eddy behind a boulder it is very easy to trip over another one! So do be very careful when wading. Try to read the water. Move slowly and concentrate.

If, however, you're unfortunate and land in deep water, don't panic. Try to bring your feet up to the surface whilst using your hands to paddle and keep your head out of the water. Work with the current guiding yourself into a quiet eddy and then get out. And don't wade when the river is in flood.

Spectacles
When fly casting, particularly in a strong wind, it's not always possible to tell where the fly is going, so wear some eye protection. It's also just as important when you're ledgering. On the occasions when a ledger weight is stuck fast on the bottom, you're bending the

rod and the line is singing under the pressure, be very careful as the weight is likely to shoot out of the water like a stray missile. In instances such as these, there have been cases of hooks spearing an eyeball. Always wear spectacles or sun shades when fishing.

Bank Erosion

In the flat areas between lakes (the land between Bassenthwaite and Derwentwater is a good example) where the river follows a twisting course through meadowland, it is possible for the bankside, on the outside of bends, to be seriously undermined. Do not walk too close to the outside edge. The bank may suddenly collapse and you'll find yourself in deep water.

Power Lines

Carbon fibre is the new wonder material from which most fishing rods and poles are made. It's ideal. It's strong, resilient and supple, but it's also a good conductor of electricity. That means that if you touch one of the overhead power lines with a pole, your body will make a perfect conductor to earth for the electric current. It's a bit like poking your finger into an electric power socket and the result will be just the same. It's not unknown for fishermen to be killed in this way. If you see any overhead power cables near where you want to fish, give them a wide berth and take heed of the signs, thoughtfully placed on the bankside, to warn of the danger.

Weil's Disease

Leptospirosis, better known as Weil's Disease, which luckily is rare in the Lake District, can be a killer. Leptospira, the organism which causes the disease, is carried by rats which in turn deposit the bacteria in stagnant water when they urinate. So it's likely to be encountered in all those places where fishermen like to go - in the quiet water at the edge of a river or pond, in the sloppy mud which always seems to cover the path to the waterside and in the eddy where you've just dropped your keepnet!

The bacteria finds its way into a human body through any open cut or abrasion or via the mouth or eyes. In its early stages the symptoms closely resemble influenza. There is a fever accompanied by shivering and muscle aches or spasms. Early treatment is vital. Get help immediately. Tell the doctor that you've been fishing and you suspect you may have been near infected water.

But prevention is always better than cure. Do not put your fingers in your mouth or eyes if they've been near suspect water and before going fishing securely cover any cuts which might come into contact with water.

Blue-green Algae

Another danger lurking in our waters is blue-green algae. The algae are a natural inhabitant of the UK and in still fresh waters they may multiply. Because they like it hot, they're active in the summer months and make their presence obvious by colouring the water a shade of blue-green. These nasty algae ferment to produce a chemical that is toxic to all mammals, including man.

Unlike Weil's Disease it's obvious from the water colour that the algae are present. Try to keep away from waters which turn blue-green in the summer. If the problem is brought to the attention of the Environment Agency, the water will be closed and notices informing everyone of the danger will be posted around the infected area.

If you notice a rash on any exposed skin which has been in contact with the algae, consult your doctor immediately. Do not drink any infected water.

Rivers & Streams

RIVER ANNAS

Only about 4 miles long, the River Annas starts its life as a group of tiny streams tumbling down the steep sides of Bootle Fell. Above Holmgate Viaduct it is small and shallow, offering little opportunity to wet-a-line, although, if you can get access to the water, the trout are lively. They are small and scare easily so tread carefully when approaching the clear water. Below the viaduct, the river slows down and lazily follows the sea shore northward before entering the Irish Sea near Selker. There's a small autumn run of salmon and sea trout (July to October) when a combination of flood water and a high tide allow the fish to get over the gravel bar near Selker Point.

Bootle (OS96:106882)
The Millom and District Angling Association controls the fishing on approximately 2 miles of the lower river, mostly on both banks, from the railway viaduct above Kiskin to the sea. The sea trout fishing is good, particularly at night, and during the day a worm trotted through the deeper pools usually brings a fish. Fly casting is easy from the open banks. No maggot fishing at any time.
Day tickets £15.00, **weekly ticket** £40.00, from the Hon. Secretary, Duddon Sports and Leisure, Millom (Tel: 01229 774405), Haverigg Post Office (Tel: 01229 772338), Broughton-in-Furness PO (Tel: 01229 716220), Waberthwaite PO (Tel: 01229 717237) and The Bridge Garage, Holmrook (Tel: 019467 24230).

RIVER BELA

Unlike the busy smaller rivers of the Lake District National Park, the River Bela is somewhat sedate as it follows a relatively flat, twisting course from its source at Lily Mere, above Killington Reservoir, to the Kent Estuary near Milnthorpe. It is not a big river and the three becks, Peasey, Stainton and Lupton, which combine to form it are generally shallow and narrow. During periods of heavy rain, particularly in winter when Killington Reservoir is full, the waterway carries a lot of muddy water. Try worm fishing then, otherwise dry

and wet fly are the best methods. In summer the water can be very clear so great care is needed not to scare the young trout. Salmon and sea trout run up to Beetham Mills. Unfortunately all the fishing is in private hands and there is no opportunity for the visiting angler to wet-a-line.
See Killington Reservoir.

Oxenholme (OS97:531901)
The fishing on St. Sunday's Beck from Deepthwaite Bridge, and on Peasey Beck, from Farleton Beck downstream to Beetham Mills, is controlled by the Milnthorpe Angling Association for members and their guests only. No day tickets.

Milnthorpe (OS97:496815)
Milnthorpe AA controls the fishing above Beetham Mills. Members only.

Fishing on the right bank from the mill downstream to Milnthorpe belongs to the Dallam Tower estate and is controlled by the Bela Anglers. The club also controls the fishing in the beautiful Dallam Tower Estate Deer Park downstream to the estuary. Members only.
See also Hall More Fishery, the Lancaster Canal and Wych Elm Fishery.

Sandside (OS97:480810)
There is some fine free fishing here in the tidal river from where the road follows the Kent Estuary shore. Ledgered sandworms are the best bait for bass, dabs and codling.

RIVERS BRATHAY AND ROTHAY
Right in the heart of tourist Lakeland, the Brathay and Rothay are typical of the streamy rivers that one finds in the Lake District National Park. Virtually dry in the summer and spectacularly turbulent in the winter, they both offer limited fishing for wild brown trout. Because the bankside is often rocky, the rivers can be difficult to fish, but if you persevere there is the chance of some really good sport. The main opportunity for fishing on both rivers is in the lower reaches where the Windermere, Ambleside and District Angling Association has water.

Ambleside (OS90:375045)

Fishing in the Langdale Becks is private.

The Windermere, Ambleside and District Angling Association controls about 3 miles on several stretches of the River Brathay, near Clappersgate, and the River Rothay upstream to Rydal Water. On the Brathay, the fishing, from the right bank only, starts about $^{1}/_{2}$ mile above Brathay Church and extends down to the point where the river meets Lake Windermere. On the Rothay, fishing rights start, on the right bank, from the outflow of Rydal Water down to a point just below Rydal Beck. Then there is a short stretch near Fox Ghyll and another even shorter stretch, near the road, between Fox How and Miller Bridge. On the left bank the fishing rights run from Rydal Beck for about $1^{1}/_{4}$ miles to Miller Bridge and then from about 50 yards below Rothay Bridge downstream to Lake Windermere.

Both rivers, feeders for Lake Windermere, offer challenging fishing for wild brown trout with the occasional late sea trout and salmon to make life interesting. Because the water tumbles over rocky boulders and outcrops into deep pools, some stretches are for the sure-footed but other areas have easy access. In winter, the rivers are often torrential and in summer almost dry, but if you can catch them when they're running off after a flood, the sport is usually good. The large deep pool on the River Brathay near where it enters Windermere is very popular with fishermen. Besides trout, it also holds pike, perch and eels. Fishing is by artificial fly and lure and shrimp, prawn worm or minnow. The brown trout season is from March 15th to September 30th, migratory fish from May 1st to October 15th and coarse fish June 16th to March 14th.

Day tickets £3.50, seniors and juniors £2.00, **seven day permits** £10.00, seniors and juniors £5.00. The nearest ticket agents are the tourist information centres in Waterhead Car Park, Ambleside (Tel: 015394 32729) and Victoria Street, Windermere (Tel: 015394 46499) and Go Fishing at Bowness-on-Windermere (Tel: 015394 47086).

RIVER CALDER

The tiny River Calder changes its character dramatically in the course of only 5 miles. It is born in high fells of western Lakeland on Kinniside Common overlooking Ennerdale Water. A multitude of small streams form the infant river which, at Side End, is further swelled by the water from Worm Gill. It then crashes and falls its way down to Calder Bridge where it flows into flat meadowland. Finally, in the last 1½ miles, it is tightly constrained in the industrial area of Sellafield before entering the Irish Sea near the mouth of the River Ehan.

Throughout its length the Calder holds a good stock of small brown trout averaging about 4 to the pound. It was once a famous sea trout river, the fish exceeding 8lb, but sport has dropped off over recent years. There is a small very late run of salmon.

Calder Bridge (OS89:040060)
The Calder Angling Association controls approximately 5 miles of the River Calder on the Calder Abbey Estate Water and the Lord Egremont Water. That is most of the fishing all the way from the upper reaches to the river mouth.
Day tickets £10.00 are issued but only for anglers accompanied by a member. From J.W.N. Holmes & Son, 45 Main Street, Egremont (Tel: 01946 820368).

RIVER DERWENT

Central Lakeland's main river system, the 30 mile long Derwent and its tributaries, offer some of the best game fishing in the area. Born on the craggy fell sides high above Borrowdale, tiny streams mingle to create the infant waterway which then flows through two of the area's loveliest lakes before heading west to Cockermouth. At Keswick, the small river meets the River Greta, itself the result of the numerous fell streams that drain the popular walking area east of the town. The Derwent then ambles through flat meadowland for a few miles before disappearing into the vastness of Bassenthwaite Lake before reappearing at Ouse Bridge. From there it flows, sometimes quickly, sometimes not, west to Cockermouth where it is joined by its major tributary, the River Cocker. A large river by Cumbrian standards, the Derwent twists, meanders and falls through lush grazing land until it joins the sea at Workington. Throughout its length, the Derwent is a lovely river, full of fine game fish. In the upper reaches, the quarry is the hard fighting wild brown trout, whilst in the middle and lower reaches salmon and sea trout are more sought after. There's still a good summer and autumn run of migratory fish, many of which get upstream as far as Ennerdale and

25

Day ticket water right in the heart of the Lake District at Keswick.
The River Derwent

Bassenthwaite, but the best salmon fishing is around Cockermouth where the river is wide and clear with long shingle runs and many good holding pools.

Borrowdale (OS90:254165)
The water here is gin clear flowing over a gravel bed, perfect conditions for the small wild brown trout that inhabit this stretch. They're easily scared and are not easy to catch except when the water is in flood and is coloured, when they will take almost any bait, although worm is the best. When the conditions are right, running an unweighted worm into the eddies created behind boulders or around bends beneath over hanging bushes will take fish. Up to 40 or 50 small trout can be expected in one session using this method. When the river is low and clear, approach very carefully and don't throw a shadow onto the water. Try a wet fly in the deeper water. Any of the northern wet fly patterns will take fish. Try Snipe and Purple, or in the early season, a March Brown.
Free fishing for holders of an Environment Agency rod licence.
See also Derwentwater Lake.

Keswick (OS90:265235)

Several miles of fishing on both banks of the Rivers Derwent and Greta, plus some tributaries, is controlled by the local Keswick Anglers' Association. Fishing, on both banks of the Derwent, is from the outflow of Derwentwater at Portinscale downstream to near the farm bridge at Long Close Farm. The Keswick AA stocks the river with $^3/_4$lb trout at the start of each season, so the brown trout fishing is better in the early months. Salmon come into the river in August. It is excellent fishing throughout especially for a wandering fly or bait angler who doesn't mind walking to find the fish. A footpath follows the river from the busy A66 but it is a long walk to some parts of the water.

Weekly ticket (salmon) £75.00, day £20.00. **Weekly (trout)** £25.00, **day** £5.00 (includes Derwentwater and River Greta). All tickets from Field and Stream, 79 Main Street, Keswick (Tel: 017687 74396) or Keswick Post Office, 48 Main Street (Tel: 017687 72600).

RIVER GRETA

The River Greta drains water from the high fells to the east of Keswick into the Derwent. The upper river, known as Glenderamackin Beck, is a tiny water, shallow and difficult to fish. It has little to offer an angler. A few small brown trout manage to survive, but they are difficult to find.

Threlkeld (OS90:320255)

The Keswick AA has fishing rights near here.

ST JOHN'S BECK

This small beck, the outflow of Thirlmere, flows for about $4^1/_2$ miles through the beautiful St John's Vale to join the River Greta near Birkett Mire. The best fishing is in the top third above Low Bridge End Farm and the last third, from Wanthwaite Bridge to the Greta. Lots of small brown trout to be had. Permission to fish is occasionally granted by farmers. An Environment Agency rod licence is required.

NEWLANDS BECK

A tiny beck rising in the Derwent Fells and flowing north into Bassenthwaite Lake. It is badly overgrown in its upper reaches. The best fishing is on the 'canalised' lower 2 miles below Braithwaite Bridge near Keswick. There are lots of small brown trout and a few perch. Access is from the public footpaths only, which run both upstream and down from Braithwaite Bridge.

Free fishing for holders of an Environment Agency rod licence.

See also Bassenthwaite Lake and Overwater Fishery.

Cockermouth (OS89:125305)
The local Cockermouth and District Angling Association owns extensive rights to fishing on the Derwent above the town. Members only.

A fine length of water, stretching through the town, can be fished by residents and visitors staying locally. The fishing, on the right bank, starts in the Memorial Gardens at Derwent Bridge and extends downstream to Harris Mill Bridge and then on the left bank from the River Cocker junction to opposite a large electricity pylon. Although overlooked and somewhat confined, it is a fine stretch of water. Long gravely glides and deeper pools offer the chance of taking a nice trout or even a good salmon in the autumn.

Weekly tickets (which also include part of the River Cocker) £7.50, juniors £2.50, from the tourist information office, the Town Hall (Tel: 01900 822634).

Cockermouth Castle Estate owns extensive fishing rights on the Derwent from Cockermouth all the way to the estuary at Workington. For information apply to The Manager, Castle Fisheries, Cockermouth Castle or Mr. Payne, bailiff (Tel: 01900 826320).

See also Cogra Moss Tarn, Ellerbeck Fishery and Mockerkin Tarn.

Brigham (OS89:085304)
Broughton Working Men's Angling Association has about 1 mile of the left bank of the Derwent near here for local working men only. No visitor's tickets.

RIVER COCKER
Flowing approximately 7 miles through the delightful Lorton

Vale between the outflow of Crummock Water and Cockermouth, the Cocker is a lovely river. With a few exceptions, the fishing is controlled by the Cockermouth and District Angling Association for the use of members only.

Local anglers, and visitors staying locally, have access to some excellent fishing on Cockermouth Town Waters. The fishing is on the left bank in Harris Park, on both banks from Victoria Jubilee Bridge to Cocker Lane and on the right bank from Waterloo Footbridge to the junction with the River Derwent. It's a great water for fly fishermen. There are some big brown trout that seem to rise well to most dry flies. Try a Black Gnat in the early season, a Greenwell's Glory in summer and don't forget the sedges. When the salmon are about, tickets can be difficult to get hold of, so book in advance.

Weekly tickets from the tourist information office in Cockermouth. *See above.*

See also Buttermere, Crummock Water and Loweswater.

RIVER DUDDON

The water from crystal clear streams flowing down craggy fellsides into Wrynose Pass, the tortuous route from Langdale to the West Coast, forms the infant River Duddon. At Cockley Beck, where Hardknott Pass continues west, the Duddon turns south and into the forest area below Harter Fell. It tumbles and falls, almost doubling back on itself, as it flows along the remaining 7 miles of the Duddon Valley to the sea at Duddon Bridge. It's a good game river. The fly fishing is excellent throughout and, in the upper reaches, it is some of the best in Lakeland. Most of the traditional patterns will take brown trout here. In the early season try a wet March Brown or Grouse and Orange. In the summer, when the water is invariably low, try Red Tag or one of the olives. There is a good run of sea trout and salmon but they arrive very late in the season. September and October are the best months.

Ulpha (OS96196936)
Most of the water is in private hands, but the Millom and District

Angling Association has fishing at Hall Bridge, Dunnerdale. This is a great length for the fly fisherman and anyone who appreciates solitude. The water is usually crystal clear so it fishes best when there is some fresh coming down. The salmon and sea trout fishing is best late in the season. No maggot fishing.

Day ticket £15.00, **weekly tickets** £40.00. The nearest ticket outlet is Broughton-in-Furness Post Office. Also from the sources listed under *River Annas*.

Duddon Bridge (OS96:196883)

The Millom and District Angling Association has about 400 yards of water through Coops Wood on the left bank downstream from Duddon Bridge. It is a productive water, for migratory fish, particularly in the autumn when there is fresh water in the river. Fly fishing is usually good, but if all else fails try running a worm into one of the deeper pools. Sea trout fishing is best at night in the summer months. No maggot fishing.

Day ticket £15.00, **weekly ticket** £40.00, from the sources listed under *River Annas*.

RIVER LICKLE

The Lickle is a tiny stream with a smallish run of sea trout and salmon plus a stock of native brown trout. Like most of the West Coast streams, the Lickle is shallow and streamy and often short of water. Migratory fish tend to wait in the lower tidal pools for floodwater to arrive to assist the passage upstream. Fishing is better in the lower reaches where the river is tidal. The best fishing method is trotting a worm into one of the deeper pools.

Broughton-in-Furness (OS96:215875)

The Millom and District Angling Association has rights to fishing on several stretches commencing just above Lower Hawthwaite and extending downstream to about 100 yards below the A595 bridge at Broughton in Furness. Fly fishing, spinning and bait fishing is permitted. No maggots to be used at any time.

Day tickets £15.00, **weekly tickets** £40.00 from the sources listed under *River Annas*.

RIVER EDEN

Yorkshire's great fishing rivers the Ure and Swale and Lancashire's River Lune all share the same source region as the River Eden. High on the lonely fells straddling the Cumbrian/Yorkshire border, tiny streams, each hardly a trickle, tumble down the sheer sides from Wild Boar and Black Moss fells, to eventually meet and create the diminutive River Eden. This is without doubt some of the most picturesque countryside in England, but the scenery is for walkers and painters, there is little up there to interest an angler. The streams are tiny and often dry in the summer and hold few fish. In the tiny Mallerstang valley, for instance, a few young trout do eke out a precarious existence in pools below waterfalls, but they are very small and difficult to catch.

The Eden has long been a renowned game fishing river and, despite the sad fact that the numbers of Atlantic salmon returning to the UK have seen a constant decrease over the last decade, it continues to maintain its position as a top salmon fishing water. Although a few spring fish, usually large, still enter the river, it is undoubtedly best to try for a salmon in the autumn, because, as the price of visitor's tickets shows, there is more chance of picking up a fish then. Most of the fish run upriver to spawn in the streams around Kirkby Stephen, but the salmon fishing is much better in the middle reaches below Appleby. There is also a good run of late sea trout which on occasions arrive close to or just after the end of the season. Whilst it is true that some anglers arrive at the Eden in search of migratory fish, many more come for the brown trout fishing which is amongst the best in the country. Native browns love this water and grow well. Fish of 2lb are common throughout and some even break the magical 4lb barrier. To be virtually certain of having a good day's fishing, it is better for a visiting angler to concentrate his/her efforts on the brown trout or, in the winter, the grayling.

Kirkby Stephen (OS91:775085)

The local Kirkby Stephen and District Angling Association controls about 20 miles of prime fishing on the main river and streams above and below the town. The club's preserves start high on the fell streams and stretch down through the town taking in much of the fishing on the Belah, Scandal and Swindale Becks and extending downstream to near Warcop. This is beautiful water, ideal for the roving angler who likes to place a dry fly in one of the small pools looking for a good brown trout. And the trout are big. In the past, the club's annual best-fish competition was won with trout over 1lb, now the winning fish is nearer 3lb. The water is stocked each year to support the stock of indigenous brown trout. A few salmon do manage to struggle up this far, but only when there has been a constant flood to lift their spirits. They tend to be exhausted anyway and hardly ever fall to a spinner of fly. It is better to try for salmon further downstream near Lazonby.

Weekly tickets £30.00 and **day tickets** £15.00 are available from '2 Ravens' 2 Market Street, Kirkby Stephen (Tel: 017683 71203) or Mr Kilvington, Solicitor, Market Square, Kirkby Stephen (Tel: 017683 71519).

See also Bessy Beck Trout Lake and Eden Valley Trout Lake.

About 2 miles downstream of Kirkby Stephen, the waters of the Eden are swelled by water from Scandal Beck, the River Belah and Swindale Beck.

SCANDAL BECK

A tiny stream draining the fellside of Ravensdale Common into the River Eden.

Ravensdale to Soulby

Good fishing for wild brown trout, particularly in the lower reaches. Almost all the fishing, on both banks, downstream through Smardale and Crosby Garrett to its junction with the Eden is controlled by the Kirkby Stephen and District AA.

Day tickets *See the Kirkby Stephen entry.*

RIVER BELAH

Although bigger than the other Eden tributaries, the River Belah is still not much more than a stream. It flows for about 5 fairly sedate miles west to join the Eden near Great Musgrave. The upper reaches are private. Approximately

1¹/₂ miles of the Belah, from the A685 bridge near Brough Sowerby downstream to the Eden, is controlled by Kirkby Stephen and District AA. Members only.

SWINDALE BECK

This is yet another tiny stream draining the northern fells into the Eden. It's a nice little trout water, particularly around Brough, but except for a short stretch held by the Kirkby Stephen and District AA for members only, the fishing is all in private hands.

Back on the River Eden at Sandford, The Sandford Arms Hotel (Tel: 017683 51121) has fishing on 5 miles of prime water on both banks, for guests only. The trout fishing is probably the best in the area and well worth a visit. Salmon run into the water late in the season. Fishing season March 15th to September 30th.
Guest tickets from the hotel.

Appleby-in-Westmoreland (OS91:685205)

Around Appleby, the fishing for late season salmon is good but some years the fish are few and far between. The brown trout fishing is far more consistent. The fish average about ³/₄lb but there is every chance of hooking one of 2¹/₂ or even 3lb. They are also free risers particularly in the evening. Best flies to try are spring Mayfly followed by sedges. Later in the year Greenwell's Glory and Iron Blues take their share of fish. Don't be afraid to try a big fly, often a size 12 will tempt one of the bigger trout when a small fly fails.

There is some free fishing here, between the bridges at Sands and at Holme Farm, for local residents only. An EA rod licence is required. It is an any-method fishery but the use of maggots is strictly prohibited.

Approximately 14 miles of excellent game fishing, mostly double bank, are controlled by the local Appleby Angling Association. This varied stretch of water extends, with a few exceptions, from Sandford in the south downstream to Temple Sowerby. It is typical upper Eden water. The river weaves its way through meadowland and bubbles over a stony bed providing some enticing holding pools and rough water for big brown trout. Each season the native stock is supported with a generous stocking of quality browns of about $3/4$lb which soon grow bigger. Access is good throughout most of the length. Fishing is mainly by traditional north country wet and dry fly, although when the river is in spate, spinning and worming are permitted. In summer, at dusk, fishing with an Alder or bustard (a traditional pattern with speckled plumage) is particularly good. Part of the water, a stretch just north of Appleby, is available for fishing on a visitor's ticket.

Day tickets £4.00 from Pigney's Ironmongers Shop, High Wiend (down the side of the Post Office) (Tel: 017683 51240) or Mr D. Richardson, Park End, Garths Head Road, Appleby (Tel: 017683 51659).

Another fine stretch of the Eden offering brilliant brown trout fly fishing, on both banks, is available above the town on the exclusive Upper Appleby water. This stretch, starting just above the town and extending upstream to near Helm Beck at Little Ormside, offers the best trout fishing on the upper reaches. It is owned and keepered by John Pape, a local fisherman who knows the water like the back of his hand. Tickets are limited to 4 rods a day, so phone ahead and book.

Day tickets £15.00 from John Pape, 12A High Wiend (down the side of the Post Office), Appleby, CA6 6RD (Tel: 017683 52148 or 0973 345342). Mr. Pape also offers fly fishing courses, on his water, covering, amongst other things, traditional fishing techniques, how to read the water, understanding fly life, and traditional Bustard fishing.

Above Bolton Bridge, on the right bank, where the river runs alongside the road, there is about $1/2$ mile of **free fishing**. It is a pleasant water but well overgrown. The deeper water, holding some good brown trout, is on the road side. An Environment Agency rod licence is required.

The Penrith Angling Association and the Appleby AA jointly control about 2 miles of salmon, trout and grayling fishing mainly on the right bank near Kirkby Thore. Members only.

Kirkby Thore (OS91:638258)

Guests at the Kings Arms Hotel, Temple Sowerby (Tel: 017683 61211) may fish on about $1^{1}/_{2}$ miles of the right bank of the main river, March 25th to September 30th. Fly fishing only. This is good fly fishing and worming water where many big browns have been taken in the past.

Tickets from the hotel for guests only.

Downstream at Temple Sowerby, The Yorkshire Fly Fishers' Club preserves about 2 miles of fishing. On the right bank from Old Bowers Bridge to the main road bridge. Members only.

On the left bank for approximately 2 miles extending below A66 road bridge the fishing belongs to the Penrith AA. Members only.

TROUTBECK

The Penrith AA controls the fishing on about 1 mile of this fine little beck between Kirkby Thore and Long Marton. It is a lovely stretch that is ideally suited to the roving fly fisherman. Use a small nymph rod, about 7 feet long, and fish small dry or west flies. Fish 'fine and far off' for the best results. The trout are not as big as their cousins on the Eden, but they are energetic and give a good account of themselves and most of the popular patterns will take them. The water can be very clear so take extra care not to cast a shadow and scare the fish.

Weekly and day tickets available. *See below, under Penrith, for availability and conditions.*

Culgaith (OS91:610297)

About 2 miles of the left bank from a few hundred yards upstream of the River Lyvennet down to the A66 road bridge is preserved for members only by the Penrith AA. No day tickets.

The Yorkshire FFC controls some excellent game fishing near Culgaith. Members only.

A lovely stretch of about $^{1}/_{2}$ mile of the right bank of the Eden above its junction with the Eamont, known as the Skirwith Abbey beat, is available for fishing by members of the Penrith AA. No day tickets.

RIVER EAMONT

The River Eamont, turbulent in its upper reaches and sedate as it flows into the Eden Valley, has its source on the eastern slopes of Helvellyn. On the inhospitable fell side, water from Grisedale and Deepdale Becks, plus that from scores of others and the outflow from Brotherswater, flow through Patterdale as Goldrill Beck. Goldrill is full of tiny trout, which are very lively and eager to take almost anything thrown into the water. Goldrill Beck flows into Ullswater and emerges, after approximately 8 miles, at Pooley Bridge as the River Eamont. The river is further swelled by water from Dacre Beck and the River Lowther as it winds its way past Penrith before meeting the River Eden at Watersmeeting.

Patterdale (OS90:339157)
There is lots of free fishing in the streams and lakes around here. The trout are tiny but they are plentiful and will greedily grab a worm or a wet fly. Almost any pattern will take fish. The fishing in Goldrill, Grisedale, Deepdale and Hartsop Becks is free but, as it often involves a climb to reach it, you will need to be fit. Goldrill Beck has much easier access and more fish. An Environment Agency rod licence is required. *See Legal section.*
See also Blea Tarn, Brotherswater Lake, Grisdale Tarn, Red Tarn and Ullswater Lake.

Penrith (OS90:514304)
The fishing on several miles of the Eamont is controlled by The Penrith Angling Association. On the left bank, commencing from the outflow of Ullswater at Pooley Bridge, the fishing rights extend, with a few exceptions, downstream for about 4 miles to Brougham Weir near Yanworth Viaduct. Then on the right bank, for almost the same distance, from Pooley Mill to Yanworth Wood. This is a fine stretch of water for a fly fisherman. Near Ullswater, the river is wild and turbulent forming many quiet pools that offer the promise of big trout. Lower downstream, the water is quiet and meanders through meadowland before bubbling over shingle slopes on its way towards the Eden. Fly fishing only is

*A good fish rising on a calm day on **Goldrill Beck** in Patterdale*

permitted, which is right for this water. In spring when the water is high, traditional wet flies take fish. Try one of the spider patterns. When the water is low and clear in summer, dry fly comes into its own. Try the smaller patterns. Early in the season, almost anything in black will take fish, then the olives are good and late in the year a Daddy Long Legs fished in the shade of a tree will often tempt a big brown. They can be over 2lb, so use a strong leader.

Weekly tickets £30.00, **day tickets** £8.00. Four fish limit per day. All fish under 10 inches to be returned carefully to the water. No coarse fishing. Tickets from Charles R. Sykes, Tackle & Guns, 4 Great Dockray, Penrith (Tel: 01768 862418) and The Punchbowl Hotel, Askham (Tel: 01931 712443).

The Penrith AA has more water on the River Eamont extending on the left bank from Eamont Bridge on the A6 downstream for approximately $^3/_4$ mile and on the right bank commencing about $^1/_4$ mile below the A6 bridge down to the junction with the River Lowther. Members only.

Approximately $1^1/_4$ miles of the right bank, from just above waters-meeting of the Eamont and Lowther, downstream to $^3/_4$ mile below the A66 bridge, the start of the Penrith AA water, is available for fishing on a weekly or daily permit. This is the Brougham Castle water, long known for the quality of its fish. There are a number of salmon holding pools and depending upon water conditions, fish are present throughout the summer and autumn. The brown trout fishing is excellent and recently a number of large 'escapee' rainbow trout have been caught. Grayling and coarse fishing is permitted in the winter.

Tickets, tackle hire and tuition from Mr. Julian F. Shaw, 2 Fell Lane, Penrith, CA11 8AA (Tel: 01768 865051 or mobile 0802 731789). Or call in person at the tackle counter of John Norris Fishing Tackle, 21 Victoria Road, Penrith. NO phone booking through John Norris.

See also Blencarn Lake, Sockbridge Mill Trout Fishery and Whins Pond.

RIVER LOWTHER

Picturesque Sleddale is the source of this small river which flows northwards to meet the River Eamont at Penrith. Its head waters have been calmed by the construction of Wet Sleddale Reservoir which in dry weather controls the flow. After several miles, at Rosegill, the Lowther is further swelled by the waters of Swindale Beck. More water enters from Haweswater Reservoir via Haweswater Beck at Brampton Grange. The river then slows down and meanders through wooded areas near Askham before joining the River Eamont. The best fishing is for the trout which average $^3/_4$lb. Salmon do run into the river but because of low water problems they tend to be very late. The few fish that do make it are large.

Brampton Grange (OS90:521180)
The Crown and Mitre Hotel at Brampton (Tel: 01931 713225) has over 3 miles of good fishing, including Haweswater Beck, and a stretch of the River Eden.
Tickets for guests only.

Further downstream, the Penrith AA holds the rights, with a few exceptions, to nearly 6 miles of prime fishing extending from Kemp Howe, south of Shap, downstream to below Whale Bridge near Askham. This is a great fly fishing water. There are lots of good brown trout, mostly wilds averaging about $^3/_4$lb with some bigger stocked fish. Most of the traditional dry and wet patterns will take fish. Some of the water is designated fly only, but bait fishing is permitted on other stretches.
Weekly tickets £20.00, **day tickets** £6.00. For ticket sources and conditions *see under Penrith.*

A stretch of water, on the left bank, commencing $^1/_4$ mile below the A6 road bridge and extending downstream to the junction with the River Eamont, is Penrith AA water for members only.

For permits for the Brougham Castle Water on the lower river *see Penrith entry above.*

Back on the River Eden, about ³/₄ mile of excellent fishing on the right bank of the river near Little Salkeld is controlled by Penrith AA. Fishing is by fly only and all the favourite patterns will attract fish. Spider patterns are particularly good when fished just under the surface. Smaller dry flies are better in summer, but when the water is up don't be afraid to use a big bushy pattern and use a strong leader because brown trout of 2lb are common.

Weekly tickets £40.00, **day tickets** £10.00. For ticket sources and conditions see under Penrith. Permits also cover Penrith AA fishing waters on River Eamont, River Lowther and Troutbeck.

The Association also has a length of Briggle Beck and a short stretch on the left bank of the Eden above Eden Lacy for members only.

Further downstream, there is some superb fishing available on approximately 1¹/₂ miles of the left bank at Eden Lacy. It is an excellent game beat with a variety of holding pools and streamy water. As with all the other salmon beats on the middle river, the best chance of a fresh run spring fish is between March and May and, if there is good water in the river, fishing remains excellent throughout the summer, peaking in October when the bigger fish arrive. Eden Lacy also boasts some of the finest brown trout fishing on the middle reaches. Fish of 1¹/₂ to 2lb are common and much bigger trout lurk in the deep pools. No bait fishing at any time. Two rods only are available on a daily basis.

Permits must be booked in advance through Julian F. Shaw, 2 Fell Lane, Penrith, Cumbria CA11 8AA. (Tel: 01768 865051 Mobile: 0802 731789 Fax: 01768 891327).

Lazonby (OS90:549397)

Lazonby has long been known as the place to go on the Eden for salmon and sea trout fishing. Indeed, the area is something of a mecca for game anglers. Unfortunately, in recent years much of the day ticket water, which once belonged to hotels, has fallen into the hands of syndicates but there is still an excellent stretch available to visiting anglers. Starting approximately ³/₄ mile upstream of Bridge End Park and extending downstream, on the left bank, for nearly a mile, to a point 200 yards downstream of Eden Bridge, the fishing rights belong to Lazonby Parish Council. It is a fine stretch of water with some shingle bars and long deeper glides, on the outside of the bend, promising the chance of a salmon or one of the big brown trout which are known to be in the river here. A wet fly drawn into the obvious holding areas on the outside of the bend is a good option. When the river is up, try a spinner. Fishing is free to residents.

Day tickets for salmon are £12.00 and for trout £10.00. **Weekly tickets** £36.00 and £30.00 respectively. An evening ticket for trout and coarse fish costs £5.00. From Lazonby Post Office (Tel: 01768 898438), The Joiners Arms (near the river) (Tel: 01768 898728) and The Midland Hotel (near the railway station) (Tel: 01768 898901). *See also Crossfield Fishery.*

Armathwaite (OS86:503462)

Most of the fishing rights in this area belong to the Lazonby Estate and are privately let although some temporary permits are available from the Estate Office at Bracken Bank Shooting Lodge, Lazonby (Tel: 01768 898241) or Castlerigg farm, Armathwaite (Tel: 01768 898337).

Guests at the Duke's Head Hotel in Armathwaite (Tel: 016974 72226) may fish for brown trout on approximately ¹/₂ mile of the right bank of the Eden below the bridge. It is a lovely dry fly water where the fish average about 1lb to 1¹/₂lb although there are some over the 3lb mark. The fishing can be challenging in the height of summer, but in the early and late season it is unsurpassed.
Permits, for guests only, from the hotel reception after June 1st.

There is excellent salmon, sea trout and brown trout fishing in the Wetheral area, but access is all preserved for members by the Yorkshire FFC.
See also East View Lake, High Stands Lakes and Lonsdale Park Lakes.

Warwick-on-Eden (OS86:470574)

One of the best stretches for salmon fishing on the lower Eden belongs to the Warwick Hall Estate (Tel: 01228 560545). The fishery, on both banks, starts at Warwick Bridge on the A69(T) and extends downstream for about 1¹/₂ miles to the junction with the River Gelt. It is most definitely a game water. There are a lot of good brown but anglers go for the salmon. Numerous holding pools make this well-maintained water a joy to fish. In keeping with the rest of the west coast rivers, this is late water, which is best fished towards the end of the season and when there is some fresh water in the river. When the water is up, a Mepps is a good bet, but fly is the preferred method. The price of tickets reflects the season, running from January 15th to October 14th. As an example:

Day tickets vary from £20.00 to £80.00. Three day and weekly tickets are also available. Phone ahead and book. This is a very popular fishery.

Carlisle (OS85:400560)
A fine stretch of water, above and below the town, is controlled by the Carlisle Angling Association. The fishing starts at the M6 flyover and extends, with a few minor exceptions, on both banks downstream through Carlisle, to about ³/₄ mile below Grinsdale and also for about 2 miles on the left bank of the tidal river opposite Rockcliffe. This is an excellent water with easy access at many points. There is a good run of salmon, sea trout and herling, particularly in the late summer and autumn. As always, runs depend upon water conditions, but as these are the first beats of the Eden it is usually a good place to pick up a fresh run fish. Throughout the season, the brown trout fishing is excellent and consistent. There are a lot of fish. Many of the browns average 1¹/₂lb and there are some over 3lb, so it worth going after these. There were once some big grayling near here but sadly none has been reported in recent years. Inevitably there are some coarse fish in the stretch, mainly big chub and dace.

Fly and worm are the best baits for the trout. Any legal method is allowed for salmon fishing, but worm is prohibited until May 1st. The best fly for salmon is undoubtedly a Shrimp imitation and the best spinners are a Devon or a Flying C.

Weekly ticket (salmon) £40.00, **day** £20.00. **Weekly ticket (trout)** £7.00, **day** £2.00 (March 15th to September 30th). **Coarse fish** (October 15th to January 14th) £1.00. Tickets from Carlisle fishing tackle outlets: McHardy's (Tel: 01228 523988), Murray's (Tel: 01228 523816) and Geoff Wilson (Tel: 01228 531542).

See also Longtown West Pond, Lough Trout Fishery, New Mills Trout Farm Fishery, Oakbank Lakes Country Park and Talkin' Tarn.

RIVER IRTHING

The Irthing rises on Grey Fell Common from where it flows west, through Gilsland, Low Row and Brampton and then joining the River Eden at Newby East near Carlisle. It's an interesting little river offering some excellent fishing for wild brown trout up to $1^{3/4}$lb. A few salmon come into the river late in the season.

Brampton (OS86:525611)
The Brampton Angling Association controls approximately 4 miles of the best fishing on the Irthing, the Gelt and the tributaries Cambeck and Kingwater. The trout fishing is particularly good in the early season. Fish average $^{1/2}$ to $^{3/4}$lb with some fish reaching $1^{3/4}$lb. They are in prime condition, hard fighters and fall readily to fly. Spider patterns or small dark flies are the most consistent fish takers.
Weekly ticket £12.00 and **day ticket** £4.00 from Brampton Sports Shop, 2 Lorne Terrace, Front Street (Tel: 016977 3795), Low Row Post Office and the White Lion Hotel, High Cross Street, Brampton (Tel: 016977 2338).

RIVER GELT

A much more exciting river than the Irthing, the River Gelt starts life in the foothills of the Pennines and flows for about 6 turbulent miles to join the Irthing near Rule Holme. For much of its life, the river twists, turns, falls and crashes along a deep gorge, making it a difficult water to fish. It can also be dangerous. Without warning, heavy rain on the Pennines will cause a flash flood further downstream. It's wise to have an escape route from the gorge when fishing the River Gelt. The river does hold a good stock of hard fighting, wild brown trout. Visitors may fish by fly only. Spider and black patterns are the best.
Weekly and day tickets available. *See entry for River Irthing above.*

RIVER PETTERIL

An attractive small river with fine trout fishing throughout but all the fishing is private.

RIVER CALDEW

With a few exceptions the Carlisle Angling Association controls most of the fishing on the Caldew. It is a small, streamy water, good for fly fishing, supporting an excellent stock of wild and stocked brown trout. Averaging about $^3/_4$lb, the fish are not as big as those on the Eden, but they every bit as lively. The Caldew is fairly shallow and the water is clear, so great care is needed. A badly placed foot or a shadow cast across the water will scare the fish. Dry fly fishermen take most of the fish. Try a Greenwell's Glory or a Black Gnat, they are always a good bet.

Day and weekly tickets are available for trout fishing only. From Dalston Hall Caravan Site (Tel: 01228 71065). *Also see above under Carlisle.*

RIVER EHEN

Great Gable, a high point of south-western Lakeland and the pinnacle of many a walker's ambition, is the starting point of the watercourse which eventually becomes the River Ehen. Tiny streams drain the rocky fellsides into a narrow wooded valley to create the River Liza, the main feeder for Ennerdale Water. Hardly worthy of the title river, the Liza is really only a beck which in summer holds little water. There are few places where fish can survive, except where it broadens close to its confluence with Ennerdale Water. The fishing is private.

Both the Ennerdale Lake Fishers and the Wath Brow and Ennerdale Angling Association have rights to fish in the lake. *See also Ennerdale Water.*

The River Ehen proper starts its life at the weir on the outflow of Ennerdale Water and flows for approximately 15 miles to the sea near Sellafield. For most of its length, it twists and turns through meadowland until the last few miles, below Beckermet, where it flows through scrub and marsh land close to the Irish Sea. Mainly because of sensible stocking policies by local angling clubs, the trout fishing is very good with brown trout averaging about $^1/_2$lb and others up to $1^1/_2$lb. The Ehen has always enjoyed a reputation as a fine sea trout river and although the fish numbers have decreased over the years, many between 2 and 3lb still find their way upstream

*The **River Ehen** and Braystones Tower*

into Ennerdale Water. On good years they are accompanied by a fair number of salmon and some herling. The salmon can be big, 20 pounders were once common here, but sadly the size and number of fish caught have reduced. It's a late river, fishing for migratory fish being better after July.

See also Meadley Reservoir.

Cleator Moor (OS89:027145)
The Wath Brow and Ennerdale Angling Association controls the rights to approximately 6¹/₂ miles of excellent water on the upper river. Fishing is mostly from both banks starting at the outflow from Ennerdale Lake and extending downstream to Briscoe Bridge just upstream of Egremont. It's mainly a brown trout water although there is a small run of sea trout and salmon late in the season. Fly fishing, spinning, prawn and shrimp fishing (depending upon the height of water) are all permitted. Also worm fishing, without weights, is allowed throughout the season, but fly fishermen have the right of way through pools. Depending upon the season and water conditions, almost any of the small river dry or wet flies will take trout, but if salmon is the quarry, try Stoats Tail, Thunder and

Lightning or a Shrimp Fly. Many of the migratory fish fall to worm though.

Weekly tickets, adult £20.00, junior £10.00. **Day tickets**, adult £5.00, junior £2.00 from J. W. N. Holmes & Son, Fishing Tackle and Firearms, 45 Main Street, Egremont (Tel: 01946 820368). Visitors must reside outside a 10 mile radius of Cleator Moor.

See also Longlands Lake.

Egremont (OS89:015108)

Almost all of the fishing on about 8 miles of lower reaches, from Briscoe Bridge, just above Egremont, on both banks down to the sea at Sellafield, is controlled by the Egremont Angling Association. This is a fine water for game fishing. High quality brown trout to $1^{1}/_{2}$lb are common. Fly fishing, spinning and worming all take their fair share of good fish. There's also a fair run of sea trout and salmon. The best salmon holding pools are on the lower beat below Beckermet. As on all of the west coast rivers, salmon numbers have drastically reduced over the years, but sea trout still come into the river in fair numbers. Fishing for these is better later in the season. No float fishing or ground baiting is permitted. The season is from May 1st to October 31st.

Weekly tickets £30.00 from the Secretary or from J.W.N. Holmes, Fishing Tackle & Firearms, 45 Main Street, Egremont (Tel: 01946 820368)

See also Silver Tarn and Tarnside Lake.

RIVER ELLEN

Following a twisting westerly course of about 11 miles from the outflow of Overwater to the sea at Maryport, the River Ellen is fairly unremarkable. It is not at all like a Cumbrian river. It is slow and ponderous, twisting through meadowland and sandy banks. However, depending upon water conditions, the fishing can be very good.

Fishing in the upper reaches, above Blennerhasset, is all in private hands but the trout are small anyway and in times of low water they are hardly worth fishing for. The trout fishing is better below the town and there is a good sea trout run. Salmon are now few and far between in the River Ellen.

See also Overwater Fishery.

Aspatria (OS85:145420)

The Aspatria Angling Association controls several good stretches above and below the town. It is mainly brown trout fishing but late in the season the night fishing for sea trout is good. Try a wet fly. Spinning is a better option when the river is in flood.

Season tickets £15.00 from Grahams Guns, Workington (Tel: 01900 605093).

Maryport (OS89:035361)

About 4 miles of fishing, on both banks, above the town is controlled by the Ellen Angling Association. If it is sea trout you're after this is probably the best place to try. Wet fly as the sun is going down is the best bet. Any of the north country patterns will take fish.

Weekly tickets £15.00 from Solway Leisure, 66 Senhouse Street, Maryport (Tel: 01900 815109).

RIVER ESK

Not to be confused with the River Esk flowing along part of the border between England and Scotland, the Cumbrian Esk is a short stream-like river that has it source near Scafell Pike. From there, it flows south-westerly for approximately 7 miles to its meeting with the estuary near Muncaster Castle. In its upper reaches, particularly around Throstle Garth where it crashes over several spectacular waterfalls, it is a turbulent river and difficult to fish. There is no road access to the upper 3 miles of river which anglers tend leave for the enjoyment of fell walkers. Further downstream, near the road from Hardknott Pass, the Esk suddenly calms down before meandering through the fertile Esk Valley to Eskholme, where it becomes tidal. The waters of the Esk are often gin clear and a careless footfall or shadow will scare the trout, although a carefully placed dry fly will often bring results. When the water is in flood, though, a worm is the best bet. Although in smaller numbers than was once the case, migratory fish continue to run the Esk, making it an important game fishing river, one of the best on the west Cumbrian coast.

Dalegarth (OS89:174008)

The Millom and District Angling Association has the fishing rights

*Irton Station Bridge on the **River Esk***

on approximately 1¹/₂ miles of the left bank through the Dalegarth Estate. There are two beats, Gill Force and Beckfoot, each with wonderful streamy water and large deep pools. Near Boot Church is Gill Force Gorge where the Esk crashes, tumbles and falls through a series of pools into a deep lagoon. It's full of fish, but extra care is needed if you are not to end your session in the maelstrom! Salmon and sea trout are in the water from about June onwards, but the fishing is better later in the year. There are some good brown trout in the pools all year. No shrimp, prawn or maggot fishing, but then fly, spinning and worm are best methods anyway.

Day tickets £15.00, **weekly tickets** £40.00. The nearest outlet for tickets is Waberthwaite Post Office (Tel: 01229 717237). *Also from the sources listed under River Annas.*
See also Burnmoor Tarn.

Eskdale Green (OS89:140002)
Fishing on the river above Eskdale Green is very patchy and it is all in private hands.

Further downstream, below the road bridge near Forge House, The

Prince Albert Angling Society has a fine stretch for members only.

Below here from Mere Beck downstream to just above the weir at Black Dub, on the right bank, plus a short stretch on the left bank, the fishing is controlled by the Millom and District AA. When the water is right there is no better stretch on the Esk. Its clear water, streamy runs, boulder strewn pools and flat banks make it ideal for fly fishing but other methods are also permitted. No shrimp or prawn fishing is allowed. Both sea trout and salmon fishing is better in late summer and autumn, providing of course that there is some extra water to help the fish get upstream.

Day tickets £15.00, **weekly tickets** £40.00 *from the sources listed above. See also Devoke Water and Knott End Tarn.*

RIVER MITE
This is a tiny streamlike river which, on the right day, offers some excellent fishing for brown and sea trout. All the fishing is in private hands.

RIVER IRT
Rainwater crashing down Wasdale Fell and Scafell Pike forms Lingmell Beck, the main feeder for Wastwater Lake and the source of the River Irt. Although a few trout do manage to survive in the clear waters of Lingmell Beck, there's little point in trying to catch them, but if you are tempted, then a worm is the best option. Lower down, from the outflow of Wastwater, the river is much more amenable to fishing and it offers the chance of catching some good wild trout. After leaving the huge lake, it follows a twisting route through quiet meadowland as it heads south-west for its meeting with the sea at Drigg. Like most of the West Cumbrian rivers it's primarily a brown trout water with the bonus of a few sea trout and salmon in the autumn. On a good year, the migratory fish run the whole length of the Irt, pass through Wastwater and spawn in the upper reaches of Lingmell Beck. They can turn up almost anywhere, so be prepared.
Fishing is not permitted in Wastwater.

Netherwasdale (OS89:125040)
The Gosforth Anglers' Club has access to some good fishing here for members only.

RIVER BLENG

A 6 mile long tributary of the Irt, the Bleng shares similar characteristics. It is very turbulent in its upper reaches, above the waterfalls in Blengdale Forest, and is hardly worth fishing, but lower down near Whin Garth, it does provide the opportunity of fly fishing trout and the occasional sea trout. Below Gosforth, the Bleng runs into flat meadowland. This is the place to pick up a salmon in the late autumn.

Gosforth (OS89:066035)
The local Gosforth AC controls most of the fishing on both banks from Blengdale Forest downstream to the Bleng's meeting with the Irt. Members only.

Holmrook (OS96:077997)
Over 5$^{1/2}$ miles of excellent fishing on both banks of the River Irt are controlled by the Lutwidge Arms Hotel. Half of the length is reserved for hotel guests, but visitor's tickets are available for the rest. This is probably the most productive stretch on the entire river. There are many good salmon holding pools and some fine fish have been taken from here in the past. Fly fishing for sea trout is particularly good at sunset and just after.
Weekly tickets £50.00, **day tickets** £10.00 from the Lutwidge Arms Hotel, Holmrook (Tel: 019467 24230).

A short stretch of water here, on the right bank, where the A595 trunk road skirts the river is **free fishing** for holders of an Environment Agency rod licence. The stretch, about $^{1/2}$ mile long, is between the A595 roadbridge and a point opposite the Lutwidge Arms Hotel, and is owned by Holmrook Town Council. It is fairly shallow, but there are some good pools and access from the road·is easy. The water offers the best chance of a fish when there is some floodwater coming down the river.

The Millom and District Angling Association has fishing on some prime stretches of water, from Holme Bridge to Bailiffs Pool and about 500 yards at Hall Carleton. Both waters are excellent for salmon, sea trout and brown trout. Late in the summer and the autumn are the optimum times to try for migratory fish. There are a few good holding pools where fish wait until the conditions are right for upstream movement. Fly, spinning and worm fishing are permitted. Fishing with maggots is prohibited. Some of the access is difficult and the water is tidal, so beware.

Day tickets £15.00, **weekly tickets** £40.00. The nearest ticket outlet is Holmrook Service Station, on the A595 just south of the bridge at Holmrook (Tel: 019467 24247). Also from the sources listed under *River Annas*.

RIVER KENT

Like so many of the Lake District's small rivers, the Kent starts its life high on the barren fells where tiny streams trickle through peat before crashing down boulder strewn hillsides into narrow valleys. In this case the streams drain remote Kentmere Common in the shadow of High Street where only the occasional walker ventures. During very dry seasons, Kentmere Reservoir holds back much of the water and, as a consequence, the River Kent can be shallow making fishing difficult, particularly in the upper reaches. The fishing is better below Staveley where the Kent is joined by the River Gowan, and the combined waters meander through meadowland and down through Kendal before finally racing towards the sea at Morecambe Bay. There is good fishing to be had right in the heart of Kendal and it continues to improve the closer one gets to Morecambe Bay. Throughout its length, the Kent fishes well for brown trout. There's also a small run of salmon, both early and late, and a good sea trout run from August onwards. On a good year, when there is some floodwater about, the fish get upstream to spawn in the tiny feeder streams above Kentmere.

Kentmere (OS90:457041)
Above the village the river is squeezed into a tight valley between the high fells of Kentmere Pike and Buck Craggs. Although it is full of smallish trout, it is turbulent and difficult to fish. Local farmers hold the fishing rights and will sometimes give permission, but don't count on it. Below, the river quietens down as it flows into the flat Kent Valley and into the natural ponds and long watercourse of the delightful Kentmere Fishery.
See also Kentmere Fishery.

Staveley (OS97:470985)

The Staveley and District Angling Association controls about 5 miles of excellent water on the Kent and Gowan. Fishing on the Kent starts near Ullthwaite Bridge in the picturesque Kentmere Valley and extends downstream through the town to Spring Hag Wood. Access is generally very easy because the road to Kentmere follows the river. In places it is turbulent with lots of small waterfalls and steep rocky outcrops. If you are very careful (the slippery rocks can be very unforgiving) it is a great place to fish. Try running a worm into the deep pools below waterfalls, especially when there is extra water in the river. Or, when it is low in summer, almost any dry fly will attract the greedy trout. Brown trout are the main target - recently a fish of $3^{3/4}$lb was taken from this water. The trout season runs from March 15th to September 30th. It's worth trying for the salmon and sea trout in September and October. Fly fishing, worm and spinning only. Maggots are strictly prohibited.

Weekly ticket £15.00 and **day tickets** £10.00 from the Membership Secretary, *see Angling Clubs section,* and D. & H. Woof, Newsagent, 22 Main Street, Staveley (Tel: 01539 821253). Woof's also sell tickets for Kentmere Fishery.

RIVER GOWAN

The Staveley and District AA has the rights to fishing on both banks of the river from the A591 Bridge downstream to where it joins the Kent. It is narrow and very shallow and often short of water but it does offer some challenging wild brown trout fishing.

Day tickets, *see entry for Staveley above.*

Burneside (OS97:505957)

About 2 miles of excellent fishing belonging to the Burneside Angling Association is available here. The fishing is from Beckmickleing Wood near Staveley downstream to just below the River Sprint junction. Fishing is from both banks and includes the mill dams at Cowan Head, Bowston and Burneside which all hold trout up to $1^{1/2}$lb, big for this area. Although salmon and sea trout run into the water from about July onwards, the fishing is better later in the season.

Weekly tickets £16.00 and **day tickets** £8.00 from the aptly named

Jolly Anglers Inn, Burneside (Tel: 01539 732552).

RIVER SPRINT

The Sprint is a tiny rivulet that tumbles south through Long Sleddale to join the Kent at Burneside. Mainly due to the shortage of water, the fishing in the upper reaches is limited. Although the trout are very small, they are wild and acrobatic, and, on the right day will give good sport.

Further downstream, where the water quietens down and the banks have become wooded, the Burneside AA has about 1 mile of water on both banks downstream to the junction with the Kent.

Another local club, the Kent Angling Association, controls the rights to about ¹/₂ mile of the left bank above the Burneside AA stretch. The brown trout are small but they are plentiful. Salmon and sea trout run into the stretch from August onwards.

Kendal (OS97:515920)

This is a good centre for the visiting angler. There's plenty of local fishing and two shops selling fishing tackle. The fishing rights within the town boundaries belong to South Lakeland District Council who make **no charge**. But you must have an Environment Agency rod licence obtainable at the Tourist Information Centre, Town Hall, New Shambles (Tel: 01539 725758). If you can ignore the noise from busy roads, it's an excellent stretch to fish and access is very easy. The water is generally fast and streamy although it is held back in places by small weirs. Mostly the fishing is for brown trout, but salmon and sea trout run through the water on their way upstream to spawn above Kentmere. In the autumn, when the water level is right, it's possible to catch salmon right in the centre of town. Try a worm in one of the quiet pools below the small weirs.

RIVER MINT

The Mint, a small stream-like river starting life as a mere trickle in Bannisdale and flanked by the high fells of Borrowdale, flows about 10 miles southerly to join the Kent just above Kendal. Fishing is very limited, particularly in the upper reaches where few fish are able to survive in the rocky stream. Large numbers of wild brown trout live in the lower river. They average about 3 or 4 to the pound and can be very acrobatic when hooked. The Kent (Westmoreland) AA has access to approximately 3 miles of water, mainly on both banks.

Day and weekly tickets *see below.*

Back on the River Kent south of Kendal, the fishing, on approximately 8 miles of water, mainly both banks, downstream to Force Bridge near Sedgewick, is controlled by the Kent (Westmoreland) Angling Association. This is a brilliant stretch of water for fly fishermen although worm and spinning are also allowed and will take their share of bigger fish during a spate. Brown trout up to $5^{1/2}$lb have been landed from this stretch but the trout usually average about $1^{1/2}$lb with a fair number of smaller fish. Salmon and sea trout fishing is best from July onwards, but after August 31st it is for season ticket holders only. Between Natland and Sedgewick bridges the river tumbles and falls through a wooded area. It's easily accessible and, because of its variety, it is an interesting place to fish. There are two weirpools, which always seem to hold fish, and, at Force Bridge, there is a deep gorge that looks particularly inviting. Be careful though - when wet the rocks can be very slippery and unforgiving. Season March 15th to October 15th. Fishing only between 0800 to 2000 hrs. No night fishing.

Weekly tickets £20.00 to May 31st then £50.00 to August 31st. **Day tickets** £7.00 to May 31st then £15.00 to August 31st from Low Park Wood Caravan Site, Sedgewick. The site is alongside the river. At the A590(T) and A591 interchange, 4 miles south of Kendal, take the Sedgewick turn off. In about 500 yards turn left onto a single track road signposted Sizergh Castle Tea Rooms. Follow the road alongside the river to the caravan site. Tickets also available in Kendal from Carlsons Fishing Tackle, 64-66 Kirkland (Tel: 01539 724867), Kendal Sports, 28-30 Stramondgate (Tel: 01539 721554) or the tourist information centre, Town Hall, Highgate, Kendal (Tel: 01539 725758).

Leven (OS97:488861)
Below Force Bridge at Sedgewick all the way downstream through Levens Park to $^{1/2}$ mile below the A6 Bridge, the fishing is private.

An excellent stretch of approximately 2 miles on the right bank from Levens Beck downstream to Morecambe Bay is available for fishing on a visitor's ticket. The river here is full and fast flowing and exciting to fish. Mostly it contains brown trout averaging about 1lb but there are much bigger fish to be had. There are also salmon and sea trout and, although the runs have decreased over the past decade, it is a productive water. Further downstream by Sampool Caravan Park the water is tidal and the sandy banks can be somewhat dangerous, so tread carefully.

Day tickets £5.00 from Mrs Parsons, Olde Peat Cotes, Sampool Lane, Leven, Nr. Kendal LA8 8EH (Tel: 015395 60096). Bed and breakfast accommodation is also available. To find the fishery from the A6/A590 trunk road, take the small road signposted to Sampool Caravan Park. Follow the road for about $1/2$ mile until it turns away from the river and Mrs Parsons' cottage is on the left.

RIVER GILPIN

Starting life as the River Pool near the village of Underbarrow, the Gilpin flows through about 4 miles of the flat fertile Lyth Valley before entering the sea at the Kent Estuary on Morecambe Bay. A favourite trout water, this lovely little stream once gave up a large salmon, but alas it is now virtually barren. Except for a few eels and dabs, in the tidal lower reaches near Sampool, there is little point in trying to get permission from local farmers to fish.

RIVER LAZY

A tiny river hardly more than 3 miles long and as the name suggests a very sluggish water. It starts life as Wincham Beck and then meanders, first westerly and then southerly, to enter the sea at Haverigg. The Lazy offers some brown trout fishing and a limited opportunity to go after sea trout and salmon.

Haverigg (OS96:160786)
The Millom and District Angling Association has the rights to about 2 miles of fishing from Hestham Farm Bridge downstream to Whitriggs Bridge at Haverigg. A drainage channel for farmland, the banks having been 'canalised' to assist the passage of floodwater, it is not a particularly attractive stretch, but, given the right conditions,

it can be productive. Some migratory fish do still enter the river although they tend to arrive very late in the year. September and October are the best months. Because the banks have been cleared, fly casting is easy, although most local anglers use a worm. No maggot fishing.

Day tickets £15.00, **weekly tickets** £40.00. The nearest outlet is Haverigg Post Office (Tel: 01229 772338). Other ticket outlets are as listed in the entry under *River Annas*.

RIVER LEVEN

A mere 5 miles long, the Leven follows a tortuous path from the outflow of Windermere Lake to the sea at Haverthwaite. It resembles a Scottish highland river and promises some splendid fishing. From the first weir, over which the Leven tumbles in its eagerness to leave Windermere, down the first mile, it crashes over waterfalls and drops into deep pools each one holding the promise of big trout. Then at Backbarrow, the river broadens and bubbles over a stony bed on its way to the sea. It's a noted brown trout fishing river, the bigger fish consistently coming from the deep pools above Backbarrow. It's also a fine sea trout water and there is the chance of a very late salmon. Except for one small stretch, all the fishing rights, on both banks, from Newby Bridge downstream to the tidal water at Greenodd, is controlled by the Leven Angling Association for members only.

Newby Bridge (OS96:370864)
The Swan Hotel, Newby Bridge (Tel: 015395 31681) issues tickets to fish the right bank downstream from the hotel for approximately $^1/_2$ mile. This is a good water suited to bait fishing or spinning. There are some big trout that occasionally fall to a float fished worm.
Day tickets £10.00, from the hotel reception.

GRIZEDALE BECK

This is a tiny beck supporting a limited number of small brown trout. The fishing around Force Mills and Rusland is let to the Hawkshead Angling Club for members only. *See Angling Clubs section.*

RIVER CRAKE

The Crake is a short river, about 4 miles long, draining Coniston water and flowing south to enter the sea at Greenodd. It is a pretty little river and is well stocked with brown trout. It also enjoys a small run of late sea trout and salmon. All the fishing is in private hands. From Spark Bridge downstream it belongs to the Penny Bridge Hall Estate and is fished by members of the Ulverston Angling Association. *See Angling Clubs section.*

RIVER EEA

A tiny river meandering through the picturesque Cartmel Valley near Grange-over-Sands, the River Eea offers some challenging fishing for wild and stocked brown trout and the chance of taking a sea trout. The wild browns are small, about 3 to the pound, but the sea trout are much larger. About 3 miles of the river from Middlefield Beck downstream to Cark and a short stretch of tidal water between Crookwheel and Sandgate Marsh are controlled by the Cark and District Angling Association for members only. For a fee, adult members are allowed two guest day tickets each season. Fly and worm fishing only. No groundbait, maggots or grub.

RIVER LUNE

Like many of the north country rivers, the Lune is born amidst the high fells on Ravenstonedale Common where dozens of crystal clear streams, their water purified and filtered by limestone, tumble down steep inclines into the narrow Lune Valley. After flowing for about 6 miles due west to Tebay, the river turns south and, mercifully keeping its distance from the M6, continues for a further 40 miles to Lancaster where it joins the Irish Sea.

High on the fells, there is little to interest an angler. The brown trout that do manage to survive in tiny pools beneath waterfalls or in deep troughs amongst the peat and heather are small, few and far between and certainly not worth the trouble of a long hike to find them. Two sizeable watercourses combine at Tebay from where the Lune turns south. One of them, flowing west from Newbiggin-on-Lune, is the infant River Lune and the other, flowing south in company with the M6, is Birk Beck. Above Tebay it is hard to distinguish between them - they both carry the same amount of water and hold similar stocks of fish. The fishing, which peaks between June and August, is mainly for native brown trout, but they are not big. A native brown of about 6 or 7 ounces is a good fish, but the stock is supplemented each season with good quality browns of approximately 1lb. A fair number of migratory fish do run up the river to spawn in the upper reaches.

Salmon and sea trout were once prolific on the River Lune, but as is sadly the case on other game rivers, the numbers of fish returning to spawn has reduced drastically. The spring run has all but disappeared and the autumn run is not what it was in the early years of this century. Depending upon water levels, sea trout start to show in the upper reaches from about June onwards and the salmon arrive about a month later, although it is better to wait until September to be almost sure of getting a fish.

Between Tebay and Sedbergh, the river starts to quieten down and flow more sedately between broad banks bordered with pastureland. Bigger trout, some over 2lb, lurk in the deeper water, especially on the bends and in pools formed by shingle bars. Near Sedbergh, the Lune is swelled with water from the River Rawthey, a fine game fishing river in its own right.

Further downstream, at Devil's Bridge, outside Kirkby Lonsdale, the river crashes through a mini gorge into a seemingly bottomless pool. A favourite with salmon fishermen, in the past 20 and 30 pounders were once landed here. It's also a scenic area where visitors line the banks and picnic. In the autumn it's still possible to stand on the bridge parapet and watch big salmon rolling in the deeps.

Below Kirkby Lonsdale, the river twists, turns and meanders through a flat fertile valley rich in grazing land. Near here it receives water from Rivers Greta and the Wenning, both excellent game fishing rivers. The fishing all along this stretch is brilliant and much of it is available to visiting anglers for the cost of a day ticket. Some of the best is between Caton and Halton where the Environment Agency owns the rights to salmon, sea trout, brown trout and coarse fishing on several miles of water. There are many good holding pools for salmon and some sizeable fish are landed from this stretch every year. The EA also hold the rights to a lovely tidal stretch through Lancaster. It's another very productive water, worth the attention of any aspiring salmon angler.

In fact throughout its length, the Lune provides some of the best game fishing in the country and much of it is available to visiting anglers.

Newbiggin-on-Lune (OS91:705052)

The fishing on the Lune is mostly in private hands until around Kelleth where a short stretch of water above the village is controlled by the Lancashire Fly Fishing Association for members only.
See also Bessy Beck Trout Lakes.

Tebay (OS91:620045)

This is an excellent centre for game fishing on the Lune. Clear gravely runs are inviting for the dry fly fishermen, whilst the inevitable deep pools offer the promise of bigger fish, usually taken on wet fly. Wild brown trout average $^1/_2$lb and stocked fish around $1^1/_2$lb. Salmon and sea trout run into this stretch late in the season and on a good year it is not unusual to take several salmon averaging about 8lb. Spinning is probably the best method. The sea trout seem to be more difficult to tempt. The M6 motorway straddles some of this water and the noise can be a bit distracting at times.

The Tebay and District Angling Association has fishing on approximately 15 miles of excellent water including the upper river and Birk, Borrow, Chapel and Raise Becks, all of which can be fished on a single permit. With a few exceptions the fishing is on both banks from 1 mile upstream of Gaisgill downstream to approximately $^1/_2$ mile above Lowgill. This is excellent fishing, particularly for the brown trout although good numbers of salmon and sea trout do get into this stretch and give good sport. Fly fishing only in April and during the night. After April, spinning is permitted. Depending upon the season, a Snipe and Purple or a dry Greenwell's Glory will attract the big brown trout. For the sea trout try a Teal Blue and Silver or a Peter Ross - they often do well. The low-water salmon flies Blue Charm and Yellow Dog are consistent throughout the season. Spinning is also productive, a quill minnow for the trout and, when there is extra water in the river, a Flying 'C' will take a salmon. Spinning is not permitted when the water is below the yellow marker. No prawn, shrimp or float fishing is permitted at any time.

Weekly ticket £25.00 from April to July and £45.00 in August and September. From Cross Keys Inn, Tebay (Tel: 015396 24240). There are no tickets in October.

See also Pinfold Lake.

Lowgill (OS97:625969)

At Lowgill, where the river and the noisy M6 finally part company, approximately 1 mile of fine fishing on both banks, extending upstream from Beck Foot Bridge to beyond Fleet Holme Farm, Low Gill, belongs to the Bowland Game Fishing Association. This is an excellent stretch of fly fishing for brown trout and fly, spinning or worm fishing for the sea trout and salmon. No ledgering allowed. Members only.

Further downstream there is more excellent fishing to be had on both banks over a 3 mile stretch. The water is well stocked with sizeable brown trout. Invariably, the salmon and sea trout fishing is best late in the season. The sea trout fishing is particularly good around Howgill. Try a Peter Ross or Silver Stoats Tail in the evening as the sun goes down.

Day tickets £10.00, or £15.00 from August, from Mr A. Barnes, Nettleport, Firbank, Cumbria LA10 5EG (Tel: 015396 20204). Firbank is on the B6257 road from Beck Foot to Sedbergh.

See also Killington Reservoir.

The massive Prince Albert Angling Society has access to approximately 1 mile of water near here for members only.

Members of the Manchester Anglers' Association fish a short stretch of the right bank at Firbank above the old railway crossing. No visitor's tickets.

Sedbergh (OS97:655921)

Thanks mainly to the Sedbergh and District Angling Association who offer over 20 miles of prime day ticket fishing on the Lune and the Rivers Clough, Dee and Rawthey, Sedbergh is a great centre for anglers. It's primarily game fishing of course. There are lots of good brown trout to be had plus the chance of salmon and sea trout later in the season. Fishing on all Sedbergh and District AA waters is by fly only until May 1st. Maggots, floats and natural minnow are banned.

Weekly tickets £50.00, and **day tickets** £10.00, between April and September, can be obtained from Lowis's Country Wear, 23/25 Main Street, Sedbergh (Tel: 015396 20446). From mid September to October 31st, only **weekly tickets**, costing £100.00, are available.

RIVER DEE

Dent (OS98:705870)

Probably the most rural of the three valleys near Sedbergh, Dentdale takes its name from its largest hamlet and offers some excellent fishing in the lower reaches for the visiting angler. Alas most of the fishing on the upper river, above the village, is in private hands but, because it's often short of water, it is difficult to fish anyway. Occasionally a friendly farmer will give permission to fish but to be certain of wetting a line try the lower reaches where the local angling club manages the water.

The Sedbergh and District Angling Association has fishing rights on both banks for about 2 miles, with a few exceptions from approximately ¹/₂ mile below Barth Bridge downstream to near Catholes. See the fishing map in the library shelter, Main Street, Sedbergh. This is great trout and grayling water, best fished with dry or wet fly. Here the Dee's waters flow quietly through farmland, with long glides between tree-lined banks offering the chance of a good trout. Atlantic salmon do get into the system but the spring run has long since disappeared and autumn fish often don't arrive until October.

The massive Prince Albert Angling Society has rights to fishing for members only on the River Dee below Catholes down to its junction with the Rawthey.

RIVERS RAWTHEY and CLOUGH

Sedbergh (OS97:655920)

The main road from Sedbergh to Wensleydale, climbing the

beautiful Garsdale, follows the River Clough to give easy access to the waterside throughout most of the river's length. The Clough is a wild river, hardly worth fishing above Garsdale hamlet, as it tumbles down the valley from its source near Garsdale Head to its meeting with the Rawthey.

Approximately one mile of fishing on both banks of the River Clough, from Danny Bridge downstream, is available for visiting anglers.

Day or weekly tickets are issued from Lowis's Country Wear in Sedbergh, *see above.*

Except for short stretches on both banks at Low Hawgarth and Lowridding, the right bank near Straight Bridge, both banks between New and Millthrop Bridges, the left bank at the Rawthey/Dee junction, the left bank at Holme Farm and both banks below Middleton Bridge to the Lune, virtually all the fishing on 8 miles of the River Rawthey is controlled by the Sedbergh and District AA who issue visitor's tickets from Lowis's Country Wear in Sedbergh. *See above.* A detailed fishing map is exhibited in the library shelter, Main Street, Sedbergh. Similar in character to the Clough, the Rawthey resembles the streamy waters of North Wales and the Lake District. It's a picturesque river, pleasant to fish for anyone who takes the trouble to use traditional wet or dry flies in the water run-offs following the small waterfalls.

A short stretch of about a quarter of a mile near Sedbergh belongs to the Prince Albert AS for members only.

Further downstream, close to the Rawthey's junction with the Lune, excellent fishing can be had for a small fee.

Day tickets, £2.00, £1.50 for children, from Holme Farm (Tel: 015396 20654).

This is a fine stretch of the River Rawthey extending over about one mile, except for a small section held by the Sedbergh and District AA, of the left bank, following a long bend across a meadow from the farm. Holme Farm is an 'Open Farm', a local tourist attraction which offers farm tours, a Roman road and stone age remains, but none of this activity interferes with the fishing. To find Holme Farm from Sedbergh take the A684 road towards Kendal and on the outskirts of Sedbergh branch left onto the A683 towards Kirkby Lonsdale. After about ³/₄ of a mile, just over Rawthey Bridge, turn sharp left onto a signposted single track road to the farm. After a further 2 miles the farm is directly in front of you.

On the right bank, fishing on the last 100 yards of the Rawthey below the A683 road bridge and extending for about 150 yards on the left bank of the River Lune belongs to the Bowland Game Fishing Association. This is a great fishery regularly producing good brown, sea trout and the occasional salmon. Fishing for brown trout is by fly only; spring olives take their fair share of fish. A Peter Ross is good for the sea trout. Fly fishing, spinning and worm are permitted for the migratory fish but no ledgering. Members only.

The Prince Albert AS has a members only stretch of approximately ¹/₂ mile of the River Lune at Killington near Sedbergh.

Kirkby Lonsdale (OS97:614785)
The Lune around Kirkby Lonsdale has long been known for the fine fish it consistently delivers. Unfortunately, in common with most of England's salmon rivers, the fishing has declined from what it used to be. However, it is still some of the best in the country. Late salmon can be big. Twenty pounders were once landed here, but now a 10 pounder is a good fish. The sea trout reach 10lb and the browns are around 1¹/₂lb.

Kirkby Lonsdale Angling Association controls the fishing on both banks for about 4 miles of the Lune extending upstream and down from Devil's Bridge. Fishing is by fly only except when the river reaches a certain height, when spinning is permitted. There is no fishing in Barbon Beck.
Five-day (Monday to Friday) permits £50.00 for people staying locally only (not anyone camping or caravaning). No visitor's permits in October. Obtainable from the tourist information centre,

24 Main Street, LA6 2EA (Tel: 015242 71437). For non-resident season tickets *see Angling Clubs section.*

Both the Lancashire and District Angling Association and the Lancashire FFA have waters below the town. Members only.

Further downstream at Whittington, a fine stretch of fishing on the right bank near the village is owned by Mr H.G. Mackereth, Whittington Farm, Whittington (Tel: 01524271286 or 0152472375). This is a really good stretch of typical Lune water, worth anyone's attention.

Day tickets £5.00, from the farm in the centre of the village.

Claughton (OS97:563665)

From Whittington all the way to Lancaster, the Lune flows through relatively flat meadowland and settles into its characteristic pattern. Long glides between sand and single banks are punctuated with sweeping bends producing superb holding pools. This much sought after water is classic salmon and sea trout fishing and when the water level is right there is no better game fishing in England. It's a late river. The salmon run through this stretch from late summer onwards. Many people would argue that the only way to catch them is on a fly, but this water lends itself to spinning. And, where they are permitted, a nice juicy prawn or lob-worm swept around one of the deep bends will take good fish. You may also pick up one of the big browns that are known to inhabit the river here.

See also Pine Lake and Redwell Carp & Coarse Lakes.

The Southport Fly Fishers have an excellent stretch of about ³/₄ mile, on the left bank, at Priory Farm downstream to the junction with the River Wenning. Members only. No day tickets.

Caton (OS97:531647)

From Wenning Foot, where the River Wenning joins the Lune, the Lancaster and District Angling Association controls the fishing on both banks of about 5 miles of the Lune downstream through Claughton to Crook 'O' Lune Bridge at Caton. This fine fishery is divided into three beats: **Upper Beat**, Claughton and Hornby; **Middle Beat**, Aughton and Swarthdale; **Bottom Beat**, Caton. Club members belong to one beat and fish approximately a third of the water. Visitors tickets are allowed on the bottom beat, the Caton water.

Day tickets from February to June 30th £10.00, from July 1st to August 31st £18.00 and September 1st to October 31st £20.00. From Mrs Curwen, Greenup Cottage, Hornby Road, Caton (Tel: 01524 770078). Day tickets only available Monday to Friday. Only 12 issued per day. Providing payment is submitted with the booking, tickets may be booked up to one week in advance.

This brilliant stretch of the Lune is ideal, depending upon water conditions, for fly, spinning or bait fishing. Fly fishing only is permitted if the river drops below $1^1/2$ feet at the marker, otherwise fly fishing, spinning and worming is allowed. Worm fishing during October is only permitted if the river reaches 3 feet or above on the marker. Of course, no maggots or grubs are permitted at any time. As can be seen from the ticket price, the salmon fishing is better later in the season. The fish caught along this stretch are usually fresh from the sea, silver and in prime condition. In October, all hen fish must be returned carefully to the water irrespective of their condition or method of capture. Devon minnows, spoons and Flying Condoms and take their share of the salmon. When the conditions are right for fly fishing, almost any of the tried and tested Scottish flies will take fish. But this is not just a salmon stretch, it is an excellent sea trout and brown trout water.

The Prince Albert Angling Society has a short stretch of the right bank downstream from the old railway bridge at Caton. Members only.
See also Bank House Fly Fishery.

Halton (OS97:505647)
Season permits are occasionally available to fish for game and coarse fish on a $1^1/4$ mile stretch, both banks, of the Lune, near Halton. As the water is not suitable for fly fishing, game anglers spin the stretch or use worm or shrimp. Limited boat permits are also available, at a small additional charge. Coarse and brown trout permits allow fishing for some of the big browns that live in the river here as well as the specimen bream. This water holds the biggest river dwelling bream in the north-west.

Season Permits are £55.00 plus a £25.00 joining fee for salmon and £25.00 for trout from The Angling Secretary, Lansil Sports & Social Club, Caton Road, Lancaster LA1 3PE. Enclose a stamped addressed envelope.

Some of the best salmon, sea trout, brown trout and coarse fishing on the lower river is accessible on permits issued by the Environment Agency. There are two beats: the Top Beat is at the Crook 'O' Lune and the Lower Beat is above the road bridge in Halton.

Top Beat: On the left bank, fishing begins at Escow Beck and extends downstream for approximately $^3/4$ mile to a point 50 yards above Forge Weir and also on the right bank, about $^1/4$ mile from just below Riverside Cottage downstream to Halton Green Beck.

Day tickets (0800 to 2000 hrs): salmon (to July 31st) £8.00, salmon (from August 1st) £15.00; brown trout £4.00 and coarse fish £4.00.
Night sea trout tickets (2000 to 0400 hrs) £7.50.

Lower Beat: On the left bank, fishing begins at a point about 50 yards below Forge Weir and runs downstream to Denny Beck and also on the right bank from Lower Halton Weir down to a point 20 yards below Old Halton Toll Bridge.

Day tickets (0800 to 2000 hrs): salmon (to July 31st) £8.00, salmon (from August 31st) £12.50. Brown trout (March 15th to May 31st) £4.00. Tickets from either Mr Shallis, Halton Newsagents, 9 St Wilfred's Park, Halton (Tel: 01524 811507) or Mrs Curwen, Greenup Cottage, Hornby Road, Caton (Tel: 01524 770078). Greenup Cottage is situated on the north side of the A683 at Caton. Permit prices do not include the EA rod licence which must be purchased separately from licence agents. Depending upon the type of permit bought the generous bag limits are 2 salmon, 6 sea trout and 6 brown trout. Fishing for sea and brown trout is by fly and worm only. No fishing with shrimp or prawn before 1400 hrs.

Lancaster (OS97:475625)
A part tidal stretch of approximately $1^1/2$ miles through Lancaster, called the Skerton Fishery, is controlled by the Environment Agency who issue day tickets. Despite the fact that this water is tidal, the brackish water runs upstream to Skerton Weir. It is an excellent stretch for game fishing. Naturally all the Lune's migratory fish have to run through this stretch and negotiate the fish pass at

Skerton Weir before heading upstream, but it is also a good brown trout and coarse fishing water.

There is very easy access to most of this fishery which extends through the town. The fishing is on both banks from Howgill Beck downstream for approximately 2 miles, to Scale Ford below Carlisle Bridge. Tickets for this fishery include the right to fish in Skerton Weir Pool. This is the first obstruction that salmon meet when coming off the sea. There is a large salmon pass which, in autumn, is very busy with migratory fish. Special rules apply to fishing in the pool. No fishing is permitted between the weir drop and the top of the island as marked by black and white marker posts. Fly fishing only is allowed between the island and river banks.

Day tickets: The fishery is effectively divided into three groups:

Howgill Beck to Scale Ford, both banks. (0800 to 2000 hrs) salmon, sea trout and brown trout. £8.00 (to July 31st) then £12.50.

Howgill Beck to Scale Ford, both banks. (2000 to 0400 hrs) sea trout and brown trout. £7.50.

Howgill Beck to Skerton Weir, both banks. Freshwater fish and eels. £4.00.

All tickets from Mr Shallis, Halton Newsagents, 9 Wilfred's Park, Halton (Tel: 01524 811507). Ticket prices do not include the EA rod licence, which must be purchased from a licence agent before fishing. Depending upon the ticket bought, the generous bag limits are 2 salmon, 6 sea trout and 6 brown trout.

See also the Lancaster Canal.

NEWLANDS BECK

A tiny beck rising in the Derwent Fells and flowing north and then into Bassenthwaite Lake. It is badly overgrown in its upper reaches. The best fishing is on the 'canalised' lower 2 miles below Braithwaite Bridge near Keswick. There are lots of small brown trout and a few perch. Access from the public footpaths only both upstream and down from Braithwaite Bridge.

Fishing is free for holder of an Environment Agency rod licence.

TROUT BECK

About 5 miles long this tiny beck starts life in the high fells near High Street and Kentmere Common and flows south through a compact valley before emptying into Windermere Lake at Calgarth Hall. As its name suggests, it holds a good head of native brown trout which scare easily. It is a fine fishery but suffers from lack of water in the summer. Fly fishing is about the only chance of taking a fish. Fish fine and be very careful not to cast a shadow on the water.

Troutbeck (OS90:409033)
The Windermere, Ambleside and District Angling Association has fishing on about 2 miles of the left bank near Long Green. Members only.

The remainder of the beck is private and is hardly ever fished.
See also Borrans Reservoir, Dubbs Reservoir and Holehird Tarn.

RIVER WAMPOOL
A collection of virtually dry streams, meandering across the flat Northwest Cumbria plane, finally come together, near Biglands, to produce the tiny River Wampool. Hardly worthy of the title 'river,' the Wampool flows for 2 crooked miles to Powhill where it becomes tidal. It then flows for an even more crooked 6 miles to the Moricambe Estuary. A few trout inhabit the area around Wampool and the odd sea trout comes into the lower reaches, but the fishing is generally poor.
Fishing is mainly free but ask permission for access to the land. An Environment Agency rod licence is required.

RIVER WAVER
A small streamy river, made up of dozens of almost dry becks, gently flowing from near Wigton to the Moricambe Estuary near Abbeytown. Not much more than a trickle in places, the Waver is fairly uninteresting. It holds some smallish native brown trout and a few sea trout and herling manage to struggle a short way upstream in the late season.
Mostly the fishing is free, but ask permission for access to the farmland. An Environment Agency rod licence is required.

Abbeytown (OS85:174508)
The local Abbeytown Angling Society has access to about 2 miles of fishing on both banks near the town for members only.

RIVER WINSTER

Compared with the dramatic scenery at the centre of the Lake District, South Lakeland is more sedate, with rich farmland and gently rolling hills reminiscent of the south of England. Indeed the upper reaches of the River Winster are similar to the trout rivers of the south. Narrow banks constrict gently flowing water that occasionally speeds up and tumbles over a pebbly bottom as it winds its way southward past grazing sheep and cattle. It then fills the tiny Helton Tarn, before setting off even more sedately towards Morecambe Bay. To assist water control, in its very bottom reaches, below Lindale, the Winster has been canalised. There is very little flow in this section except when there are dangerously high tides forecast and the sluice gate is opened. The water backs up along this length and can rise by several feet in a very short space of time.

Most of the fishing is private except for a short stretch near to where the river flows into Morecambe Bay.

Witherslack (OS97:433839)
A short stretch of fishing on both banks above the A590 is controlled by the Wigan and District Angling Association, for members only.

Meathop (OS97:425795)
About 600 yards of the right bank downstream to the tidal sluice is controlled by the Kendal and District Angling Club. It is easy to find. From the A590 Kendal to Barrow road at Lindale roundabout, turn left. Take the first left towards Meathop village and then the next right. Follow the road until it crosses the river at the tidal sluice.

This is a canalised stretch of water which Norfolk anglers will recognise as a 'drain'. It's not as big, as deep (about 4 feet) or as productive as some in Norfolk, but the fishing is good. Bream, dace, eels, perch, roach, rudd and tench are all resident in good numbers, so expect some fairly heavy mixed bags. Extra care is needed when fishing here because the river level varies with the tide. At high tide the estuary sluice gate closes and the river water backs up, even appearing to flow upstream! It's a popular venue with pole anglers who, using maggots and groundbait, make short work of the shoals of roach and rudd. Some of the bream are fairly heavy at 4lb, if you can find them. An interesting and frustrating time is when the mullet come into the water. They lazily swim along taking everything

South Lakeland's 'Fenland drain', the River Winster near Grange-over-Sands

thrown into the water, except when it's on a hook that is! On the right day, with patience, you may tempt them with a bread crust, but don't count on it. The closed season is March 15th to June 15th inclusive.

Day ticket £3.00, senior citizens and juniors £2.00. **Weekly ticket** £8.00, senior citizens and juniors £4.00. Obtainable from the Post Office at Witherslack (Tel: 015395 52221), The Fishing Hut, Grange-over-Sands (Tel: 015395 32854), Carlsons Fishing Tackle, Kendal (Tel: 01539 724867) and Go Fishing in Bowness-on-Windermere (Tel: 015394 47086).

Still Waters

This section lists 101 still water fisheries ranging in size from the vast lakes of Central Lakeland down to the tiny farm waters of the Eden Valley. Somewhere in this list you should find just the water and the fish you're looking for. There are brown and rainbow trout, char, schelley and virtually every species of coarse fish swimming in remote tarns, spectacular lakes, reservoirs, ex gravel pits and purpose built fisheries right across the area. There are fisheries with a single lake, multiple lakes, shallow lakes, deep lakes, clear water and peaty water. In fact there is almost any combination that takes your fancy.

Where the fishery is a day ticket water, comprehensive details have been included, not only of the ticket prices, but also the ease of access, the quality of the banks, fishery facilities and, where possible, full information on the baits or flies that normally bring success. If the still water is fished as a members only fishery, a description is included to help readers who anticipate joining the appropriate fishing club to get access to the venue. Fishing is not permitted on a few of the listed waters. They have been included because they exist and in order to save you wasting time finding out that you can't fish them anyway.

All the waters are listed alphabetically and the location of all the day ticket fisheries is included on the fishing maps.

Coarse Fishing Still Waters

Banks Pond, Kendal.	Day tickets
Bassenthwaite Lake.	Day tickets
Beacon Tarn, Coniston.	Free
Bigland Hall Tarn, Newby Bridge.	Day tickets
Blea Tarn, Langdale.	Free
Blea Water, Haweswater.	Free
Blelham Tarn, Hawkshead.	Day tickets
Borwick Lake, Carnforth.	Day tickets
Brayton Park Lake, Aspatria.	Day tickets
Brotherswater.	Free
Burnmoor Tarn, Boot.	Free

Buttermere.	Day tickets
Cleabarrow Tarn, Windermere.	Day tickets
Coniston Water.	Day tickets
Crofton Lake, Carlisle.	Season tickets
Crossfield Farm Fishery, Kirkoswald.	Day tickets
Crummock Water.	Day tickets
Derwentwater.	Day tickets
Easdale Tarn, Grasmere.	Free
East View Fishery, Carlisle.	Day tickets
Ellerbeck Coarse Fishery, Cockermouth.	Day tickets
Gatebeck Reservoir, Oxenholme.	Day tickets
Grasmere Lake.	Day tickets
Hallmore Fishery, Hale.	Day tickets
High Dam, Finsthwaite.	Free
High Stand Lakes, Cotehill.	Day tickets
Holehird Tarn, Windermere.	Day tickets
Killington Reservoir, Oxenholme.	Day tickets
Littledale Hall Coarse Fishery, Caton.	Day tickets
Longtown West Pond, Longtown.	Day tickets
Lonsdale Park Lakes, Cumwhinton.	Day tickets
Loughrigg Tarn, Skelwith Bridge.	Day tickets
Loweswater.	Day tickets
Mecklin Tarn, Gosforth.	Day tickets
Mill Beck Fishery, Barrow.	Day tickets
Mockerkin Tarn, Cockermouth.	Day tickets
Oakbank Lakes Country Park, Longtown.	Day tickets
Pine Lake, Carnforth.	Day tickets
Ratherheath Tarn, Kendal.	Day tickets
Redwell Carp & Coarse Lake, Carnforth.	Day tickets
Roanhead Lakes, Barrow-in-Furness.	Day tickets
Rydal Water.	Day tickets
Silver Tarn, Sellafield.	Free
Skelsmergh Tarn, Kendal.	Free
Small Water Tarn, Haweswater.	Free
Talkin' Tarn Country Park, Brampton.	Day tickets
Tarnside Caravan Park Lake, Sellafield.	Day tickets
Thirlmere.	Free
Ullswater.	Free
Urswick Tarn, Ulverston.	Day tickets

Whins Pond Coarse Fishery, Penrith.	Day tickets
Windermere.	Free
Witherslack Hall Tarn, Witherslack.	Day tickets

Trout Fishing Still Waters

Bank House Fly Fishery, Caton.	Day tickets
Bassenthwaite Lake.	Day tickets
Baystone Bank Reservoir, Millom.	Day tickets
Beacon Tarn, Coniston.	Free
Bessy Beck Lakes, Newbiggin-on-Lune.	Day tickets
Bigland Hall Trout Fishery, Newby Bridge.	Day tickets
Blea Tarn, Langdale.	Free
Blea Tarn, Watendlath.	Free
Blea Water, Haweswater.	Free
Blelham Tarn, Hawkshead.	Day tickets
Blencarn Lake, Penrith.	Day tickets
Brotherswater.	Free
Burnmoor Tarn, Boot.	Free
Buttermere.	Day tickets
Codale Tarn, Grasmere.	Free
Cogra Moss Fishery, Lamplugh.	Day tickets
Coniston Water.	Free
Crummock Water.	Day tickets
Derwentwater.	Day tickets
Devoke Water, Eskdale.	Day tickets
Drunken Duck Tarn, Hawkshead.	Day tickets
Dubbs Tarn, Windermere.	Day tickets
Easdale Tarn, Grasmere.	Free
Eden Valley Trout Lake, Little Musgrave.	Day tickets
Ennerdale Water.	Day tickets
Esthwaite Water.	Day tickets
Fisher Tarn, Kendal.	Day tickets
Ghyll Head Reservoir, Windermere.	Day tickets
Gilcrux Springs Fishery, Gilcrux.	Day tickets
Grasmere.	Day tickets
Grisdale Tarn, Grasmere.	Free
Harlock Reservoir, Barrow-in-Furness.	Day tickets
Haweswater Reservoir.	Free
Hayeswater Reservoir, Patterdale.	Day tickets

High Arnside Tarn, Hawkshead.	Day tickets
High Newton Reservoir, Newby Bridge.	Day tickets
Kentmere Fishery, Kentmere.	Day tickets
Killington Reservoir, Oxenholme.	Day tickets
Knott End Farm, Ravenglass.	Day tickets
Levenswater, Coniston.	Free
Longlands Lake, Cleator Moor.	Day tickets
Lough Trout Fishery, Thurstonfield.	Day tickets
Loweswater.	Day tickets
Meadley Reservoir, Cleator Moor.	Day tickets
Mecklin Tarn, Gosforth.	Day tickets
Moss Eccles Tarn, Near Sawrey.	Day tickets
New Mills Trout Fishery, Brampton.	Day tickets
Oakbank Lakes Country Park, Longtown.	Day tickets
Overwater Fishery, Uldale.	Day tickets
Pennington Reservoir, Barrow-in-Furness.	Day tickets
Pinfold Lake, Raisbeck.	Day tickets
Poaka Beck Reservoir, Barrow-in-Furness.	Day tickets
Red Tarn, Helvellyn.	Free
Roanhead Lakes, Barrow-in-Furness.	Day tickets
Roosecote Reservoir, Barrow-in-Furness.	Day tickets
Rydal Water.	Day tickets
School Knott Tarn, Windermere.	Day tickets
Small Water Tarn, Haweswater.	Free
Sockbridge Mill Trout Farm, Penrith.	Day tickets
Thirlmere.	Free
Ullswater.	Free
Watendlath Trout Fishery, Watendlath.	Day tickets
Whins Trout Fishery, Penrith.	Day tickets
Windermere.	Free
Wych Elm Fishery, Carnforth.	Day tickets
Yew Tree Tarn, Coniston.	Day tickets

ABBOTS MOSS LAKE

Location (OS86:510426)

About 10 miles north-east of Penrith in Eastern Cumbria. From
Penrith take the A6 north. In about 8 miles, turn right onto a small
road signposted Lazonby and, after another mile, turn left. After a
further 1¹/₂ miles, Abbots Moss Lake is on the righthand side.

Fishery Controller
Not known.
Water and Stock
This 3 acre attractive lake was once a rainbow trout fishery, but now it is a nature reserve. No fishing.
Ticket Prices
None.

ALCOCK TARN

Location (OS90:348079)
Alcock Tarn is situated high in the fells, about 1¹/₂ miles east of Grasmere. To find it, take the public footpath via Hollens Farm up Greenhead Gill.
Fishery Controller
Lake District National Park Authority.
Water and Stock
A tiny hill tarn holding small brown trout.
Ticket Prices
Free fishing for holders of an Environment Agency rod licence.
Opening Times
April 1st to September 30th from dawn to dusk.
Description
A delightful, shallow, upland tarn set in the hills and holding a good stock of mostly small, very wild, brown trout. The tarn is very remote so you'll need to be energetic to get to it. If you intend to fish it, travel light and, as it is exposed to the vagaries of the weather, which in Lakeland can close in very quickly, be prepared. Although fly fishing and spinning are allowed, the best bait is worm. On the right day, expect to catch a lot of trout, but they will be small.
Fishery Rules
None.
Facilities on Site
None.

BANK HOUSE FLY FISHERY

Location (OS97:528648)
Alongside the River Lune at Caton. From Lancaster, take the A683 to Caton. On the outskirts of the village, turn left at the fishery sign. The lake is on the right in about 100 yards. Park on the left.

Fishery Controller

Jan Dobson, Bank House Fly Fishery, Low Mill, Lancaster Road, Caton, Lancs (Tel: 01524 770412).

Water and Stock

A 2 acre pond well stocked with brown and triploid rainbow trout averaging about 2lb.

Ticket Prices

Day £20.00 for 4 fish, half day £12.50 for 2 fish and junior £7.00 for 1 fish. Full day sporting ticket £12.50 and half day £8.00. Season tickets: full day (26 visits) £480.00, half day £293.00.

Opening Times

All year from dawn to dusk.

Description

Something of an unusual water, this dam is the only remaining one of four which once supplied water to the Mills of Caton. Now it has been thoughtfully landscaped with several islands and peninsulas providing interesting areas to fish and provide some seclusion. Solid paths make access to the entire water easy and casting jetties open up most of the water so distance casting is not necessary. Disabled anglers have priority access to some of the jetties. Bank House is run very much on a put-and-take basis with the water being stocked regularly according to how many fish are taken. The policy aims to maintain a generous stock of about 150 fish per acre. They average 2lb with some larger browns and rainbows up to about 6lb. It is not a very deep water, dropping to 10 feet in front of the anglers cabin, so there is no need for fast sinking lines. In the spring when the fish are on the bottom, use a sink tip and retrieve a Black Pennell, or similar, close to the lake bed. When the fish are moving just below the surface, Gold Ribbed Hares Ears and Damsel nymphs are a good bet. In the heat of the day, buzzers can't be beaten. Try them in black or olive or the new gold head patterns.

Fishery Rules

Single hooks only, size 10 or smaller. No long shank hooks. No lures. Catch and release is permitted after limit taken.

Facilities on Site

Car park. Pine fishing lodge with access for wheelchairs. Toilet. Kitchen facilities. Fishing flies and hire of equipment. Tuition.

BANKS POND

Location (OS97:576868)

From Kendal, take the A65(T) road towards Endmoor. Turn left onto the B6254 to Oxenholme and continue through the village. Go through Old Hutton and under the M6. In about 1$^{1}/_{2}$ miles, facing the entrance to Crosslands Farm, turn left, go through the metal five-bar gate and park about 50 yards up the track. The pond is about 200 yards up the hill on the left.

Fishery Controller

Kendal and District Angling Club. *See Angling Clubs section.*

Water and Stock

A tiny pond holding some good bream, carp, chub, perch, roach and tench and a few gudgeon.

Ticket Prices

Day ticket £3.00, senior citizens and juniors £2.00. Weekly ticket £8.00, senior citizens and juniors £4.00. From Carlsons Fishing Tackle in Kendal (Tel: 01539 724867), Go Fishing in Bowness-on-Windermere (Tel: 01539447086), Witherslack Post Office (Tel: 015395 52221) and The Fishing Hut in Grange-over-Sands (Tel: 015395 32854).

Opening Times

All year from dawn to dusk.

Description

A small, fairly shallow, man-made pond, situated in pleasant countryside. It's not very old, around 15 years, but it has been landscaped and now looks completely natural. There are 18 pegs and rarely ever more than a couple of anglers so there is plenty of room to move and find the fish. Most anglers aim for the deeper water, around 6 feet, near the island where the better carp and tench are taken. There are carp to 16lb but the average is nearer 5lb. Tench run to about 4lb, the bream to about 7lb and they are prolific. Best baits are luncheon meat, trout pellets or maggots usually float fished right up against the island fringe. It's a favourite water with pole anglers who on a good day have some good bags of roach, perch and gudgeon with the occasional big bream making the day interesting. It is somewhat exposed, so try and visit on a day when there is little wind. There is no suitable access for disabled anglers.

Fishery Rules

Large bream and carp are not to be kept in nets. Tickets must be

purchased before going to the water.
Facilities on Site
None.

BASSENTHWAITE LAKE

Location (OS90:215295)
Alongside the A66 trunk road between Keswick and Cockermouth.
Fishery Controller
Fishery Manager, Leconfield Estates Company, Cockermouth, Cumbria.
Water and Stock
At over 4 miles long and $^1/_2$ mile wide, Bassenthwaite is huge. It holds big perch, pike, eels, roach and the rare vendace. There are also brown trout and the very occasional salmon.
Ticket Prices
Season tickets £38.00, weekly tickets £9.00 and day tickets £2.50. Half price for senior citizens, the disabled and the unemployed. Free fishing for the under 16s. Day ticket plus launching of own boat £4.50. Nearest ticket sales are at the Swan Hotel, Thornthwaite (Tel: 017687 78256), Mr & Mrs Pepper, Beckstones Farm, Thornthwaite and Mrs Cheesbrough, Bassenthwaite. Tickets also from Field & Stream, Keswick (Tel: 017687 74396), Grahams Guns and Sports, Workington (Tel: 01900 605093), the Compleat Angler, Whitehaven (Tel: 01946 695322), Geoff Wilson, Carlisle (Tel: 01228 531542), Cockermouth tourist information centre (Tel: 01900 822634) and Keswick tourist information centre (Tel: 017687 72645).
Opening Times
Salmon: February 1st to October 31st. Trout: March 15th to September 30th. Coarse fish: open all year. No night fishing.
Description
Bassenthwaite is the fourth largest lake in the National Park and one of the area's legendary pike fisheries. Access is very easy to the west and north banks, all of which can be fished on a day ticket, but most of the east bank belongs to farms and is private land. Very big fish lurk in the depths which can be over 70 feet, but the lake generally much shallower, especially at the southern end and in the many bays. Pike over 20lb are common although they average about half that. Almost all of the good fish fall to dead sprat or herring fished well out, although it is possible to tempt a big scavenging fish with

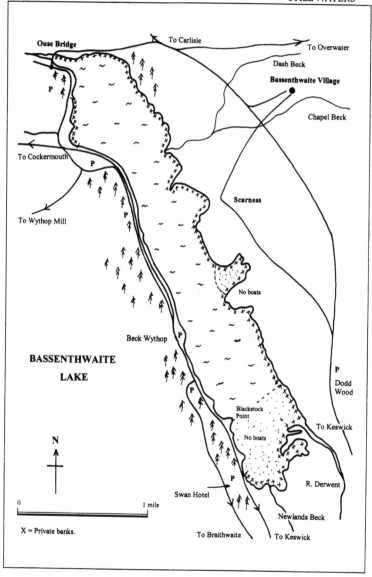

a flashy spoon or spinner pulled through the reedy margins. Many fishermen come here just for the perch. They can be over 2$^{1/2}$lb, substantial for this hard fighting predator, but they are more likely to be nearer 1$^{1/2}$lb. They also move in large shoals - interest one, and you're sure to have a good day. A ledgered lobworm will usually attract the bigger fish.

On the right day, the trout fishing can be brilliant. Some of the native browns run large and they live in the deeper water so spinning from a boat is the best method, but not before the coarse season opens. It's a fly fishing only water until June 16th. Bassenthwaite is not an easy lake to fish with a fly. Once again you'll need to go deep for the bigger fish. Big black and white marabou lures, fished on a lead-cored line, will take some of the better browns. You may also get a surprise at Bassenthwaite. A rare species, the vendace, more commonly found in the lakes of north-west Europe, seems to like it here. Looking a bit like a cross between a dace and a herring, it grows to about 12 inches in length. It's also very rare and should be returned to the water with extreme care if caught. Derwentwater is the only other lake in the area where the vendace has found a home.

Own boats can be launched from the slipway near where the A66(T) crosses the road to Dubwath, close to the yacht club. Bassenthwaite is a popular sailing water but yachts usually stay well out in the lake and rarely interfere with the fishing.

Fishery Rules
Fly fishing only for trout until the opening of the coarse season on June 16th.

Facilities on Site
Car parking at various points along the A66 and at Hursthole Point. The most convenient is a lay-by alongside the lake where the road splits into a dual carriageway.

BAYSTONE BANK RESERVOIR
Location (OS96:172860)
Situated about 8 miles north of Millom, close to Hallthwaites village on the A595. Take the A595 west from Hallthwaites. In about $^{1/2}$ mile turn right at a signpost indicating Whirlpippin Farm and Baystone Bank Farm. Drive up the track to the indicated car parking area. The reservoir is a further $^{1/4}$ mile up the track.

Fishery Controller
Millom and District Angling Association on behalf of North West Water. *See Angling Clubs section.*

Water and Stock
A small sheltered reservoir holding a good head of rainbow trout plus a few native browns.

Ticket Prices
Day ticket £15.00 for 3 fish, weekly ticket £40.00 only from the Hon. Secretary. Ticket numbers are strictly limited on a daily basis.

Opening Times
Dawn to dusk during the trout fishing season.

Description
This little known gem is tucked away in a narrow valley between Gray Stones Fell and Knott Hill in south-western Cumbria. It's a small man-made reservoir with a deep dam wall at the southern end and a wooded area to the north. It is very deep and the rocky shores are steep so great care must be taken when clambering around the eastern side in the shadow of Baystone Bank. Because it's well protected from the worst of the weather, winds are not a major problem. Also the water warms up quickly when in direct sunlight, so the fish tend to be free risers. The fishing day is equally divided into two sessions: dawn to 1400 hrs and from 1400 hrs until dusk. Only 8 rods are permitted in each session so there is virtually unlimited bank space. Inevitably the wall attracts anglers as does the wooded area at the top where a small beck enters. Baystone Bank is stocked with rainbow trout that thrive in the cool clear water. They will quite happily take a lure fished on a sinking line. In the early season try a Viva or similar along the dam wall. When retrieved very slowly, a Viva will often attract a big fish. As the water warms up and the rainbows start to feed on sub-surface insects buzzers and gold-heads are very good. During the height of summer when there is a slight breeze it's always worth trying a big surface fly, like a Walker Wake Fly, in the ripple. Expect a savage take, because a fish will come from the depths at great speed to take such an offering. Use a strong leader. The use of barbless hooks is encouraged. Anyone using them may return fish after the limit is taken. Anyone not using barbless hooks must cease fishing after three fish are caught.

Fishery Rules

Fly fishing only. Park only in the indicated car park. No cars are allowed near the reservoir.

Facilities on site

Car park and the dramatic scenery.

BEACON TARN

Location (OS97:274900)

Beacon Tarn is to the west of Coniston Water. Take the A5084 from Torver southwards towards Penny Bridge. In approximately 5 miles, after passing the southern end of Coniston Water, at Water Yeat, turn right. Follow the road to Greenholme Farm. Park carefully and then follow the public footpath north-westwards to the tarn a distance of about 1 mile.

Fishery Controller

Lake District National Park Authority.

Water and Stock

An 11 acre upland tarn holding small brown trout, perch and pike.

Ticket Prices

Free fishing for holders of an Environment Agency rod licence.

Opening Times

April 1st to September 30th from dawn to dusk.

Description

A delightful, shallow, upland tarn with a good stock of mostly small, very wild, brown trout. The tarn is very remote so you'll need to be energetic to get to it. It's also very exposed to the vagaries of the weather, which in Lakeland can close in very quickly. Be prepared. Worm, fly or spinning are the best methods for the both the trout and perch. On the right day, expect to catch a lot of them. There have been no reported catches of char recently although it's likely that this scarce fish still resides in the tarn.

Fishery Rules

None.

Facilities on Site

None.

BESSY BECK TROUT LAKES

Location (OS91:703052)

At Newbiggin-on-Lune. The fishery is best approached from the M6. Leave at junction 38 and take the A685 towards Kirkby Stephen.

Bessy Beck Trout Lakes *in the Lune Valley offer good trout fishing*

In approximately 6 miles, on the outskirts of Newbiggin-on-Lune, turn right into the fishery.

Fishery Controller
Mr Simon Ballantyne, Bessy Beck Trout Farm, Newbiggin-on-Lune, Cumbria CA17 4LY (Tel: 01539 623303).

Water and Stock
Three lakes of varying sizes up to $1^{1}/_{2}$ acres and well stocked with trout.

Ticket Prices
Rainbow Lake: Day £12.00 for 3 fish; four hour ticket £5.00 for 1 fish. Further fish can be purchased at £1.50 per lb. Brown Lake: Day £17.00 for 3 fish; four hour ticket £5.00 for 3 fish. Further fish at £3.25 per lb. Small Rainbow Lake: Day £5.00; six hour ticket £1.50. Pay for all fish caught. No catch and release.

Opening Times
All year, 0800 to 2000 hrs or sunset.

Description
Several streams, from the Howgill Fells, bring clear, clean water to Bessy Beck Fishery before continuing their flow into the upper

reaches of the tiny River Lune. The same water also brings with it the insect life needed to maintain the high level of stock in the three lakes on site. Rainbow Lake, as you would expect, holds only rainbow trout. They average about 1½lb but there are bigger fish up to 6lb. Brown Lake holds brown trout up to about 5lb. The smallest lake is an any method water holding both browns and rainbows. All the lakes have been sensibly constructed, with plenty of open space and raised banks making back-casting very easy. Access throughout is good and disabled anglers should have no difficulty getting at the fish in both the Rainbow Lake and the any method lake. This is not a fishery for lead cored lines. Depth of the lakes varies between 7 feet and 10 feet so it's best to use a floating line with a sinking leader. Fishing on the surface is usually productive and there's often a good evening rise. In the early season though, try near the bottom. Any of the small lures in black, such as Viva or Black Marabou take fish. On the warmer days, try near the surface. Buzzers in orange, olive or black, Hares Ear or any of the gold heads will also take fish. When the wind becomes a problem, move to get it at your back and try a big bushy fly on the surface. Daddy Long Legs are good in season, as are the brown sedges.

Fishery Rules

Fly fishing only. No bigger than size 10 hook. Catch and release is not permitted. Fishing must stop when limit is reached. Extra tickets may be purchased.

Facilities on Site

Car park. Toilet. Fishing lodge. Refreshments.

BIGLAND HALL TROUT FISHERY

Location (OS97:355830)

Take the A590(T) from Newby Bridge at the base of Lake Windermere and head for Barrow-in-Furness. In about 2 miles, at Backbarrow, turn left. Go through the village and continue through Brow Edge. About 500 yards further on turn left again. The entrance to the trout fishery is about 1 mile further, on the left.

Fishery Controller

Tony Myers, Bigland Hall Estates, Backbarrow, Newby Bridge, Cumbria LA12 8PB (Tel: 015395 31728 or 01229 812001 or mobile 0585 732444).

Water and Stock

*Fishing a quiet corner of **Bigland Hall Trout Fishery***

One 16 acre lake well stocked with rainbows averaging about 2lb with some fish reaching 16lb.

Ticket Prices

Day ticket £15.00 for 4 fish; any six hours £10.00 for 2 fish; sporting ticket £8.50. Rod hire £8.50 per day and instruction £10.00 per hour. Fun fishing ticket, including rod hire and bait, £4.00. Tickets on site from the fishing lodge.

Opening Times

All year from 0900 hrs until sunset. Early morning fishing, by prior arrangement.

Description

Bigland trout lake is a beautiful part natural water that has been developed into an interesting fishery. There are several islands, three of which are accessible for fishing, rocky outcrops and a long peninsula jutting into the water near the fishing lodge. The crystal clear water is on average 6 feet deep but it drops to nearly 18 feet near the dam wall. Good well-worn rocky paths and open banks allow access to the whole water but it would be difficult for disabled anglers. Favourite spots are between the islands and, in the deeper water, near the dam. Bigland is stocked weekly with quality rainbows from about 1¹/₂lb into double figures and they are free rises. Also, because the water is so clear, fish can often be seen cruising in the shallower margins and near the rocky islands. When you see them, try a weighted tadpole imitation and drop it right in front of a cruising trout. In the early season, though, when the water is cold, a Viva or similar retrieved slowly close to the bottom will bring results. When it warms up a bit, buzzers, nymphs, shrimps and corixa all take lots of fish. Rod averages of five to six fish are common with many of the regulars landing as many as twenty in one session! In the late summer, sedges do well as do Daddy Long Legs. Try one when there is a ripple on the water. Grease the fly well and cast it across the wind. Give it a tweek every so often and wait. When a take comes it will be violent.

There's also a small beginner's pond called Lomonds Loch, aimed at newcomers to the sport. It's well stocked with 2lb trout, easily accessible and tackle and bait are included in the price. A great place to catch a first trout.

Fishery Rules

Fly only. Barbless hooks only. No flashabou or waggies. Bank fishing only. Limited to 20 anglers at any one time.

Facilities on Site

Car park. Anglers' lodge. Riding. Clay pigeon shooting. Archery. Deer watching. Deer stalking. Pheasant shooting.

BIGLAND HALL TARN

Location (OS97:355830)

Take the A590(T) from Newby Bridge at the bottom of Lake Windermere and head for Barrow-in-Furness. In about 2 miles, at Backbarrow, turn left. Go through the village and continue through Brow Edge. About 500 yards further go straight ahead into Bigland Hall Estate. The tarn is about 500 yards up the track.

Fishery Controller

Tony Myers, Bigland Hall Estates, Backbarrow, Newby Bridge, Cumbria LA12 8PB (Tel: 015395 31728 or 01229 812001 or mobile 0585 732444).

Water and Stock

One 13 acre natural tarn stocked with bream, carp, eels, perch, pike, roach, rudd and tench.

Ticket Prices

Twenty-four hour ticket (by appointment) £7.00, day ticket £4.00, seniors and juniors £2.00. Rod hire £8.50 per day and instruction £10.00 an hour. Tickets are on sale at the fishing lodge.

Opening Times

All year from 0900 hrs until sunset. Overnight fishing by prior arrangement.

Description

Bigland Tarn, a mature 16 acre upland lake overlooked by the old hall and teeming with most species of coarse fish, is arguably the best coarse fishing venue in southern Lakeland. It's not a deep water, about 4 feet at the bottom of the meadow by the car park, dropping to 15 feet at the far end, but it certainly is productive. A favourite spot is the lefthand side where the water is sheltered with woodland. Access is easiest to the righthand bank, closest to the old hall, where tall reeds and some lily pads grow. This is the best place to try for the carp. They average about 5lb, but can reach 15lbs and the biggest fish to date is a beauty of nearly 27$^{1/2}$lb. Try boilies - tutti-fruiti, strawberry or chocolate flavours all take fish as do the more traditional pork luncheon meat and bread baits. As a bonus, night fishing is also permitted, along with tents and bivouacs, provided you book in advance. Try the same area for the tench that will take similar baits and can be pushing the 7lb barrier. Added to this there are loads of bream, huge shoals of roach and rudd swimming along the lefthand shore in the shade of the wooded hillside. With all these fish around it's not surprising that the pike grow big. If you're a pike enthusiast this is a dream water. There are plenty of Jacks around, many others into the 20lb bracket and fish nudging the 30lb mark. A dead herring or similar on the edge of the weedy area will bring results. A jetty has been constructed for wheelchair anglers but some assistance will be needed to get to it from the car park.

Fishery Rules

Night fishing by prior appointment.

Facilities on Site

Car park. Anglers' lodge. Horse riding. Clay pigeon shooting. Archery. Deer watching. Deer stalking. Pheasant shooting.

BLEA TARN, LANGDALE

Location (OS90:293043)

From Ambleside, take the road towards Skelwith Bridge and the

Langdales. Follow the road through Elterwater into Great Langdale and continue on the B5343 until the road climbs the steep hill out of the valley. Keep going to the top. Blea Tarn lies in the valley ahead.

Fishery Controller

The National Trust, North West Region, The Hollens, Grasmere, Ambleside, Cumbria LA22 9QZ (Tel: 015394 35599).

Water and Stock

A tiny moorland tarn of about 1 acre with plenty of tiny wild brown trout and a few perch.

Ticket Prices

Day ticket £2.50 from Mrs Myers, Blea Tarn Farm, at the southern end of the lake (Tel: 015394 37614).

Opening Times

Dawn to dusk, during the trout season.

Description

Blea Tarn in Langdales should not be confused with the numerous other more remote Blea tarns or lakes in Lakeland. This one lies in a natural amphitheatre nestling beneath the highest point on the tourist circular route from Skelwith Bridge through Great and Little Langdale. Although seen by many, it is visited by few, which is a pity because on a good day, when the sun is shining and there is a gentle breeze, the fishing is great. The trout are small but they are lively when hooked and there are plenty of them. Try throwing a worm out into the deeper water beyond the shallow rim and wait. The takes will be strong. For fly anglers try a brown or black buzzer in the ripple or traditional wet flies a few feet down. Forget the flashy lures.

Fishery Rules

No boats are permitted.

Facilities on Site

The spectacular scenery. Bed and breakfast and camping at Blea Tarn Farm.

BLEA TARN, WATENDLATH

Location (OS90:293142)

High in the Borrowdale Fells above Watendlath.

Fishery Controller

The National Trust, North West Region, The Hollens, Grasmere, Ambleside, Cumbria LA22 9QZ (Tel: 015394 35599).

Water and Stock

One small moorland tarn of approximately 1 acre with plenty of tiny wild brown trout.

Ticket Prices

Fishing is free for holders of an Environment Agency licence.

Opening Times

Dawn to dusk, during the trout season.

Description

On its day, this remote tarn, usually only seen by intrepid walkers, provides some exciting fishing for wild brown trout. The fish are small but acrobatic when hooked. Because of its remoteness, it is hardly ever fished so the sport is good especially if you can catch it on a day with sunshine and a gentle breeze. Try throwing a worm out into the deeper water beyond the shallow rim and wait. The takes will be strong. For fly anglers try a brown or black buzzer in the ripple or one of the traditional wet flies fished a few feet down. Leave the big flashy lures at home.

Fishery Rules

No boats are permitted.

Facilities on Site

None, except for the spectacular scenery!

BLEA WATER

Location (OS90:450108)

Blea Water feeds Haweswater reservoir. Take the dead-end road alongside Haweswater right to the car park at the end. Then take the footpath to the feeder stream. Follow the righthand branch up into the high fells and you will find Blea Water.

Fishery Controller

The Lake District National Park Authority.

Water and Stock

A 20 acre upland tarn holding small brown trout, perch and pike.

Ticket Prices

Free fishing for holders of an Environment Agency rod licence.

Opening Times

April 1st to September 30th from dawn to dusk.

Description

Yet another remote water with the name 'Blea', the ancient Norse word for blue, Blea Water is a strikingly pretty upland tarn nestling

89

in a natural amphitheatre below High Street. It's only for the energetic fisherman. A couple of hours of strenuous exercise is needed to get to it, but the trip is worth it. It's grossly under-fished. Just to see an angler there is surprising and two would be a crowd! Its clear 'blue' water teems with small trout and perch and they can be very greedy. They'll readily fall to worm, fly or spinner, although worm probably takes more fish. Blea Water is very exposed to the vagaries of the weather, which in Lakeland can close in very quickly. Don't take chances and be prepared.

Fishery Rules
None.
Facilities on Site
None.

BLELHAM TARN

Location (OS90:365005)
Situated at the north-western end of Lake Windermere. Take the B5286 from Clappersgate towards Coniston. In approximately 2 miles turn left to Low Wray. About 1 mile along this road, park in the layby and take the footpath through the fields to Blelham Tarn.
Fishery Controller
Windermere, Ambleside and District Angling Association on behalf of The National Trust.
Water and Stock
A 25 acre tarn holding a good head of roach, plus perch, pike and eels.
Ticket Prices
Day £3.00, junior £1.50 from the sources listed in the Angling Clubs section.
Opening Times
All year from 0900 hrs to dusk.
Description
Nestling in a tiny valley in a popular part of the Lake District, Blelham Tarn is not the easiest water to get to. It's a long walk, although a pretty one, from the road to the water's edge. Although Blelham holds perch, pike, roach and eels, it is undoubtedly the roach that attracts anglers. Many of the fish run to 1¹/₂lb and they are fairly prolific. Maggots, casters or seed are good baits to try on a floating rig in the shallower water near the edges. Don't ignore the

pike - though there are plenty of them around and you can have a good day laying a dead bait in the edge of the deeper water. Occasionally, when the fish fry are around, a pike over 20lb takes a flashy spinner pulled across the reedy margins. Blelham shelves gently from a few feet at the edge down to around 45 feet in the centre. It has a fairly even bottom except right out in the middle where several old research tanks lie, but unless you're trolling from a boat they pose no problem. In common with most Lakeland tarns, Blelham holds native brown trout. They are hardly ever fished so it is not known how big they run. There could be a monster lurking in the depths!

Fishery Rules
None.

Facilities on Site
The lovely scenery!

BLENCARN LAKE

Location (OS91:640315)
From Penrith, take the A66 road towards Appleby-in-Westmoreland. After crossing the River Eden, turn first left to Culgaith. In the village, turn right towards Skirwith. Follow this road for about 2¹/₂ miles and then take a sharp left turn to Blencarn. Go through the village towards Kirkland and the lake is on the right after a few hundred yards.

Fishery Controller
Mr J. K. Stamper, Blencarn Hall, Blencarn, Penrith, Cumbria (Tel: 01768 88284).

Water and Stock
A 15 acre trout lake stocked with high quality browns and rainbows averaging 1¹/₂lb.

Ticket Prices
Day ticket £16 for 4 fish, 5 hour ticket £10.00 for 2 fish. Ten rods only per day so booking is advisable.

Opening Times
April 1st to September 30th from 0830 hrs until sunset.

Description
Blencarn Lake is a beautiful spring fed water nestling in scenic meadowland in the foothills of the Pennines. It's quiet and secluded, an ideal place for anyone looking to catch some really good fish in

splendid surroundings. It's also a traditional fly fisherman's water. Leave the lead cored sinking lines at home and use a floater or at most a sink tip. Blencarn is well stocked with full-tailed browns and rainbows averaging $1^1/_2$lb and many others up to 8lb. There are also bigger grown-on fish, particularly the browns, so use a good strong leader and lots of backing. There is plenty of bankspace and most of it is accessible and, because only 10 rods are permitted each day, there is no chance of being crowded out.

In the early season when the cold winds sweep off the Pennines, it's best to try lures. A Cat's Whisker, a Viva, Tadpoles or any of the orange lures will attract the rainbows. The browns often like something a bit different. Try a Black, or Grey Ghost. For most of the season, though, when the fish tend to be in the upper water, buzzers and emergers do well. When the trout are obviously rising, any of the traditional patterns will attract them. Olives are very popular here. In the late summer when the fish get fussy, try tiny black midges and fish, very carefully, to a rising trout. A Corixa fished in the margins is also popular at this time.

Fishery Rules
Fly fishing only. No wading. All fish caught are to be killed. Catch-and-release fishing is not permitted. Additional permits may be purchased.

Facilities on Site
Car park.

BORRANS RESERVOIR

Location (OS90:430010)
From Windermere, take the A591 Kendal road. In about 1 mile turn left to The Common. Go through the village and turn right at the next T junction. After about $^3/_4$ mile, turn left onto a small road to High Borrans.

Fishery Controller
North Tyneside M.B.C.

Water and Stock
A $3^1/_2$ acre moorland reservoir set high on the fellside overlooking Windermere and holding brown trout. It is a lovely water although it does suffer in the wind, especially when a south-westerly blows. Currently, fishing is not permitted.

Ticket Prices
No fishing.

BRAYTON PARK LAKE

Location (OS85:163423)

Near Aspatria in north-western Cumbria. The lake is easily found from the A596 trunk road between Maryport and Carlisle. In Aspatria turn onto the B5299 road towards Mealsgate. In about 1 mile turn left onto a gravel track signposted to Lakeside Inn Golf Course. Follow the track to the end.

Fishery Controller

Mr J. B. Ward, 'The Garth' Home Farm, Brayton, Aspatria, Cumbria CA5 3SX (Tel: 016973 23539).

Water and Stock

A lovely lake of approximately 7 acres supporting a fine stock of common, crucian and wild carp.

Ticket Prices

Day ticket £10.00 in advance of fishing from the kiosk in the Lakeside Inn car park. Only three rods maximum per day, so advance booking is advised.

Opening Times

All year from dawn to dusk.

Description

Probably the oldest established carp fishery in Cumbria and one of the few remaining wild carp waters in Great Britain, Brayton Park is a must for carp anglers. Although the carp are not massive by southern standards, averaging about 8lb, they are prolific and readily feed on the popular baits. There are much bigger fish of course and the inevitable rumours of a monster that cruises, when the sun is shining, near the reeds. It is possible that such a fish will take a floating bread crust, during a hot summer evening, but don't count on it. Most anglers use pork luncheon meat, sweetcorn or flavoured boilies. Depending upon conditions, local fishermen tend to fish in the end close to the inn, or from the raised bank alongside the drive, and cast towards the deeper water in the middle. It really doesn't matter where you try from because the fish move freely throughout the whole lake. And you won't be crowded out. With about 7 acres of water and only 3 rods a day, there's plenty of room to move around and follow your instincts. On a good day it is not uncommon to take a dozen or more fish. The pond has a good bottom for ledgering and shelves away to about 15 feet near the centre. In addition to carp, it holds a sizeable colony of eels, all of which must be carefully returned to the water.

Fishery Rules

No boats, bait boats, guns, bent hooks, fixed leads, tether rigs or peanuts. No carp over 4lb or 18 inches in length to be kept in keepnets. All fish to be returned to the water as soon as possible. Do not kill eels. Unhooking mats to be used for large fish.

Facilities on Site

Car parking. Toilets. Refreshments in the inn.

BROTHERSWATER

Location (OS90:402128)

At the foot of Kirkstone Pass in Patterdale, alongside the A592 road from Windermere to Ullswater.

Fishery Controller

The National Trust, North West Region, The Hollens, Grasmere, Ambleside, Cumbria LA22 9QZ (Tel: 015394 35599).

Water and Stock

An attractive lake of about 2 acres holding mainly brown trout and a few perch and pike.

Ticket Prices

Free fishing for holders of an Environment Agency rod licence.

Opening Times

During the trout fishing season.

Description

Few anglers visiting the Lake District can fail to be captivated by Brotherswater. Not only is this beautiful lake surrounded by magnificent scenery, it is teeming with wild brown trout. On favourable days, when the sun is shining and there is a slight ripple on the water, these acrobatic fish seem to fall on the hook! They're not very big, averaging about 4 to the pound, but they are lively. And on a good day you may catch twenty or thirty fish. They scare easily though and the water is crystal clear, so approach the lakeside carefully. Try fishing a wet fly into the deep pool, from the shingle bar, at the south end of the lake where Dovedale Beck enters. Fishing a worm on a floating rig is particularly fruitful. In the height of summer, try the area along the western shore, in the shade of the trees.

Fishery Rules

No boats are permitted.

Facilities on Site
The spectacular scenery.

BURNMOOR TARN

Location (OS89:183045)
Burnmoor Tarn is in western Lakeland, south of Wastwater. Take Hardknott Pass westward. Drop down from the pass to meet the River Esk and continue towards Dalegarth railway station. Just before the station turn right to Boot. Park in the village and then follow the path northward some 3¹/₂ miles to Burnmoor Tarn.

Fishery Controller
Lake District National Park Authority.

Water and Stock
An 12 acre upland tarn holding small brown trout, perch and pike.

Ticket Prices
Free fishing for holders of an Environment Agency rod licence.

Opening Times
April 1st to September 30th from dawn to dusk.

Description
Set high in the Eskdale fells, this water is big and one not easy to get at. It is over 3¹/₂ miles from the nearest civilisation and demands strenuous exercise to get to the fishing, but when you do it's excellent. It teems with small trout and perch, particularly at the northern end where Whillan Beck flows out. At times the fish are very greedy and will readily fall to worm, fly or spinning. Take some light tackle and remember to be prepared for the weather. Burnmoor Tarn is very exposed and conditions can deteriorate quickly. If you want to be alone and combine fell-walking with fishing, Burnmoor is a good choice.

Fishery Rules
None.

Facilities on Site
None, except the wild remote scenery.

BUTTERMERE

Location (OS89:180160)
From Keswick follow the road into Borrowdale. Continue over the spectacular Honister Pass to Gatesgarth. Buttermere is on the left.

Fishery Controller

The National Trust, North West Region, The Hollens, Grasmere, Ambleside, Cumbria LA22 9QZ (Tel: 015394 35599).

Water and Stock

Buttermere, approximately 2 miles long and ¹/₂ mile wide, holds plenty of trout, char, pike and perch.

Ticket Prices

Season ticket £35.00, week £10.00 and day £3.00. Senior citizens and under 17s: season £15.00, week £4.00 and day £1.00. Tickets also cover Crummock Water and Loweswater. Day charge for launching own boat (no powered craft) £1.50. Hire boats: weekly rate for boat and rod £60.00; daily rate, boat and rod £15.00 (£10.00 afternoon); boat only, £5.00 per hour. Returnable deposit of £5.00 per boat. All permits and boats from Mr & Mrs Parker, Dalegarth Guest House, Buttermere (Tel: 017687 70233). Permits also from Graham's Guns, Workington (Tel: 01900 605093).

Opening Times

Dawn to dusk, March 15th to September 30th.

Description

Sandwiched between the 800m High Stile and the 550m Buttermere Fell, Buttermere lake is a delight for fishermen, photographers and walkers alike. All walkers will know of the route over High Stile, all photographers the pine trees along the shoreline and all fishermen the perfectly marked brown trout which swim in the clear waters. In short Buttermere is a delight. The brown trout are numerous and some of them are big. And from about May to September they feed ferociously. Probably the best way to fish the lake is by boat and the favourite spots are along the south-western tree-lined shore, near to where the stream leaves the lake for Crummock Water, and at the south-east end near Gatesgarth. The biggest trout are caught by trolling in the deeper water, but most fish are taken on fly or worm. The valley is a sun trap and in summer most of the favourite dry flies will take fish from the surface. When the inevitable wind blows try a big brown fly like a Walker's Sedge in the wind ripples. For bank fishermen the easiest access is along the north-eastern shore where the B5289 skirts the water, or follow the track from Buttermere village until it crosses the outflow and fish up from there. Buttermere is also home to some fine pike and perch although they are not fished for very often. There are undoubtedly some big pike in the deeps and they can be caught on a dead bait laid on the edge of the

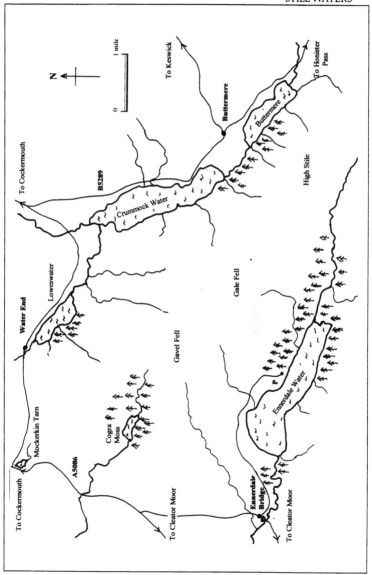

gravel bed where it suddenly drops sharply away into the depths.

Fishery Rules

Fly only until June 16th then worm or spinning is allowed.

Facilities on Site

Car parking at Gatesgarth and Buttermere village.

CLEABARROW TARN

Location (OS97:425962)

From Bowness-on-Windermere, take the A5074 south. In about 1¹/₂ miles turn left onto the B5284 for Crook and Kendal. Follow the road for about 2 miles and the tarn is on the left, approximately 150 metres after the entrance to Windermere Golf Club. Park in the lay-by on the B5284.

Fishery Controller

Windermere, Ambleside and District Angling Association. *See Angling Clubs section.*

Water and Stock

A tiny 'squarish' tarn holding lots of small gudgeon, roach, rudd and golden rudd. There are also a few carp and tench.

Ticket Prices

Day tickets £3.00, juniors £1.50 from Plantation Bridge Filling Station, near Staveley on the A591 (Tel: 01539 821753). Also from Go Fishing, Gillys Landing, Glebe Road, Bowness-on-Windermere (Tel: 015394 47086) and tourist information centres.

Opening Times

All year from dawn to dusk.

Description

Cleabarrow, a tiny, shallow tarn overstocked with fish, is popular with juniors and pleasure anglers. It has a maximum depth of around 4¹/₂ feet near the islands, rising to only 2 feet in the margins. It's well wooded on one side and a gravel path gives easy access to all the marked pegs. Twenty good pegs have been provided on three sides, the other side is virtually impossible to get at because of overhanging trees and the prolific weed. Pegged areas are regularly cleared of weed so it's not a problem for fishermen. A strong inflow of water from feeder streams causes the lake clarity to change with the seasons. Fishing is much better when the water has a bit of colour in it. Cleabarrow is popular with pole fishermen who, on a good day, manage to get heavy bags of roach and rudd with the occasional 4 or 5lb carp making life interesting. Corn or maggots are good baits, fished on a ledger rig out near one of the islands.

Fishery Rules

No night fishing. Only four visitor tickets in any one day.

Facilities on Site

Car park in the B5284 lay-by.

CODALE TARN

Location (OS90:295088)

About 4 miles north-west of Grasmere. From the village follow the road into Easdale. Continue to Easdale Tarn and then follow the feeder stream for about 1 mile to Codale Tarn.

Fishery Controller

Lake District National Park Authority.

Water and Stock

A classic Lakeland tarn holding small brown trout.

Ticket Prices

Free fishing for holders of an Environment Agency rod licence.

Opening Times

April 1st to September 30th from dawn to dusk.

Description

A lovely natural upland tarn, Codale is very remote, wild and unfished. It's full of wild brown trout and they just love worms. Catch it on a good day and you could well land hundreds of fish. The water is a long way from civilisation. Be prepared for the weather. Remember that it can deteriorate very rapidly.

Fishery Rules

None

Facilities on Site

None

COGRA MOSS FISHERY

Location (OS89:095196) See map p97

On Lamplugh Fell, approximately 1¹/₂ miles east of the A5086 near Crossgate. At Crossgate, take the road to Lamplugh. In the village, turn right to Felldyke. Park in Felldyke and follow the track for about ³/₄ mile to Cogra Moss.

Fishery Controller

Cockermouth and District Angling Association. *See Angling Clubs section.*

Water and Stock

A natural tarn of about 40 acres nestling in a wooded area on Lamplugh Fell. It holds brown trout averaging about $1^{1}/_{2}$lb with some wild fish up to about 4lb.

Ticket Prices

Day ticket £10.00 for 3 fish, junior £6.00. Evening (1700 hrs to dusk) £6.00 for 2 fish. Weekly ticket £40.00 for 3 fish per day. Junior £25.00. Eight month ticket £100.00.

From Inglenook Caravan Site at Lamplugh or Miss Stevens whose house is at the bottom of the track leading to the lake. Look for a sign in the porch window.

Opening Times

March 30th to October 31st from dawn to sunset.

Description

One of Lakeland's beautiful tarns, Cogra Moss is hardly ever seen by visiting anglers. This is mainly because it is a long walk from the car to the water's edge, but it is worth it. The lake, bordered by trees on three of its sides, offers some brilliant fishing in lovely surroundings. Once at the lakeside access is easy. A favourite area is the south side, in the shade of the trees, beneath Murton Fell. In the summer there are almost always fish to be seen moving. As you would expect, beetles are favourite, as are green pie weevils. Almost anything in black and green will take fish. When the water has a gentle ripple and the Daddies are in season a good artificial can be a killer. If you have the energy to walk to the eastern end, where a tiny lake and feeder stream feeds the main water, you're almost sure to take fish.

Fishery Rules

Fly only. Three fish limit. Stop fishing after third fish caught.

Facilities on Site

None.

CONISTON WATER

Location (OS97:300940)

Coniston Water is easily found. It is approximately 5 miles west of Windermere. Take any road signposted to Coniston.

Fishery Controller

The Lake District National Park, The National Trust and private landowners.

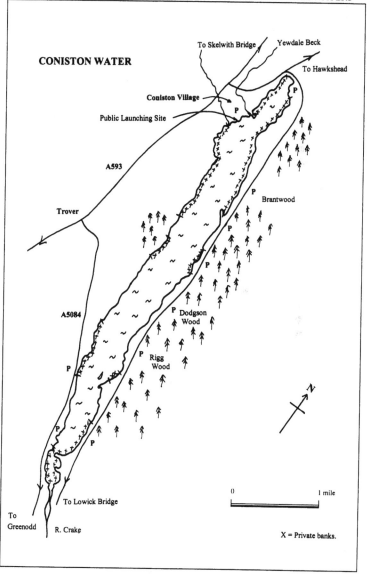

CONISTON WATER

To Skelwith Bridge
Yewdale Beck
To Hawkshead

Coniston Village

Public Launching Site

A593

Trover

Brantwood

A5084

Dodgson Wood

Rigg Wood

N

To Lowick Bridge

To Greenodd   R. Crake

0   1 mile

X = Private banks.

101

Water and Stock
Approximately 5 miles long and ¼ mile wide, Coniston Water holds plenty of trout, pike and perch and a few salmon and sea trout.

Ticket Prices
Free to holders of an Environment Agency rod licence. Fish only from the public bankside.

Boats
Boats can be hired from Coniston Boating Centre at Coniston (Tel: 015394 41366). For a fee, own boats can also be launched from the centre. Non-powered craft can be launched from Brown Howe Car Park on the A5084.

Opening Times
All year during the appropriate season.

Description
Coniston Water is a long, thin lake sitting in pleasant meadowland. It is often placid, and by no means as spectacular as many others in Lakeland but it is very popular with those who enjoy wildlife watching or sailing. It also provides a fine opportunity for fishing. There are some good brown trout to be had, plus large numbers of perch and pike. It is also said that char are here in big numbers, although they have been very scarce recently. No char fishing from November 1st to April 30th. The best flies are a Black Gnat, a Coachman or any of the spiders. In the autumn, salmon enter the water from the River Crake. The lakeside at Coniston village is always very busy so, unless you plan to launch a boat there, it's best to give it a miss. Access is easiest from one of the many parking areas on the east side. The Dodgson and Rigg Wood areas are mostly open for fishing, but large areas in the north and south are private. The best baits for perch and trout are maggots and worms although either fish will take a lure fished near the bottom. Coniston is not a deep water, so a sink tip or floating line will be sufficient. Occasionally pike have been landed using this method but if it's pike that you're after, try a dead bait laid on the bottom or a flashy spinner pulled through the weeds. The fish are not big, a 10 pounder is a good one, but there are lots of them.

Fishery Rules
All method fishing.

Facilities on Site
Car parks at various sites around the lake. *See the map p101.*

CROFTON LAKE

Location (OS85:306500)

Approximately 7 miles south-west of Carlisle. Take the A595 towards Cockermouth. In about 7 miles, just before crossing the River Wampool, turn right to Crofton. The lake is on the right.

Fishery Controller

Carlisle and District Coarse Angling Club. *See Angling Clubs section.*

Water and Stock

An 8 acre lake with a fine stock of coarse fish including, bream, carp, perch, roach, rudd and tench.

Ticket Prices

Permits for members' friends only from the Hon. Secretary. *See Angling Clubs section.*

Opening Times

May 1st to March 15th from dawn to dusk.

Description

Crofton Lake is a shallow, 8 acre estate lake set in pleasant agricultural land. There are 44 easily accessible pegs, all of which provide the opportunity of getting amongst the fish. Carp are one of the main targets. Both commons and mirrors run to over 15lb and there's a good stock of wild fish around 10lb. Best baits are luncheon meat and boilies. The bream average 5 or 6lb and the tench 3 to 4lb and they are in Crofton in good numbers. Sweetcorn or the old faithful maggot will take heavy bags of these two fish. Maggots, pinkies or casters will always attract the shoals of rudd, roach and perch. The fish are not particularly big but they are very plentiful and they seem always to be willing to take a bait.

Fishery Rules

No bait restrictions. Carp are not to be kept in keepnets.

Facilities on Site

Car parking area.

CROSSFIELD FISHERY

Location (OS86:545436)

Situated in the Eden Valley, about 8 miles south-east of Armathwaite. From the village, cross the Eden and turn first right. Continue along the road to Staffield. The fishery is on the outskirts of the village.

Fishery Controller

Mr Massingham, Crossfield Cottages and Leisure Fishing, Staffield,

Kirkoswald, Cumbria CA10 1EU (Tel: 01768 898711, 24 hrs, for a brochure or 01768 896275, 0800 to 2000 hrs daily, to make a booking).

Water and Stock

Two pools of approximately 2 acres each, one holding mainly carp and the other bream, plus a selection of other coarse species.

Ticket Prices

Day ticket £10.00, weekly ticket £35.00. Permits must be booked in advance. They cannot be purchased on the day. Reduced rates for holiday cottage guests.

Opening Times

All year from dawn to dusk.

Description

Crossfield Fishery has two clear water lakes set near holiday cottages and bordered by a stream. Carp lake is heavily stocked with good quality commons and mirrors averaging 6 to 7lb with some fish up to 13lb. It's a square lake with very easy access to all the bankspace. Open banks enable easy casting and the shingle lake-bed lends itself to laying-on a carp rig. The water shelves quite quickly, from shallow margins, to about 15 to 18 feet deep. Sweetcorn is good for the carp. It's worth trying the new flavours - strawberry is a good bet. Boilies are also a great bait. Again strawberry or the ever popular tutti-frutti will take fish. On the right day it's not uncommon to land several fish in one session. Bream Lake, slightly smaller and with a landscaped island, is just as prolific as its neighbour. There are large numbers of good quality bream averaging about 4lb, but many top the 6lb mark. Maggots, casters, pinkies or bread fished on a pole or waggler rig will bring fish. Bream Lake also holds roach, rudd and tench and it is possible to have some really heavy catches here. Both lakes were once trout fisheries and still hold some heavy trout as well as the unusual ide. In fact the British ide record, a fish of 3lb 4oz, is held by this water.

Disabled anglers will have no difficulty in getting to the solid bankside of either lake and the car park is very close to the entrance.

Fishery Rules

Carefully return all fish to the water.

Facilities on Site

Four holiday cottages to let. Toilet. Refreshments. Disabled facilities. Caravans and camper vans accommodated. Pets welcome.

CRUMMOCK WATER

Location (OS89:155190) See map p97

From Cockermouth taken the B5292 Keswick road. In about $4^1/_2$ miles turn right onto the B5289 to Buttermere. The road follows the lakeside. Woodhouse, where permits and boats can be obtained, is signposted from this road at the southern end of the lake.

Fishery Controller

The National Trust, North West Region, The Hollens, Grasmere, Ambleside, Cumbria LA22 9QZ (Tel: 015394 35599).

Water and Stock

Crummock Water, approximately $2^1/_2$ miles long and up to a $^1/_4$ mile wide, holds plenty of trout, char, pike and perch. Salmon and sea trout enter the lake from late July.

Ticket Prices

Season ticket £35.00, weekly £10.00 and day £3.00. Senior citizens and children under 17: season £15.00, week £4.00 and day £1.00. Tickets also cover Buttermere and Loweswater. Day charge for launching own boat (no powered craft) £1.50. Hire boats: weekly rate for boat and rod £60.00; daily rate, boat and rod £15.00 (£10.00 after noon); boat only, £5.00 per hour. Returnable deposit of £5.00 per boat. All permits and boats from Mr & Mrs McKenzie, Woodhouse, Buttermere (Tel: 017687 70208). Tickets also from Graham's Guns, Workington (Tel: 01900 605093).

Opening Times

Dawn to dusk, March 15th to September 30th.

Description

The middle one of three of Lakeland's most beautiful waters, Crummock Water can look somewhat daunting to a visiting angler wondering where to start. Probably the first place to try is the easiest one to get at! A scenic road, the B5289 from Keswick to Cockermouth, occasionally running perilously close to the water in places, skirts the eastern shore. There are even a few tiny parking areas along the road and if you're lucky you will be able to squeeze into one, but do not count on it. In contrast, the opposite side of the lake is remote. It is accessible only by a rough footpath entered from each end of the lake. It's also precarious in places, so if you choose to fish this side be careful and be prepared - the weather can deteriorate very quickly. Access is easiest from a boat. Most fishermen hire one from Woodhouse at the southern tip of Crummock and fish the hotspots around the islands. The more adventurous row their boat to the craggy western shore, in the region of Ling Crags, and try trolling for the bigger browns. This is also the way to pick up one of Lakeland's beautiful char. Some big browns in excess of 4lb have been caught near Ling Crags, but you are more likely to catch fish between $^3/_4$lb and $1^1/_2$lb and, on a good day, you should get plenty of them. In the early season the fish will be deep down, then it's a good time to try the bigger lures or Scottish Loch wet flies on a sinking line. In the late summer, try nearer the surface at the northern end where the beck from Loweswater enters and the River Cocker leaves the lake. You could make contact with one of the sea trout or salmon coming in off the Cocker, but don't count on it. Crummock holds some big perch. They'll take almost anything and, on the right day, you should catch dozens of them. Pike anglers seem to be few at Crummock which is surprising because it undoubtedly holds some monster fish. However you fish this big water, keep an eye on the weather. If you decide to take a boat out, dress well and wear a life preserver. When a strong northerly wind blows the water can become rough and it can be very unforgiving.

Fishery Rules

Fly only until June 16th then worm or spinning is allowed.

Facilities on Site

None.

DERWENTWATER

Location (OS90:260200)

Extending southward from Keswick.

Fishery Controller

Keswick Angling Association on behalf of The National Trust. *See Angling Clubs section.*

Water and Stock

At $3^1/_2$ miles long and $^1/_2$ mile wide, Derwentwater is one of the National Park's major lakes. It holds eels, perch, pike, roach, brown trout, salmon and the unique vendace.

Ticket Prices

Weekly tickets, salmon, £75.00, day £20.00. Weekly, trout, £25.00, day £5.00. Weekly, pike and coarse fish, £12.00, day £3.00. Concessions for junior, senior and disabled anglers. Tickets include fishing on all Keswick AA waters. Nearest outlets are Field &

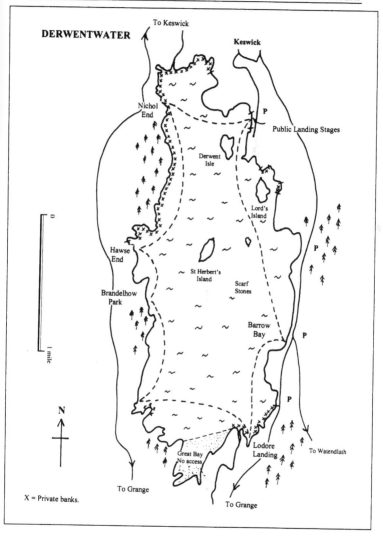

DERWENTWATER

To Keswick

Keswick

Nichol End

Public Landing Stages

P

Derwent Isle

Lord's Island

0

Hawse End

Brandelhow Park

St Herbert's Island

Scarf Stones

Barrow Bay

P

P

1 mile

N

Great Bay No access

Lodore Landing

To Watendlath

To Grange

To Grange

X = Private banks.

Stream, 79 Main Street, Keswick (Tel: 017687 74396), the tourist information office, Moor Hall, Market Square, Keswick (Tel:017687 72645) and Keswick Post Office, 48 Main Street (Tel: 017687 72269).

Boats

Boats can be hired from Nicol End and Keswick landings. Rowing boats are available from the Keswick Launch Company, Lakeside, Keswick. Permits are not required for launching own unpowered boats but there may be a launching charge. Launching sites are at Derwentwater Marina, Nichol End Marina, Allerdale Council campsite, Lakeside Caravan Site and the public landing stages at Lake Road.

Opening Times

Salmon: February 1st to October 31st. Trout: March 15th to September 30th. Coarse fish: open all year. No night fishing.

Description

Derwentwater is ideally situated and easily accessible for a visiting fisherman. Accommodation is easy to find in Keswick, which also has an excellent fishing tackle shop. Access to the bankside is easy, especially in the summer when ferries run from Keswick to several points around the shore. It's not a deep lake. Shallow at the edges, the water gently drops away to about 20 feet around the islands where much of the best fishing is to be had. Of course you will need to hire a boat to reach it. Some of the biggest pike, about 20lb, are taken on deadbait near the islands, but a lot of fish are caught on a spinner in the weedy margins at the south end. The perch, which grow to over 2lb, can be taken almost anywhere. Worm is the best bait, either ledgered or on a floating rig. Derwentwater is home to the unique vendace, now an endangered species, although very few fish have been reported over the past decade. It's a slender silver scaled fish which grows to about 12 inches long. If one is caught it should be returned carefully to the water.

Keswick AA stocks annually with over a thousand 12 inch brown trout to support the native stock. Many of these grow on to become fairly substantial. Fish over 3lb have been taken, by boat anglers, from the shelving water close-in to the islands. Worm is a good bait for the brown trout and the best place to try for these is at the south end where the fledgling River Derwent enters from Grange. The trout fishing can be spectacular at Mayfly time. Take a boat out in late May and try a big bushy imitation Mayfly. Be ready for some savage takes. After heavy rain the flooded river brings a lot of insect life into Derwentwater. This is another good time to try the southern end of the lake, but remember fishing is not permitted in Great Bay.

In the autumn, there is a small run of salmon up the River Derwent into the lake, but they often arrive late and sometimes only after the end of the season.

Fishery Rules
No night fishing.

Facilities on Site
Car parking at various points around the lake. Car park and toilets at Lakeside, Keswick.

DEVOKE WATER

Location (OS96:155970)
This remote water is best approached from Duddon Bridge on the A595(T). Take the road north to Bank End and follow the River Duddon to Ulpha. Turn left on the road up Birker Fell towards Eskdale. In approximately 5 miles, turn left onto a single track road to the tarn.

Fishery Controller
Millom and District Angling Association. *See Angling Clubs section.*

Water and Stock
A remote lake of about 25 acres supporting a good stock of wild brown trout and some perch.

Ticket Prices
Day ticket £15.00 for 6 fish, weekly ticket £40.00, from the Hon. Secretary, Haverigg Post Office (Tel: 01229 772338), Broughton-in-Furness Post Office (Tel: 01229 716220) Waberthwaite Post Office (Tel 01229 717237) and Holmrook Service Station (Tel: 019467 242756).
Tickets for launching rowing boats (five only per day) are 50p only from the Hon. Secretary. *See Angling Clubs section.*

Opening Times
Dawn to dusk during the trout fishing season.

Description
Lakeland's largest tarn, Devoke Water, set in unspoilt beautiful surroundings, over 760 feet above sea level, is a delight to fish. Catch it on a day when the sun is shining and the surface is rippled by a

gentle breeze and all the effort of getting to the waterside is worthwhile. Devoke Water is about ³/₄ mile from the Eskdale to Ulpha road and it is a strenuous, but pleasant walk, unless of course you're carrying a boat! The tarn is over 40 feet deep near the middle rising steadily to a few inches at the north side. Along the south bank the water depth drops fairly sharply to over 10 feet. Most fishermen favour the southern bank where the feeder streams from White Pike enter. Other favourite spots are in the west where Linbeck Gill runs down into Eskdale, and near the boathouse. If you intend to fish from a boat, landing is not permitted on the island, but the water surrounding its rugged shores is often alive with trout. The fish are as wild as the scenery. Hook one of these acrobatic wild browns and be treated to an aerobatic display. They average about ¹/₂lb and there are much bigger fish swimming in the clear depths so sinking lines and lures can be good. When visiting Devoke Water, travel light. Take a lightweight fly rod and just a selection of favourite patterns. In the spring, Scottish Loch flies, like a Butcher or a Dunkeld, will often tempt a trout. Later in the year when the water has warmed up a bit, buzzers are always a good bet. Try the black or green tyings. On the days in the early summer when there is a good rise, try a dry Gold Ribbed Hares Ear or Greenwell's. Later in the summer an Iron Blue Dun is worth a try. If all else fails a humble worm on a light floating rig will bring a reaction. Ledgering is difficult due to the lake bottom being covered with stones and boulders.

Fishery Rules

No maggots allowed. Park off the track. Do not land on the island. No camping.

Facilities on Site

The dramatic scenery.

DRUNKEN DUCK TARN

Location (OS90:350010)

From Ambleside, take the A593 road towards Skelwith Bridge. At Clappersgate, turn left onto the B5286. In approximately 1¹/₂ miles turn right. The Drunken Duck Inn and Tarn are at the next crossroads.

Fishery Controller

Drunken Duck Inn, Barn Gates, Ambleside, Cumbria LA22 0NG (Tel: 015394 36347).

Water and Stock
A beautiful secluded tarn holding a good stock of rainbow trout averaging about $1^1/2$lb, and some wild browns.
Ticket Prices
Day ticket £12.00, half day £7.00 and evening £5.00 from the hotel.
Opening Times
March to September, fishing from dawn to dusk.
Description
This is a beautiful Lakeland tarn set in woodland close to the splendidly named Drunken Duck Inn. This is not a big water and the trout are not large but they are obliging and it is a delight to fish. Whilst having easy access, it's very secluded and well protected from the prevailing winds. The fish, both browns and rainbows, are free risers and a prolific amount of flylife, from the bankside vegetation, finds its way onto the water. Traditional fly fishing methods with a floating line bring the best results. In the early season, when the water is still cold, most of the northern wet flies are good - any of the Mallard range for the wild browns, Invicta or Alexandra for the rainbows. As the water warms up, a winged Black Gnat, or a Hawthorn fly often brings results. On the hotter days, smaller sizes and fine leaders are needed. There are extensive reeds and weedy margins, ideal for trying a Corixa or similar water boatman imitation. Also in the height of summer, when the trout are chasing minnows and other fry, an imitation tadpole is a good attractor.
Fishery Rules
Maximum of 4 rods only.
Facilities on Site
Car park. Accomodation in the Inn

DUBBS TROUT FISHERY

Location (OS90:421018)
From Windermere, take the A591 Kendal Road. In about 1 mile turn left to The Common. Go through the village and turn left at the next T junction. After about 300 yards, turn right onto a single track rough road to the Dubbs Tarn. The fishery is about $^1/2$ mile up the track.
Fishery Controller
Windermere, Ambleside and District Angling Association. *See*

Angling Clubs section.

Water and Stock

An 8 acre moorland reservoir holding native brown trout to 2lb and stocked with rainbow trout averaging $1^{1/2}$lb with some bigger fish up to about 10lb.

Ticket Prices

Day ticket £8.50 for 2 fish. The nearest ticket outlet is the tourist information centre in Victoria Street, Windermere (Tel: 015394 46499). Also from Ings Service Station on the A591, Go Fishing at Bowness-on-Windermere (Tel: 015394 47086), Carlsons Fishing Tackle, Kendal (Tel: 01539 724867), the Kendal Sports Shop (Tel: 01539 721554) and other tourist information centres.

Opening Times

March 15th to December 31st from dawn to dusk.

Description

Dubbs is a man-made reservoir bearing a remarkable similarity to the wild Pennine reservoirs of the Yorkshire Dales. It's not as deep as you might expect at first glance. The water shelves fairly gently from the north side, where the feeder stream enters, down to the dam wall. Imagine the bed to be saucer shaped, like the 'concrete bowl' reservoirs of the south of England and the best method to employ is a sink tip line with a long leader and a weighted fly, probably a nymph or a shrimp pattern. When the wind blows, as it so often does here, it's worth keeping an eye out for rising fish. It's not uncommon for big rainbows to come up from the bottom after flies that have been blown onto the water. Especially during the summer and early autumn try a large (size10) Daddy Long Legs or Sedge in the waves. Tug it occasionally and wait for the take. It will be violent so use a strong leader. The native brown trout usually take the more traditional wet patterns. Any of the north country flies will attract fish, but it is not always easy fishing. Patience is a virtue. Try Black and Peacock Spider, Gold Ribbed Hares Ear, March Brown or Mallard and Claret. Catch and release fishing is encouraged using barbless hooks.

Fishery Rules

Catch and release permitted. Barbless hooks only.

Facilities on Site

Car parking at the reservoir. Toilet.

EASEDALE TARN

Location (OS90:309088)

From Grasmere village take the road about ¹/₂ mile north to Lancrigg. Park where you can and then take the footpath up Sour Mill Gill for about 2¹/₂ miles to the tarn.

Fishery Controller

The National Trust, North West Region, The Hollens, Grasmere, Ambleside, Cumbria LA22 9QZ (Tel: 015394 35599).

Water and Stock

A wild moorland tarn holding mostly pike and perch. There are a few native brown trout.

Ticket Prices

Fishing is free for holders of a valid Environment Agency rod licence.

Opening Times

Dawn to dusk during the coarse fishing season.

Description

Anyone thinking of fishing Easedale Tarn will need to be fit and well. It is remote, something like 2¹/₂ miles uphill from Grasmere, but, when you eventually get there, it is beautiful. Be prepared, consult the weather forecast and if the day looks right, then go. Take light tackle and expect to get a lot of fish because Easedale is hardly ever fished. The tarn is teeming with perch, but they tend to be fairly small as do the pike. Worm is the best bait, fished on a floating rig, although a flashy spinner occasionally does well. Easedale Tarn is a fishery for those people who like to be alone!

Fishery Rules

No boats are permitted.

Facilities on Site

None.

EAST VIEW FISHERY

Location (OS85:411463)

Approximately 6 miles south of Carlisle. From Carlisle centre, take the road signposted to the racecourse. Continue past the course towards Penrith. After about 5 miles, turn left at the Crown Inn. The fishery is the first farm on the right.

Fishery Controller

Mrs Lancaster, East View Farm, Broadfield, Southwaite, Cumbria

(Tel: 016974 73324).

Water and Stock

A single lake of about 1 acre holding bream, carp, eels, roach, tench and a few pike.

Ticket Prices

Day tickets £2.00, juniors under 16 £1.50, from the farm house. Also from Geoff Wilson Fishing Tackle in Carlisle (Tel: 01228 31542).

Opening Times

All year fishing from dawn to dusk. Night fishing by prior appointment.

Description

This is a 1 acre former gravel pit pleasantly situated in grazing land close to the farm. As with most gravel pits it is deep, dropping to nearly 20 feet in the centre and with depths of 10 feet close-in to the bank. It's a popular pole venue with fairly easy access to most of the 18 pegs, although the side nearest the road is overhung and difficult to get at. A favourite hot spot is the furthest point from the farm where a small headland juts into the deeper water. Carp to 16lb and bream to 7lb are not uncommon so, if you intend to use a pole rig, use strong elastic. Luncheon meat and boilies are the favourite baits - local anglers wouldn't be without milk chocolate flavour. Maggots, casters and worms are all good for the roach and perch. Try feeding with hemp seed to attract a shoal. In the winter the pike fishing comes into its own. The fish are big for the size of the water. Ten pounders are fairly common and some top the scales at 15lb. Dead bait is by far the best bet.

Fishery Rules

None.

Facilities on Site

Car park at the farm.

EDEN VALLEY TROUT LAKE

Location (OS91:762125)

From Kirkby Stephen, take the A685 towards Brough. In approximately 1 mile by the Eden Bridge, turn left onto the B6259 road to Warcop. In about $2^{1}/_{2}$ miles, after twice crossing the river, turn left to Little Musgrave and then left again. The fishery is approximately 1 mile on the left.

Fishery Controller

*The attractive **Eden Valley Trout Lake** day ticket water*

Norman or Liz Hughes, Bersett, Rowgate Avenue, Kirkby Stephen, Cumbria CA17 4SR (Tel: 017683 71489 or 071683 51428).

Water and Stock

An attractive small lake holding a good stock of brown and rainbows to about 8lb.

Ticket Prices

Day ticket £18.00 for 3 fish; half day £13.00 for 2 fish. Sporting ticket £20.00 full day.

Maximum 5 rods. Purchase tickets in advance from Bersett, Rowgate Avenue, Kirkby Stephen approximately 200 yards on the left past the Croglin Castle Hotel.

Opening Times

April 1st to October 31st from 0700 to 1900 hrs.

Description

This attractively landscaped man-made lake of approximately 1 acre is set in some of the Eden Valley's prettiest countryside. Sensible planting of shrubs and water plants has created an attractive and secluded fishery. The lake is stocked with both brown and rainbows, averaging $1^{1/2}$lb with fish up to 8lb, which, because of the prolific insect life, thrive in the clear water. This is not a big water so you won't need fast sinking lines. A floater or at most a sink tip would be better. In the summer when the tadpoles are about, rainbows can often be seen cruising in the shallower water close to the side nearest the lodge. That's the time to try a good tadpole imitation or a corixa alongside the weeds. Be very careful not to cast a shadow onto the water, the fish scare easily. In the spring, or on the hottest summer days the rainbows tend to be with the browns in the deepest water alongside the island on the far bank. There, in front of the fishing platform where the water drops away to around 10 feet, is a good place to try a deep fished nymph. A Pheasant Tail or Gold Ribbed Hares Ear will take fish. There is usually a good evening rise. Try a variety of olive patterns or if they fail, Greenwell's Glory is always a killer.

Fishery Rules
Fly only. No wading. Maximum 5 rods.

Facilities on Site
Toilet. Refreshments. Fishing lodge. Boats. Tackle for hire. Caravan and camping facilities.

ELLERBECK COARSE FISHERY

Location (OS89:091299)
From the centre of Cockermouth take the A5086 Cleator Moor road to the bypass. Turn right towards Workington, then in about ³/₄ mile turn left towards Brigham village. Ellerbeck Farm and fishery is on the left on the outskirts of the village. Or alternatively follow the coarse fishing signs from the A66.

Fishery Controller
Taylor and Judith Lawson, Ellerbeck Farm, Brigham, Cockermouth (Tel: 01900 825268).

Water and Stock
Two ponds holding a large stock of bream, common and crucian carp, perch, roach, rudd, tench and trout.

Ticket Prices
Day ticket £4.00, evening £2.00. Children under 10 half price. Available on the bank or from the farmhouse.

Opening Times
All year, fishing from dawn to dusk.

Description
Two nicely landscaped lakes, set in an attractive area on the edge of

a working farm, have been well stocked with a variety of coarse fish to create a fine coarse fishery. The larger lake, approximately ²/₃ acre, is arranged with 43 pegs, 18 of which are specifically adapted for disabled anglers. There is easy access from the car park to all the bankspace which has been sensibly landscaped to allow easy casting and comfortable fishing. The water is about 12 feet deep near the islands rising to 4 feet at the fringes and is teeming with fish, so expect some pretty heavy bags. Carp to 10lb are common, the bream can reach 9lb and roach 2lb and they are prolific, as are the rudd. Coloured maggots are the favourite, but try also pinkies and squats on a pole rig. For carp and tench, which like a big mouthful, luncheon meat is undoubtedly the bait. Boilies and bloodworm are banned, but you don't need them anyway. Quarry Lake is much smaller and has a completely different character. As the name suggests, it is a quarry pond of unknown depth in places, although it's thought to be about 15 feet deep alongside the quarry face. The water is clear and dark and it's easy to imagine monsters lurking in the cold depths. In fact the common carp run to about 20lb, although much bigger fish have been seen cruising near the rock face. There are also crucians, perch and tench. One angler managed to take over 60 crucians in one afternoon which is pretty good by any standards. Disabled anglers can get easy access to two of the 5 pegs on Quarry Lake.

Fishery Rules

Barbless hooks only. Dip nets in tubs before approaching the lakes. No carp to be kept in nets. No boilies or bloodworm.

Facilities on Site

Toilet with ramp and wide door. Car parking near big lake. Some of the pegs on big lake are adapted for disabled and wheelchair anglers. En-suite bed and breakfast accommodation. Refreshments available at the farm house. Site for 5 touring caravans. A 4 berth luxury static caravan for hire. Scenic woodland walk.

ELTERWATER

Location (OS90:330041)

From Skelwith Bridge, take the B5354 road towards Elterwater. The lake is on the left.

Fishery Controller

The National Trust, North West Region, The Hollens, Grasmere,

Ambleside, Cumbria LA22 9QZ (Tel: 015394 35599).

Water and Stock

A beautiful clear water tarn fed by Little and Great Langdale Becks. It is full of small wild brown trout, but because it is in a wildlife conservation area, no fishing is allowed.

Ticket Prices

No fishing.

ENNERDALE WATER

Location (OS89:105150) See map p97

Situated beneath Ennerdale Fell in western Lakeland. Public car parks are situated at Bowness Knott and Broadmoor. To find the fisherman's car park, continue past the Broadmoor turnoff and take the next right to How Hall Farm. Go through the farm and down a gated track to the lakeside.

Fishery Controller

Ennerdale Lake Fishery, a joint venture between the Egremont Angling Association and the Wath Brow & Ennerdale Angling Association. *See Angling Clubs section.*

Water and Stock

One of the National Park's major lakes, Ennerdale is approximately 3 miles long by $3/4$ mile wide holding mainly wild brown trout and char.

Ticket Prices

Season ticket £12.00 and weekly tickets £6.00, juniors half price, from Wath Brow Post Office, Cleator Moor, Cumbria (Tel: 01946 810377). The ticket also includes fishing on the Ehan. *See entry under River Ehan.*

Opening Times

Dawn to dusk, during the trout fishing season.

Description

Ennerdale Water is an ideal venue for anglers who appreciate beautiful surroundings and don't mind having the odd blank day. The water is well stocked with good quality fish, but they are not easy to find on a single outing, although if you catch it when the conditions are right, you'll have a terrific day. A flat calm is no good nor is a howling gale. Ennerdale is best fished when a gentle northerly wind blows with just enough strength to ripple the water. Access to the remote areas at the eastern end is really only for

*Typical Lakeland scenery at **Ennerdale**, a lovely day ticket fishing water*

energetic anglers who don't mind a long stroll. Footpaths, from the two public car parks, one on the north bank at Bowness Knott and the other not far from the outflow weir of the River Ehen, hug most of the bankside. With something like 8 miles of bankspace available for anglers, Ennerdale is never overfished, although the wooded area to the north and east is very popular with fishermen. In the early season, when the water is still cold, spinning is the best bet. Go fairly deep for the bigger browns which will take Devons, Quills or a spoon. Use something fairly large for the big old browns - they like a mouthful! A ledgered worm sometimes picks up a good brown and occasionally a char. As the water warms up try fly fishing with traditional north country wet flies. Almost anything dressed in black will take fish. From May onwards, read the surface and whenever the fish are showing, try a dry in one of the wind lanes. There is a small run of salmon and sea trout into Ennerdale, but they're impossible to find and fishing for them is not permitted anyway.

Fishery Rules

Fly fishing, spinning, worm only. No groundbaiting. No maggots. No boats. Use bubble floats only.

Facilities on Site
Car park.

ESTHWAITE WATER

Location (OS97:360965) Also see map p195
Esthwaite is west of Lake Windermere, sandwiched between the
B5285 from Hawkshead to Bowness-on-Windermere (via ferry)
and the Hawkshead to Newby Bridge road. To find Hawkshead
Trout Farm, where fishing tickets can be purchased, from Hawkshead
follow the road to Newby Bridge. In approximately 2 miles turn left
into the farm.

Fishery Controller
Hawkshead Trout Farm, The Boat House, Ridding Wood,
Hawkshead, Ambleside, Cumbria LA22 0QF (Tel: 015394 36541).

Water and Stock
A beautiful lake over 250 acres holding a good stock of brown and
rainbow trout, roach and some of the biggest pike in the Lake
District.

Ticket Prices
Hawkshead Fisheries offer a huge range of tickets and prices. A few
examples are listed here. Day tickets £15.50 for 6 fish, evening ticket
(after 1600 hrs) £15.50 for 6 fish, any method £15.50 for 6 fish.
Concessionary rates for senior citizen and junior anglers. Reduced
charges for winter fishing from November 31st to February 28th
inclusive. Boats (with electric outboard motors), day £21.00 and
evening £13.00. Catch-your-own tickets £7.00, or £6.00 using own
rod for 2 fish.

Opening Times
All year from 0800 hrs to dusk.

Description
Loch style fishing in Lakeland! Take a boat out on a bright summer
day and gaze around at the lovely scenery. It's like a tiny part of
Scotland has moved south. But don't waste too much time because
there are a lot of big fish waiting to be caught. Esthwaite is a
biologically rich lake which means that the stocked browns and
rainbows grow-on very quickly and soon become hard fighting
monsters. Each season it receives an initial stocking of some 3$\frac{1}{2}$ tons
of trout! That's a lot of fish. As the season progresses it is restocked
as required with the odd $\frac{1}{2}$ ton up to about 12$\frac{1}{2}$lb. Rod catch

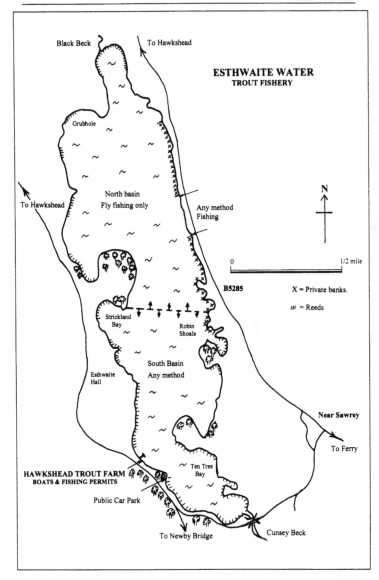

averages are some of the best in the country. Recently it has been 5.4 fish and this figure is typical. Many anglers do much better, with catches in excess of 20 fish being reported. Good over-wintered fish over 8lb are common. The record rainbow is currently 16lb and the brown a wee bit smaller. It's an any-method water (no maggots) but fly tends to outfish bait. The North Basin is exclusively for fly fishing only and this is where some of the best sport is enjoyed. Heavy hatches of black buzzer in April/May account for most of the big bags. In the summer months, when there is surface activity, try Black Gnat, Hawthorn Fly or beetles. When it is too hot, and the fish go deep, one of the flashy lures will do well. Almost anything with orange in the tying is a good bet. In the late season static nymphs, buzzers and pheasant tails, fished on a long leader, can be deadly. For those anglers who brave the winter months, any of the big black lures fished deep should take fish. In general boat fishermen cover the lake by drifting with the wind. The best drifts are over mid-water shallows, but remember to lift the outboard motor when drifting in shallow water.

To keep the family happy, there is a small 'catch your own' area where children are virtually guaranteed to catch a trout, near the shop.

Pike fishing

Although, at over 250 acres, Esthwaite Water can look a bit overwhelming it is advisable to persevere because this is arguably the best water in the whole of England for big pike. It is hardly surprising the pike grow big because the lake is well stocked with trout and there are masses of coarse fish. The lake is known to hold thousands of 'doubles', many more over 20lb, some over 30lb and specimen fish tipping the scales at over 40lb. And in the cold winter months, when pike fishing is allowed and it is the best time to fish for pike anyway, they are very lively. When there is a nip in the air and no wind, take a boat out and try dead bait fishing along the weedy fringes of the bays. There are also known hot spots in the southern end near the car park. A static ledgered dead bait fished almost anywhere in that area will attract a take.

Fishery Rules (Trout)

Catch and release after limit taken. Barbless hooks only. No maggot fishing.

Fishery Rules (Pike)
No live bait fishing.
Facilities on Site
Car park. Toilet. Boats available. Adapted boat for wheelchair anglers. Tackle and flies for sale. Tuition from bank or boat. Special competition arrangements for groups or clubs. Fish farm and shop on site. Dead bait sold on site.

FISHER TARN

Location (OS97:550928)
Approximately 5 miles east of Kendal on the A684 road to Sedbergh.
Fishery Controller
North West Water Authority.
Water and Stock
A lovely 3 acre drinking water supply reservoir, holding both brown trout and rainbow trout.
Ticket Prices
Contact Kendal Sports Shop, 30 Stramongate, Kendal (Tel: 01539 721554).
Opening Times
During the trout fishing season from sunrise to 1800 hrs.
Description
North West Water's Fisher Tarn, actually a 3 acre drinking water supply reservoir for Kendal, is fished by a small private syndicate. The water holds some smallish brown and rainbow trout with few bigger grown-on fish. Most of the popular lake flies will take fish. In the early season try a Silver March Brown or a Black and Silver. From late May onwards the fish come to the surface. A Greenwell's or a Black Gnat are the favourites then. It's also worth trying a Black and Peacock Spider, especially by the reeds.
Fishery Rules
Fly fishing only. No spinning, worm or ledger. No wading. No dogs.
Facilities on Site
Small car parking area.

GATEBECK RESERVOIR

Location (OS97:565862)
From Kendal, take the A65(T) road towards Endmoor. Turn left

onto the B6254 to Oxenholme and continue through the village. Go through Old Hutton and under the M6. In about 1$^{1}/_{2}$ miles, turn right on the small road to Gatebeck. The reservoir is about 500 yards down the road on the right.

Fishery Controller

Kendal and District Angling Club. *See Angling Clubs section.*

Water and Stock

A small mad-made reservoir holding a good stock of carp, minnow, perch, roach, tench and trout.

Ticket Prices

Day ticket £3.00, senior citizens and juniors £2.00. Weekly ticket £8.00, senior citizens and juniors £4.00. From Carlsons Fishing Tackle in Kendal (Tel: 01539 724867), Go Fishing in Bowness-on-Windermere (Tel: 015394 47086), The Fishing Hut in Grange-over-Sands (Tel: 015395 32854) and Witherslack Post Office (Tel: 015395 52221).

Opening Times

All year from dawn to dusk.

Description

Gatebeck is a tiny water with room for only about 3 anglers and is relatively unfished. In fact it is so rarely visited it's difficult to know what is swimming in the shallow weedy water. It's known that there are carp in Gatebeck, but they are not very big, plenty of roach and perch, some tench and the inevitable brown trout. Float fishing is the best method to use and bread, sweetcorn or worm are the favourite baits. This is a perfect venue for a solitary angler looking to catch fish in quiet surroundings and, who knows, you may just catch a monster carp! There is no access for disabled anglers.

Fishery Rules

None.

Facilities on Site

Car park on the road at the western end.

GHYLL HEAD RESERVOIR

Location (OS97:398922)

From Bowness-on-Windermere, take the A592 south towards Newby Bridge. After about 2 miles, turn left onto the small lane, Cartmel Fell Road. In approximately $^{1}/_{2}$ mile, the lake is on the right. There is ample car parking near the entrance gate.

*Fly fishing at the popular **Ghyll Head Reservoir** overlooking
Lake Windermere*

Fishery Controller
Windermere, Ambleside and District Angling Association. *See
Angling Clubs section.*

Water and Stock
A long, thin Lakeland reservoir of about 11 acres stocked with
rainbow trout averaging about $1^{1}/_{2}$lb and some up to 8lb. There are
also a few native brown trout.

Ticket Prices
Day ticket £8.50 for 2 fish. The nearest outlets are the Beech Hill
Hotel on the A592 just south of the turnoff to Ghyll Head (Tel: 01539
724867) and Go Fishing, Gilly's Landing, Glebe Road, Bowness-on-
Windermere (Tel: 015394 47086). Tickets also from other local
fishing tackle shops and tourist information centres.

Opening Times
Season 15th March to December 31st (brown trout season March
15th to September 30th). Fishing from dawn to dusk.

Description
The Lake District abounds with beautiful lakes and to say Ghyll
Head is one of them does not really do it justice. It's actually a man

made reservoir set in lovely surroundings and commanding fine views over Windermere. The grassy bankside is beautifully maintained (by the grazing sheep) and there are just enough trees to give some shade in the summer. Surprisingly it's not a wild water to fish. Except when a westerly gale blows, the lake is sheltered from the worst of the weather. It's long and thin, almost tooth-shaped and is very deep particularly near the western end by the dam wall where the water drops away to near 20 feet. At the top end, where the feeder beck enters, it's only about 2 feet deep and in summer it is very weedy. Around this area and in the shallow bays, there are shoals of minnows to keep the rainbow trout active. Watch the shallow edges for signs of feeding rainbows. At the right time of year, a fry imitation, pulled across the nose of a big trout, will induce a take. In the summer months a Corixa, or a tadpole imitation fished on the edge of the weeds often attracts a rainbow. Early in the season, try a Viva or Marabou pattern on a sinking or sink tip line. Fish fairly deep and expect a savage take. In early summer the Damsel patterns, buzzers, small goldheads and traditional nymphs should do well. Some tagged fish have been released to encourage catch and release fishing. They must be returned if caught before September 30th.

Fishery Rules

Fly fishing only. Two fish limit. No wading. Catch and release permitted.

Facilities on Site

Car parking.

GILCRUX FISHERY

Location (OS89:117385)

About 8 miles east of Maryport in north-western Cumbria. From Maryport take the A596(T) road towards Carlisle. In about 4 miles, at Crosby Villa, turn right towards Bullgill. Go through the village and take the next left to Gilcrux. Turn left in Gilcrux to the lakes.

Fishery Controller

Mr Gilbert and Helen Pyke, Rydal Mount, Gilcrux, Cumbria (Tel: 016973 22488 or 22971).

Water and Stock

Two lakes, one holding a variety of trout and the other, rainbow trout only.

Ticket Prices
Fly fishing lake: eight hours £15.00 for 5 fish, four hours £10.00 for
3 fish. Bait fishing lake: day £6.00 for 2 fish. Additional tickets may
be purchased. Season tickets are available. All permits are available
from the farm house at the top of the gravel track. Not from the
bungalow overlooking the fishery.

Opening Times
All year from 0800 to 2030 hrs or dawn to dusk.

Description
There are two small lakes on site, one for fly fishing only and the
other for the bait fisherman. Both have been excavated in a quiet
area on the edge of a trout farm and both have open bankspace to
allow easy casting. The fly fishing lake holds a selection of species
including brook trout, brown trout, golden trout, rainbows and
char. It's unusual to find char stocked in a small fishery. It's
becoming very rare and is more commonly found in the deeper
lakes of Cumbria. It is a member of the salmon family, beautifully
coloured and a hard fighter, so it's well worth trying for one. You
will probably need to fish close to the bottom and use a flashy lure.
Golden trout and American brook trout are also unusual fish to find
in a put-and-take fishery. It's good to see them and, on the right day,
they can be just as greedy as common rainbows. All the trout will
respond well in the early season to lures, but the lake is not very
deep so leave the lead-cored lines at home and use a floater with a
longish leader. In summer, try buzzers or a Gold Ribbed Hares Ear
nymph. Use a strong leader because some of the rainbows are over
10lb, the takes can be savage and the fish acrobatic when hooked.
The bait pool is somewhat larger than the fly pool and holds
rainbows averaging about 2lb up to over 5lb.

Fishery Rules
Catch and release is permitted if barbless hooks are used. Return
all golden and brown trout.

Facilities on Site
Car park.

GRASMERE LAKE

Location (OS90:335065)
Alongside the A591 Ambleside to Keswick road approximately
3¹/₂ miles north-west of Ambleside.

Fishery Controller
Windermere, Ambleside and District Angling Association *(see Angling Clubs section)* on behalf of The National Trust.

Water and Stock
Over a mile long and ¹/₂ mile wide holding some good pike, perch, eels and roach. There are also some excellent brown trout and a very few late sea trout and salmon.

Ticket Prices
Week £10.00, senior citizen and junior £5.00 and day £3.50, senior citizen and juniors £2.00. Tickets, which also permit fishing on many WADAA waters, from Go Fishing, Gilly's Landing, Glebe Road, Bowness-on-Windermere (Tel: 015394 47086), other fishing tackle shops and tourist information offices. Boats can be hired from Allonby's Boatyard, opposite Kelbarrow house on the road to Loughrigg. One person per hour £4.00, two people per hour £6.00 etc. Launching own boat from site £8.00 per day plus parking.

Opening Times
Open all year, but from March 15th to June 15th inclusive the only permitted fishing methods are lures and fly, spinners or worms. Positively no fish baits during this period.

Grasmere, one of Lakelands best known waters, is a fine fishery

Description

About three-quarters of the bankside fishing on Grasmere is controlled by the WADAA and the remainder is private. The Association's water starts on the east bank, from the point where the A591 leaves the shore, near the Prince of Wales Hotel, and continues down towards the outflow, across the footbridge and then up the west side until the public footpath strikes away from the water's edge. The rest of the bank, that is all of the northern end, is strictly private. Despite having miles of bankspace available for fishing, it is difficult to find solitude here. It gets very busy with walkers and bikers and there doesn't seem to be a season for them! But the fishing is brilliant. If it's pike that you're after, this is the place to be. The fish are generally bigger than those downstream in Rydal Water and more prolific. There are plenty of fish in the range 8 to 10lb, lots more up to 20lb and some, to make your mouth water, over the magical 30lb barrier. Some of the best fish come from the deep water alongside the A591 on the eastern side. Try laying a dead herring or golden sprat on the shingle bottom. Be patient but move it every so often to make sure it's not hidden by weed. Some of the local anglers use a section of dead eel as bait both here and downstream in Rydal. It is not surprising that the pike go for it - there are a lot of eels in Grasmere.

The perch fishing is also great. Maggots on a floating rig is the most consistent method, but perch readily take a spinner. Try one and you might even pick up one of the big brown trout. Don't count on it though, there seem to be fewer of them now than was once the case. But if you're lucky and get into one over 4lb they run far and fast so make sure you have good strong tackle. The salmon run has dropped off over the last couple of decades. But if you intend to try for a fish don't forget that you will need a different EA rod licence and it is more expensive.

In summer it's wise to stay clear of the south-western side - it gets packed with families enjoying a picnic and swimming in the clear water. For a quieter day out, hire a boat from Allonby's Boat Yard in Grasmere.

Fishery Rules

No night fishing or camping. Strictly no live bait fishing. No access to the island or the north shore. Carefully return all coarse fish, to the water, alive - this includes pike.

Facilities on Site
One boat, for the use of members only. Other boats can be hired from the boatyard at the northern end of the lake. Car parking in the village, White Moss Common and in the lay-bys alongside the A591.

GRISEDALE TARN

Location (OS90:350120)
Situated about 2 miles south-east of Thirlmere. Park on the A591 and follow the footpath up the fell to Grisedale Hause. The tarn is a little further uphill.

Fishery Controller
The National Trust.

Water and Stock
Another classic Lakeland Tarn holding small brown trout.

Ticket Prices
Free fishing for holders of an Environment Agency rod licence.

Opening Times
April 1st to September 30th from dawn to dusk.

Description
Grisedale is a beautiful water, but sitting as it does nearly 1,800 feet above sea level, it is wild and often difficult to fish. It's deep in places, dropping to over 60 feet, the water is clear and as you might expect it's full of native brown trout. Travel light and wear something warm, even in summer, as it can be cold at high altitude. The fish readily take worms, but they can also be tempted with a fly. Any of the northern patterns will take them, especially when there is some sun on the water.

Fishery Rules
None.

Facilities on Site
None.

HALLMORE FISHERY

Location (OS97:501770)
From Milnthorpe take the A6 south. In about 5 miles turn right onto a road signposted to Arnside, Silverdale and the Wildlife Oasis and caravan site. Follow the signs to Hallmore Fishery.

Fishery Controller

Geoff and Michelle Campbell, Lakeside, Hallmore Farm, Hale, Cumbria LA7 7BP

(Tel: Lake 015395 64400, farm 01524 420073 or mobile 0467 304584).

Water and Stock

One $2^{1}/_{2}$ acre lake holding some big carp and lots of roach and rudd.

Ticket Prices

Season ticket £75.00, junior £40.00. Day/night ticket £5.00, junior £3.00. Second rod £2.00. Tickets obtainable at the farm, the fishing hut or from the bailiff Mr Pat Foster.

Opening Times

All year from dawn to dusk. Night fishing by prior arrangement. Juniors must be accompanied by an adult when night fishing.

Description

This 15-year-old mature lake is squarish in design with one large shrub-covered island. All the bankspace is accessible and it is easy to find a nice quiet spot to settle down with a floater or ledger rig between the weeds and lily beds. The water varies in depth from about 6 feet to 10 feet and is generally clear. Unusually for this area, the emphasis at Hallmore is definitely on carp. But that's not surprising as the owner is a carp enthusiast. And he is a man who knows his fish and knows what carp anglers are looking for. Under his guidance, Hallmore is rapidly becoming a top northern carp fishery. It's sensibly run and the carp are big. There are grass carp to 26+lb, commons to 15+lb and mirrors and leathers to 20+lb and they like boilies. There is no doubt that this is the favourite bait. A variety of boilies, plus other concoctions, is on sale in the caravan which doubles as a fishing hut. The popular flavours are multivitamin, plum and stench! Maggots or lob worms will also take their fair share of fish as will floating crust, particularly on the hot summer's evening. The lake also holds large shoals of both roach and rudd to about $1^{1}/_{2}$lb.

Disabled access from the car park is easy and there is an area in front of the fishing hut reserved for wheelchair anglers.

Fishery Rules

All nets must be dipped before fishing. Barbless hooks only. No bloodworm or joker. Groundbait in moderation. No large fish to be kept in nets, return to water immediately after weighing and taking photos. Use unhooking mats. No fires.

Facilities on Site

Disabled access. Free coffee and tea for anglers. Toilet. Fishing tackle and bait for sale. Tuition can be arranged.

HARLOCK RESERVOIR

Location (OS96:249791)

From Barrow-in-Furness, take the A590 road towards Ulverston. At Lindal-in-Furness, turn left to Marton. In the village turn right and follow the road uphill to the reservoir.

Fishery Controller

Barrow Angling Association on behalf of North West Water. *See Angling Clubs section.*

Water and Stock

A very large upland reservoir holding a good head of native and stocked brown trout.

Ticket Prices

Day ticket £12.00 for 3 fish from Mr J. R. Jones, 69 Prince Street, Dalton-in-Furness (Tel: 01229 462955). Ticket also covers Pennington, Poaka Beck and Roosecote Reservoirs.

Opening Times

Dawn to dusk from March 15th to September 30th.

Description

One of three reservoirs set high on a hillside overlooking Morecambe Bay, Harlock can be a wild place to fish. It is higher on the hillside than its neighbours and consequently is more open to the strong winds. Indeed, there are days when it's better to move to Poaka Beck or Pennington than try to battle with the elements. On most days though, when the wind is not blowing from the south, it's relatively sheltered and easy to get at. The banks are solid and a road circumnavigates the water. At first sight these big reservoirs can appear somewhat daunting. It seems that just finding the fish will be a problem. Not so here. Poaka Beck is stocked monthly with good quality brown trout, and because the insect life is prolific, they feed well and grow on quickly. When the wind blows from the south try a black lure - a Viva is the favourite - on a slow retrieve along the stony bottom near the dam wall. Black is also a good colour when there is a flat calm. A Black and Peacock Spider can be a killer as can a tiny Black Gnat. In the autumn try a big bushy dry fly, something like a Daddy Long Legs or Walker Sedge and be prepared for violent takes. A Toby is the best spinner.

Fishery Rules
Fly fishing and spinning only. Barbless hooks only. No trebles.
Catch and release operates but fishing must stop after killing three
fish.
Facilities on Site
Car park.

HAWESWATER RESERVOIR

Location (OS90:480140)
Haweswater is situated to the east of High Street in eastern Lakeland.
It is easily found from the A6 at Shap. Take the road to Rosegill and
Brampton Grange. Turn left in the village to the reservoir.
Fishery Controller
Northern Estates Management Team, North West Water Ltd, The
Old Sawmill, Thirlmere, Keswick, Cumbria (Tel: 01768 772334).
Water and Stock
A massive stretch of water holding a good stock of native brown
trout and char. There are also some pike and perch.
Ticket Prices
The fishing is free to holders of an Environment Agency rod licence.
Opening Times
March 15th to September 30th.
Description
At some $5^{1}/_2$ miles long by $^{1}/_2$ mile wide, Haweswater can be
daunting, not it is not really that bad. To begin with it is beautiful.
Surrounded by steep rugged fells, it is a classic Lakeland water. It
can be difficult to fish though, particularly when the strong winds
blow. The trick is to dress warmly, wear strong boots and take some
provisions. Unless you enjoy an energetic walk, stick to the south
bank where a road follows the shore line. The fishing is good all
round the water and the access is better from this road. Don't expect
to catch fish on the first visit. The lake is not stocked. All the fish are
wild but they are very lively. Mostly it's better to try worms,
although on the right day sunken lures on a fast sinking fly line will
attract the browns. When the fish are showing on top, buzzers are
a good bet. During the Daddy Long Legs season, try a good artificial
in one of the wind lanes. If there is no immediate take, jerk it every
so often and wait for the crash. You'll also catch a lot of perch. They
can run to 2lb but they are mostly smaller. If it's the pike you're after,

a dead sprat or similar fished near one of the shallower areas is a good bet. Sadly there have been no reported catches of char for some time.

Fishery Rules

Char must be returned to the water unharmed. No maggots or loose feed to be used.

Facilities on Site

Car parks at various points along the eastern shore on the dead-end road leading to the southern end of the reservoir. Large car park at the end.

HAYESWATER RESERVOIR

Location (OS90:430120)

From Windermere, take the A592 road towards Ullswater and Penrith. Follow the road up and over Kirkstone Pass to Brotherswater and Hartsop village. Leave your car in the car park and take the pass up Hayeswater Gill, about 1¹/₂ miles, to the reservoir.

Fishery Controller

Windermere, Ambleside and District Angling Association on behalf of North West Water.

Water and Stock

A man-made reservoir of nearly 35 acres holding brown trout, char and schelley.

Ticket Prices

Week £10.00, seniors and juniors £5.00. Day £3.50, seniors and juniors £2.00. Tickets also cover fishing on many WADAA waters. *See Angling Clubs section.* The nearest outlets are the tourist information centres in Glenridding (Tel: 017684 82414), Grasmere and Ambleside (Tel: 015394 32582). Also from local fishing tackle shops and other tourist information centres.

Opening Times

March 15th to September 30th from dawn to dusk.

Description

Huddled in a tiny valley on top of the world near High Street, 1,400 feet above sea level, this is a wild water to fish. It also demands a lengthy hike to get to it, so it's really only for the fleet of foot. Remember also to dress warmly as most of the time it is windy and cold and the low cloud and drizzle can move in pretty quickly. Because of its remoteness, Hayeswater is very under-fished, but for any energetic fisherman who takes sensible precautions, it is a great place to fish. There are thousands of wild brown trout, some char and the unusual schelley to be caught. Treat it as a day out. If the fish are not feeding, just sit back and admire the views, some of the finest in Lakeland. Fishing for brown trout is the best bet. Most of the upland wet flies take fish. In the early season, when you probably won't see another fisherman, try Invicta, Dunkeld, any of the Claret range or possibly a Zulu. In summer, especially on the calm days, buzzers and nymphs will take fish. When there is a gentle breeze, as opposed to a howling gale, blowing across the water, try a big bushy fly in the wind ripples.

Fishery Rules

Fly fishing only. Two fish limit. Catch and release encouraged using barbless hooks. No boats.

Facilities on Site

The beautiful unspoilt scenery.

HIGH ARNSIDE TARN

Location (OS90:331011)

This tiny tarn is best found from Skelwith Bridge. Take the A593, over the River Brathay, towards Coniston. In approximately 1¹/₂ miles a small track on the left, marked Cumbria Way, leads to High Arnside Farm and Tarn Howes. The fishery is a few hundred yards up the track. Cars are not allowed. Park in the lay-by on the opposite side of the A593.

Fishery Controller

Windermere, Ambleside and District Angling Association (*see Angling Clubs section*) on behalf of the National Trust.

Water and Stock

A tiny lake of approximately 1¹/₂ acres holding native brown trout and stocked rainbows.

Ticket Prices

Weekly ticket £10.00 (seniors and under 17s £5.00). Daily ticket £3.50 (seniors and under 17s £2.00). Tickets from Go Fishing, Gilly's Landing, Glebe Road, Bowness-on-Windermere (Tel: 01539447086) and most tourist information centres.

Opening Times

March 15th to September 30th from dawn to dusk.

Description

Set in delightful surroundings, this tiny tarn offers some interesting fishing for rainbow trout. It's unusual in Lakeland to have rainbow trout stocked into such a small lake but they seem to like the water and grow-on well. Fish in excess of 3lb are present and because the water is rich in insect life there are likely to be bigger fish around. Unfortunately High Arnside, lying in a sheltered sun trap, is fairly shallow and consequently suffers with the weed in summer, but then it can be an interesting time to fish. At times rainbows can be seen attacking the shoals of tiny minnows which swim in the weedy areas. On those days, use a strong leader and a fry imitation and you should have a good day. In the early season it's best to try lures. Anything in black is usually good. Viva or flouro-green bearded Montana both take their share of fish.

Fishery Rules

Two fish limit. Catch and release encouraged using barbless hooks. No boats.

Facilities on Site

Car parking in the lay-by on the A593 facing Cumbria Way.

HIGH DAM

Location (OS97:362888) See map p195

At the southern end of Lake Windermere. From Newby Bridge take the A590(T) towards Ulverston. In a $^1/_4$ mile turn right over the River Leven towards Lakeside. Go through the village and in $^3/_4$ mile, take left at a T junction. The car park for Bobbin Hill is on the right as you drive towards Finsthwaite.

Fishery Controller

The Lake District National Park Authority.

Water and Stock

A 10 acre dam holding perch, pike, rudd and trout.

Ticket Prices

Free fishing for holders of a valid Environment Agency rod licence.

Opening Times

All year. No night fishing.

Description

It's a long and difficult climb from the car park to this mature water, but it's worth it. This is a lovely lake, set in beautiful wooded surroundings not far from the shores of Lake Windermere and it is full of fish. Probably the best fishing is for the perch and pike. As always they will take almost anything. Maggots are good for the perch and rudd and the pike will fall to a small dead sprat ledgered alongside the weeds. The rudd tend to be prolific and fairly large shoals can be seen in the shallows. Attract one of these and a keepnet can be filled quickly. There's also a good stock of small brown trout averaging about four to the pound and they will take maggots or worms. Try float fishing in the top end where the tiny feeder stream comes in. Or alternatively the deeper water near the overflow will often hold a bigger fish. Although in the summer there are rising fish, open bankspace is at a premium and back casting is virtually impossible, so fly fishing is very difficult. The area is a renowned beauty spot and consequently it gets very crowded in the warm summer months.

Fishery Rules

None.

Facilities on Site

None.

HIGH NEWTON TROUT FISHERY

Location (OS96:400840)

From Newby Bridge, at the outflow of Windermere Lake, take the A590(T) road towards Levens and Kendal. In 2¹/₄ miles at Ayside Village turn left onto a narrow road into the village. After a short distance, turn left again onto the single track lane leading up a steep hill to the reservoir. It is a gated road. Please close them.

Fishery Controller

Windermere, Ambleside and District Angling Association on behalf of North West Water. *See Angling Clubs section.*

Water and Stock

A 10¹/₂ acre reservoir with a good head of natural brown trout and stocked rainbow trout averaging 1¹/₂lb with a few fish growing on to nearly 10lb.

Ticket Prices

Day ticket £8.50 for 2 fish from Newby Bridge Motor Services on the A590 (Tel: 015395 31253) and Carlsons Fishing Tackle, Kendal (Tel: 01539 724867), Kendal Sports Shop (Tel: 01539 721554). Also from other fishing tackle shops and tourist information centres.

Opening Times

March 15th to December 31st (brown trout season March 15th to

September 30th). Fishing is from dawn to dusk.

Description

Situated on a hillside overlooking Morecambe Bay, High Newton can be a wild fishery, especially when a south-westerly wind blows, but it is one of southern Lakeland's beautiful places and well worth a visit. All the bankside is accessible, especially on the dam wall and the adjoining sides. At the top end, where the feeder streams enter, the banks are craggy and the water depth drops away very quickly. This is a popular area for anyone fishing a lure on a sinking line. The crystal clear water is very deceptive though. Don't be tempted to wade in to land a fish - water which looks to be only a few inches deep can often be over several feet. High Newton is a popular early season venue, but it can be very cold fishing it then. Dress up warmly before you start and when a cold southerly wind blows, keep it at your back and fish the deeper water by the dam wall. A sunken line with one of the flashy Fritze's or Montanas, cast out into the 12ft deep water, should induce a take. Later in the season the fish move into the shallower water on the northern side and will take the ubiquitous buzzers in black or green, almost any tying of goldhead and olive or brown shrimps. When the days are warm, there's usually a prolific hatch of flies and the rainbow trout gorge themselves on the surface. During the day small black flies are good, in the evening switch to a brown hackled fly such as a medium brown sedge. If it's the wild brown trout you're after, try the traditional northern wet fly patterns - Invicta, Butcher, Grouse and Orange - in the area by the craggy banks at the top end.

Catch and release fishing is positively encouraged here. Use barbless hooks and be careful how you return the trout. Unhook the fish whilst still in the net and release from there. The water is stocked every two weeks. Some specimen sized tagged rainbow trout are stocked at the opening of every season for catch and release sport fishing. These fish are in addition to the normal stocking and, if caught before September 30th must be returned alive.

Fishery Rules

Fly fishing only. Two fish limit. Catch and release operates. Barbless hooks only. No boobies on sunken lines.

Facilities on Site

Car parking in several lay-bys along the eastern side.

HIGH STANDS LAKES

Location (OS86:482501)

Situated in the Eden Valley approximately 4 miles south-east of Wetheral. From the A69 Carlisle to Brampton road, take the B6263 to Wetheral. Go through the town and in about 1¹/₂ miles turn left for Armathwaite. Half a mile after crossing the railway line, turn right towards Cotehill. On the edge of the village, turn left into High Stand Plantation. Follow the unmade track for about 2 miles, into the forest, to the lakes.

Fishery Controller

Bigwater Angling Club on behalf of the Forestry Commission.

Water and Stock

Three small lakes with a variety of coarse fish.

Ticket Prices

Season tickets only £15.50 from Geoff Wilson, Tackle Shop, 36 Portland Place, Carlisle (Tel: 01228 531542).

Opening Times

All year from dawn to dusk.

Description

Three very pretty, tiny lakes on the edge of the massive High Stand Plantation offer some excellent coarse fishing in secluded surroundings. The lakes are well hidden from view. Even after driving nearly 2 miles into the forest and getting to within a few yards of the water, they are not easy to find, but once there you'll have plenty open bankspace to set up a rig. This is definitely a fishery for an angler who likes to be alone. One who likes to catch a lot of fish in a secluded and very beautiful setting. It's also a good place to visit on windy days. When it's impossible to get a line out at some other venues, High Stand Lakes are so well protected that the surface of the water will be flat calm. And there are plenty of fish to be had. One of the lakes is teeming with tench. The fish are not massive, averaging about 3 to 4lb, but some do go over 5lb and they are exceedingly obliging. They will take most of the popular baits and they love sweetcorn, maggots and bread, although red worms are especially good. Large bags are the order of the day with some anglers taking 20 to 30 fish in one session. As always the weedy corners offer the best chance of a fish. Try sweet corn on a floating rig, near the bottom and as close to the reeds as possible. The other lakes are better known for their shoals of roach, rudd and perch and

139

are a favourite with pole anglers. Maggots, pinkies, casters and squats all take fish.

Fishery Rules
No night fishing.

Facilities on Site
Small car parking area.

HOLEHIRD TARN

Location (OS90:408009)
From Windermere, take the A592 towards Kirkstone Pass. Holehird Estate lies about 2 miles outside Windermere. The entrance is clearly marked on the righthand side of the road. The anglers' car park is signposted just inside the entrance to Holehird Hall, a Cheshire Home. It is approximately 200 metres from the car park to the fishery.

Fishery Controller
Windermere, Ambleside and District Angling Association, *see Angling Clubs section.*

Water and Stock
A kidney shaped lake of about 3 acres holding some good carp, bream, chub, gudgeon, roach, rudd and tench.

Ticket Prices
Day ticket £3.00, juniors £1.50. Only four permits are allowed and they must be obtained in advance from Go Fishing, Gilly's Landing, Glebe Road, Bowness-on-Windermere (Tel: 015394 47086) or from other fishing tackle shops and tourist information centres.

Opening Times
June 16th to March 14th. Fishing from one hour before sunrise to one hour after sunset.

Description
Southern anglers will find it easy to bond with this fishery. It's a man-made feature pond set in the beautiful 19th century grounds of Holehird Hall, now a Cheshire Home. The water is fairly shallow, about 6 feet at its deepest point near the dam, rising to only 2 feet deep near the inflow. As you would expect, the parkland that surrounds it has been beautifully landscaped with no expense spared on trees and shrubs. One side of the lake is wooded whereas the other, where the boathouse is situated, is formed of well-shorn grass. There are currently 13 pegs giving access to most of the water,

except those areas where it is nearly impossible to fish because of weedy margins and overhanging trees. Only 10 anglers are permitted at any one time, including only 4 visitor permits, so there's always room to move around. It's primarily a carp water, and a good one. The fish are not big by southern standards, but they are plentiful. Expect commons to about 15lb with a lot more in the 6 to 8lb bracket. They will take most of the popular baits. If you are after the bream (up to 6lb), the tench (4lb), the roach (1½lb), the rudd (1lb) or the big chub (5lb), try the old faithful maggots, casters, pinkies and squats. Feed lightly with hemp.

Fishery Rules
No night fishing. Four visitor tickets only in any one day.

Facilities on Site
Car park.

KENTMERE FISHERY

Location (OS90:455032)
From the A591 Windermere to Kendal trunk road turn left to Staveley. After purchasing a fishing ticket in Staveley, take the road running alongside the River Kent, towards Kentmere. Follow this road up the ever narrowing valley until, about ½ mile short of Kentmere village the fishery is signposted on the left.

Fishery Controller
Mrs Harrison (Tel: mobile 0585 560706 or evenings 01768 88263).

Water and Stock
Two beautiful lakes, one of 30 acres and the other 4 acres, holding brown and rainbow trout. Salmon run into the larger lake in the autumn.

Ticket Prices
Day ticket £16.00 for 4 fish; half day (5 hours) £10.00 for 2 fish. Sporting day ticket £10.00, sporting half day £6.00. Evening ticket, after 1700 hrs £7.00 for 1 fish. Tickets, which permit fishing in both lakes, must be obtained prior to fishing from D. & H. Woof, Newsagents, 22 Main Street, Staveley (Tel: 01539 821253).

Opening Times
Season March 15th to October 31st. Fishing from 0800 hrs to dusk.

Description
Kentmere is an unusual fishery located in the upper Kent Valley close to the river. Indeed, the River Kent flows through part of the

fishery and brings with it an abundant supply of clean water and insect life. The Main Lake, a natural water extending to nearly 20 acres, looks like a lowland tarn with clear water, reed fringed edges and perfectly conditioned trout. Natural imitations are the best flies to try here. Buzzers and pheasant tails are always good as, in season, are Damsel Nymphs and Mayfly Nymph. At certain times a Black and Peacock Spider, fished a few inches below the surface, is a killer. When there's a good rise, try an Alder or Gold Ribbed Hares Ear. There are some big browns and rainbows in the lake and because of its size and depth, dropping to 15 feet, they have a lot of space to run into when hooked. Use a good strong leader especially if you are fishing in the late season when you may hook one of the salmon that run through the lake on their way to the spawning grounds. Depending upon water levels, the first salmon arrive in early August. It is advisable to book in advance for this lake when the salmon are about.

East Bay Lake, approximately 4 acres, is deep and very clear providing a good home for the big trout that are stocked. They average about 1^{1}/$_{2}$lb but fish over 13lb have been taken in the past. This is another terrific fly fishing water, clear in the margins yet with just enough cover to permit fish stalking. A weighted tadpole imitation is always good for this method of fishing. When there is a ripple on the water, the fish rise well to sedges and other bushy flies. Nymphs or buzzers do well in the surface film. On some days the fish can be seen chasing the large shoals of minnows that swim in the margins. When you see them, try an imitation minnow.

Fishery Rules

Fly fishing only. Catch and release permitted after limit taken. Use barbless hooks.

Facilities on Site

None.

KILLINGTON RESERVOIR

Location (OS997:590910)

Alongside the Killington Service Area on the southbound side of the M6. It's best approached by leaving the M6 at junction 37 northbound and crossing the motorway on the A684 towards Sedbergh. In about 500 yards turn right onto an unmarked road and follow it to the reservoir.

Fishery Controller

Kent Angling Association on behalf of British Waterways. *See Angling Clubs section.*

Water and Stock

A very large reservoir extending to nearly 80 acres with a good stock of perch, pike, wild brown trout and a few rainbows.

Ticket Prices

Weekly ticket £4.50 and day £2.00 from the reservoir keeper, Mutton Hall Farm, 200 yards from the water, Carlson's Fishing Tackle, Kendal (Tel: 01539 724867) or Kendal Sports Shop (Tel: 01539 721554).

Opening Times

March 15th to September 30th for trout and all year for coarse fish. Fishing is from dawn to dusk.

Description

Acres of water and miles of bankspace make this an excellent venue for anglers who don't like to be crowded. It's very quiet and peaceful, if you stay clear of the west bank and the M6 motorway, that is. It is also under-fished and well worth a visit. Killington is primarily a trout fishery holding some fine fish. It supports a good stock of native browns ranging from 1/2lb up to over 5lb and stocked rainbows of much the same size. Perch are also present in big numbers and there are some large pike, many over 20lb. Huge numbers of 'Jacks' between 6 and 8lb, roam at will and keep the small fish population down. This water is a feeder reservoir for the Lancaster Canal and consequently its level will fall from time to time. It's not deep, 20 feet seems to be the maximum near the dam wall rising to only a few feet in the weedy bays at the north-east end. Fishing from the wall is prohibited. Depending upon the wind direction, the best places to try are in the shallower margins and the weedy bays. During the summer when the minnows are on the move, it's usually easy to tempt rainbows with a fry imitation or a black tadpole. Watch the water for turbulence as the fish gorge themselves on small fry! Access is easiest from the eastern side where a small road skirts the reservoir. Fishing along any of this bankspace is popular. The pike fishing is good throughout the year but most anglers only fish for them outside the trout season. Favourite methods are dead bait laid on the edge of the weeds or spinning a flashy spoon in the northern bays.

Fishery Rules
Fly only until June 16th, then any method. No maggot fishing.
Facilities on Site
None.

KNOTT END TARN

Location (OS96:133977)
This water sits alongside the River Esk and is best found from
Ravenglass. Take the A595(T) east and south until it crosses the
River Esk. Turn first left, signposted and continue to Knott End. The
tarn is on the left.
Fishery Controller
Mr W. Arnold, Knott End Estate, Ravenglass, Cumbria CA18 1RT
(Tel: 01229 717255).
Water and Stock
A beautiful 3^1/$_2$ acre tarn stocked with brown trout averaging ^{3}/$_4$lb
and some fish to 4lb.
Ticket Prices
Day ticket £12.00 for 2 fish or 4 hours' fishing. Available on site.
Opening Times
Dawn to dusk during the trout fishing season.
Description
In an area of the country where beautiful lakes are easy to find,
Knott End, with its landscaped islands and banks, is one of the best.
A mature tarn, approximately 3^1/$_2$ acres, sitting neatly in the beautiful
Esk Valley, it blends well into the countryside. The banks are well
tended and fishing stages have been constructed to give easy access.
It's a purist fly fishing water where traditional dry flies and methods
work best. And a place where, on the odd occasions when the trout
are not interested, it's nice to pause and admire the spectacular
scenery. Remember the tarn is stocked with brown trout. Leave the
flashy flies at home. In the early season try the old faithful Black
Gnat (the winged variety) and as the season progresses try Gold
Ribbed Hares Ear or an Iron Blue. In the late summer when the
Daddy Long Legs are about the sport can be furious. If there is a
wind, cast one into a ripple and wait for the take. It will be savage.
Because of the prolific fly life, there's hardly a day when the trout are
not rising. But of course there will be days when they are 'tailing',
showing a tail on the surface as they go after the emerging nymphs.

On these days try buzzers or caddis. It is also worth trying a Corixa when you see fish tails. Take your time at this water - it is clear, so a carelessly cast shadow will scare the fish. Use barbless hooks and return the smaller fish carefully.

Fishery Rules
Maximum size 12 short shank hook. Full floating line only. No line trays. No stripping. No lures of any type are permitted. All fish over 12 inches must be returned carefully to the water.

Facilities on Site
Car park. Fly casting tuition available including tackle.

LEVENS WATER

Location (OS97:280992)
Situated about 2 miles north of Coniston Village. From the village, follow the track leading to the old mine workings. Levens Water is approximately 1 mile further on up the track.

Fishery Controller
The National Trust.

Water and Stock
A small lake supporting an abundance of tiny trout.

Ticket Prices
Free fishing for holders of an Environment Agency rod licence.

Opening Times
April 1st to September 30th from dawn to dusk.

Description
Now about 5 acres in size, Levens Water is a natural lake that was once extended by building a dam. It is a pleasant water, clear and fairly deep in the middle, set in attractive moorland and very secluded. It's very rare to see anyone fishing here which is a pity because there are lots of hard fighting wild trout to be caught and they can be large, up to 1lb. Best fishing is from the dam wall and the favourite method is a float fished worm.

Fishery Rules
None.

Facilities on Site
None.

LILY MERE

Location (OS97:604915)

Situated close to Killington Reservoir alongside the M6. Take junction 37 from the motorway and follow the A684 towards Sedbergh. Lily Mere is on the right in about 1¹/₂ miles.

Fishery Controller
British Waterways.

Water and Stock
A beautiful and secluded lake feeding Killington Reservoir. The mere and Tarn Moss in which it sits is a wildlife conservation area. No fishing is permitted.

Ticket Prices
No fishing.

LITTLE LANGDALE TARN

Location (OS90:310032)
From Ambleside, take the road to Skelwith Bridge and continue on the A593 towards Coniston. Turn right to Little Langdale - the tarn is in the valley near the village.

Fishery Controller
The National Trust, North West Region, The Hollens, Grasmere, Ambleside, Cumbria LA22 9QZ (Tel: 015394 35599).

Water and Stock
A beautiful small tarn of about 1 acre in the diminutive Little Langdale valley. There are plenty of tiny wild brown trout and a few perch.

Ticket Prices
No fishing is permitted.

LITTLEDALE HALL COARSE FISHERY

Location (OS97:567620)
About 6 miles due east of Lancaster. Take the A683 towards Kirkby Lonsdale. In Caton village, turn right at the Black Bull Inn and follow the road to Littledale Hall.

Fishery Controller
Morecambe Angling Centre. (Tel: 01524 832332)

Water and Stock
An attractive 1 acre lake holding a variety of coarse fish, including bream, carp, roach and tench.

Ticket Prices
Day ticket £3.00 or, at weekends, £4.00 from the Morecambe Angling

Centre, Grange Garage, Thornton Road (Tel: 01524 832332).

Opening Times
All year from dawn to dusk.

Description
A pretty, landscaped lake in the grounds of a fine old house make this an ideal water for those anglers who appreciate the combination of pleasant surroundings and good fishing. It's a long and narrow lake with plenty of bankspace and has relatively easy access to the whole water. Only 14 rods are permitted, so the banks never get overcrowded. Big carp are the main goal for many anglers here. Commons of 26$^{1/2}$lb have been recorded and there are many fish in the middle range, around 12 to 14lb. There is also a fair stock of crucians. The carp go for sweetcorn and luncheon meat as well as the ever popular boilies. Every carp fisherman has a winning flavour. For the best one to try here ask Howard Barker at the Morecambe Angling Centre when you buy a ticket. He knows the water better than anyone else. Maggots, casters and pinkies will all take their fair share of the bream, roach and tench as will the trusty traditional bread crust. As an added bonus, you may get a surprise and land one of the cat-fish.

Fishery Rules
No ground baiting. No night fishing. No carp or anything over 3lb to be kept in nets.

Facilities on Site
Car park.

LONGLANDS LAKE

Location (OS89:013128)
From the centre of Egremont, take the A595 towards Whitehaven. After about 1$^{1/2}$ miles turn right onto the A5086 to Cleator Moor. In approximately 1$^{1/2}$ miles turn right at a signpost indicating Longlands Lake. Follow the track alongside the garage to the car park. Cross the suspension bridge, over the River Ehen, to the lake.

Fishery Controller
Wath Brow and Ennerdale Angling Association. *See Angling Clubs section.*

Water and Stock
A 3$^{1/2}$ acre pond with stocked rainbow trout, averaging about 1lb, and some wild browns.

147

Ticket Prices

Day ticket (visitor) £9.00, (member) £5.00. Stop after 3 fish limit is reached. Only 1 ticket per person per day. From Wath Brow Stores and Post Office, 121-122 Ennerdale Road, Wath Brow, Cleator Moor (Tel: 01946 810377) and J. W. N. Holmes and Son, Fishing Tackle and Firearms, 45 Main Street, Egremont (Tel: 01946 820368).

Opening Times

Dawn to dusk, during the brown trout season.

Description

An attractive lake, set in pleasant scrubland alongside the River Ehen. It's a popular spot for local dog walkers and visitors so it can get busy in the summer. At first glance, Longlands looks like a coarse fishery but in fact, apart from a few pike, it's stocked with both brown and rainbow trout. On the right day, when the sun is shining and there is a gentle breeze to ripple the water, the sport can be outstanding. On most other days it can be frustratingly quiet. It's quite a shallow lake so there is no need for sinking lines. A sink tip or floater with a longish leader will suffice. In early season try a lure near the lake bed. There are some submerged branches and shrubs along the side near the River Ehen so expect to lose a few flies. Almost any of the popular patterns will attract fish. Orange is usually a good colour and marabou a good material. The Fritz range will also attract the rainbows. Because it's shallow, Longlands warms up quickly. When the sun is on the water it's best to try buzzers or dry flies. The weedy margins are a good place to go after the rainbows. Try a black tadpole imitation.

Fishery Rules

Fly fishing only. No other baits or methods permitted. No returning fish to the water. No wading. One permit only per day.

Facilities on Site

Car park.

LONGTOWN WEST POND

Location (OS85:372689)

North of Carlisle near where the A7 crosses the River Esk at Longtown. Immediately after crossing the river, the flooded gravel pits are on the left. Turn left onto the A6071 Gretna Road, go over the railway bridge and turn immediately left into the fishery.

Fishery Controller

Mr Chris Bowman, Crosshill Cottage, Blackford, Carlisle CA6 4DU (Tel: 01228 74519).

Water and Stock

One large lake holding specimen coarse fish including bream, carp, chub, perch and pike.

Ticket Prices

Season permit £40.00, day tickets £4.00 from Mr & Mrs Yeomans, 3 Smalmstown Terrace, Longtown (adjacent to the pond), Chris Bowman at the address above and Geoff Wilson Fishing Tackle, Carlisle. Permits **must** be obtained before fishing.

Opening Times

From dawn to dusk all year except for one Saturday in July when the water is closed for swan ringing.

Description

There are three lakes on site but only the largest, and the best, one is open for fishing.

The West Pond, an ex-gravel pit of 20 acres, is run by a small syndicate as a specimen fishery. Because of low fish density, weed growth and variety of depths, it has the reputation of being a difficult water but what it lacks in quantity it makes up for in quality. This does mean that visitors will be unlikely to find the fish on a single visit. It will take time to learn about the water and discover the best baits. But once you've got to grips with it you'll soon realise that it's a great fishery. The water regularly delivers some fine specimen fish. Bream to 11lb, carp to 24lb and chub over $5^{1}/_{2}$lb have been recorded recently and, because all fish, except small pike, must be returned, there could be bigger fish lurking in the depths. To maintain fish quality, there is a strict no keepnets rule, although specimen fish may be sacked until photographs have been taken. The favourite baits are boilies, sweetcorn, potato, maggots and worms.

West Pond holds a lot of pike. In an attempt to increase the average weight of the pike stock, all fish less than 6lbs are to be removed from the fishery. All other pike must be returned to the water as soon as possible. No live baiting for pike.

Fishery Rules

No bent hook rigs allowed. No live baiting. No keepnets.

Facilities on Site

Car park.

LONSDALE PARK LAKES

Location (OS86:465515)

North-east of Carlisle in the beautiful Eden Valley. From junction 42 on the M6 south of Carlisle take the B6263 road to Cumwhinton village. Turn right towards Cotehill. In approximately $1^{1}/_{2}$ miles, at the Lonsdale Park sign, turn left. Follow the road, under the railway line, into the park.

Fishery Controller

Lonsdale Park, Nr. Cotehill, Cumwhinton, Carlisle CA4 0AY (Tel: 01228 573375 or mobile 0370 825896).

Water and Stock

Five lakes of 10 acres in total, each holding specimen coarse fish.

Ticket Prices

Fishing is free for guests staying in the lakeside cottages or static mobile homes. A limited number of day tickets at £4.50 are issued for Arches Lake.

Opening Times

All year from dawn to dusk.

Description

Lonsdale Park is a beautiful natural mature park of some 30 acres situated in the Eden Valley. It's a dream location for both dedicated coarse fishermen and novice anglers. There are five lakes each of which holds some big coarse fish and each of which is under-fished. There is approximately 10 acres of water - that's almost an acre for each holiday chalet, so it never gets crowded and the chalets are at the lakeside so there is no time lost in getting to the fishing. Some of the cottages are equipped for disabled anglers who have direct access to their own reserved fishing pegs on Lonsdale Lake, the largest water. It's $4^{1}/_{2}$ acres in size and a carp fisherman's dream. Fish of 30lb+ have been landed here in the past. There are also ghost carp to 18lb and grass carp to 20lb and lots more over 10lb. The tench fishing is brilliant. Fish up to 9lb have been taken in the past. There are also perch to $3^{1}/_{2}$lb, roach over the magical 2lb and chub over 4lb. If all that isn't enough, the pike are massive. If you try for one, be prepared for a thirty pounder. As its name suggests Reed Lake, a former nature reserve of $2^{1}/_{2}$ acres, has numerous reedy bays beloved of carp. It is a good stalking water. It also holds tench, roach and perch. Deer Lake is famed for its ghosties, wildies and mirrors. Plenty of fish to 17lb are ready for the taking. There are also some big tench, roach, chub and perch. Birch Lake, really a small pool, is unusual. It's aimed at novices and young children. The fish are not big, the carp rarely exceed 4lb, but they are plentiful and there are lots of tench and roach to keep young minds occupied. Last but by no means least is the 2 acre Arches Lake which is available for fishing on a day ticket. Numbers are limited so phone in advance. It's a pretty lake with easy access, particularly along the open banks facing the wooded area, and it's full of carp, tench, perch and roach. They all respond well to the usual proprietary baits.

Fishery Rules

Two rods per person. Barbless hooks only, minimum size 8 for carp. No fixed leads. Minimum breaking strain 8lb for carp, 3lb otherwise. No particle baits, except hemp and sweetcorn. No keepnets. Carp sacks only to be used for 20lb+ fish. Unhooking mats to be used for all large fish. Night fishing by arrangement.

Facilities on Site

Car park. Various types of accommodation. Tackle for sale.

LOUGH TROUT FISHERY

Location (OS85:320563)

From the centre of Carlisle, take the A595 Workington Road. About 500 yards after crossing the River Caldew, at Willow Holme roundabout, take the B5307 towards Kirkbampton. In approximately 5 miles, after going through Moorhouse village, on the outskirts of Thurstonfield, turn left into Thurstonfield Lodge and the fishery.

Fishery Controller

Raymond Potter, Lough Trout Fishery, Thurstonfield, Carlisle, Cumbria (Tel: 01228 576552).

Water and Stock

One 25 acre lake stocked with rainbows.

Ticket Prices

Day ticket (0900 to 1700 hrs) £18.00 for 4 fish. Part day (0900 to 1300 hrs or 1300 to 1700 hrs) or evening (1700 to 2100 hrs or dusk), £9.00 for 2 fish. Rowing boats: Day £6.00, morning or afternoon £3.00, evening £4.00.

Opening Times

March 15th to October 31st from 0900 to dusk. Ticket office closes at 1800 hrs. Opening hours vary at weekends and on bank holidays. It is advisable to book in advance (Tel: 01228 576552).

Description

The Lough, a 25 acre stream fed lake, is a natural water set in 50 acres of beautiful woodland designated as a Site of Special Scientific Interest. To preserve the many rare plants, grasses and wildlife that exist around the lake, landing is not allowed. Fishing is permitted only from specially constructed boats that will easily and safely carry two anglers. The Lough is exceptionally well stocked with full tailed rainbow trout at around 90 to 100lb of fish per acre. Because of the nature of the wooded area, fly life abounds. There are consistent fly hatches throughout the summer and autumn bringing rainbows to the surface at almost any time of day. When there is a good rise on the water, most of the popular patterns will take fish. On the inevitable windy days, try a Walkers Wake fly or any of the big bushy sedges in the wind lanes. It's surprising just how often a large rainbow comes from the depths to take one of these flies when it is skittered across the ripples. In the early season one of the black lures, Marabou Viva, Ace of Spades or similar, will usually take fish. There is good wheelchair access via a loading ramp onto a 'Wheely Boat' specifically designed for disabled anglers. It has been supplied by the Country Landowners Charitable Trust and is available for disabled visitor booking.

Fishery Rules

Boat fishing only. Fly only, less than size 10. Maximum 16 anglers. All anglers must carry a landing net and a priest. All fish caught to be killed.

Facilities on Site

Disabled 'Wheely Boat' available. Toilets. Refreshments. Flies for sale. Scandinavian pine bungalows, overlooking the lake, for hire.

LOUGHRIGG TARN

Location (OS90:345043)

From Ambleside follow the A593 towards Coniston. At Skelwith Bridge, turn right onto a minor road leading up a steep hill to Tarn Foot. Loughrigg Tarn lies in the tiny valley below Loughrigg Fell.

Fishery Controller

The National Trust, North West Region, The Hollens, Grasmere, Ambleside, Cumbria LA22 9QZ (Tel: 015394 35599).

Water and Stock

A small picturesque tarn holding mostly roach, pike and perch and a few native brown trout.

Ticket Prices

Day ticket £1.00 from Mr Murphy, Tarn Foot Farm (a few hundred yards south of the lake) (Tel: 015394 32596).

Opening Times

All year for coarse fishing. Brown trout fishing between March 15th and September 30th.

Description

Undoubtedly one of the prettiest and most accessible tarns, Loughrigg offers some really good fishing. It sits in a natural 'bowl' in a tiny valley between Grasmere and Elterwater, at the meeting of some popular lowland walking paths, and consequently the area can be very busy at times. But there is no official access to the waterside, unless you buy a ticket. The tarn is almost circular and because the natural slope of the surrounding fells continues into the water, its depth shelves quickly from a few inches at the edge to around 50 feet at the centre. All the bankspace is accessible to anglers, but the easiest part to get at is close to the farm and it's a good place to start. This is a fine coarse fishing venue. There are plenty of perch and roach. Worm is the best bait, although coloured maggots, casters and sweetcorn will all take fish. Try float fishing - waggler or slider methods tend to be best. As with most Lakeland tarns, Loughrigg holds a lot of pike. They're not big, anything over 10lb is a good fish, but they are prolific. There are also a huge number of 'Jacks' of 5 or 6lb, and they seem to like a small dead bait laid in the deeper water just off the reeds. This is also a good method for taking the bigger perch and you may just make contact with one of the large native brown trout. There are some beautiful brown trout in Loughrigg and they do fall regularly to bait fishermen. Few anglers bother fly fishing, but a roach fry or similar imitation fished on a sinking line is worth a try.

Fishery Rules

No boats are permitted.

Facilities on Site

Limited car parking in the farmyard.

LOWESWATER

Location (OS89:125215) See map p97

Loweswater is easy to find. From Cockermouth take the B5292

Keswick road. In about $4^1/_2$ miles turn right onto the B5289 to Buttermere. After a further 3 miles turn right to Loweswater and continue through the village until the road meets the lake.

Fishery Controller

The National Trust, North West Region, The Hollens, Grasmere, Ambleside, Cumbria LA22 9QZ (Tel: 015394 35599).

Water and Stock

Loweswater holds mainly wild brown trout although there are a few perch and pike.

Ticket Prices

Season ticket £35.00, week £10.00 and day £3.00. Senior citizens and children under 17 years old, season £15.00, week £4.00 and day £1.00. Tickets also cover Buttermere and Crummock Water. Rowing boat hire £15.00 per day, £10.00 after 1200 hrs and £6.00 after 1700 hrs. All tickets from Mr and Mrs Leck, Water End Farm, Loweswater (Tel: 01946 861465) and Grahams Guns, Workington (Tel: 01900 605093).

Opening Times

Dawn to dusk, March 15th to October 30th.

Description

Smallest of three lakes, sharing a compact valley in the north-east of the Lake District National Park, Loweswater is the most fertile. Beautiful, comparatively shallow (up to 30 feet), often placid, sometimes, when a strong north-westerly blows, choppy, its character constantly changes and it can be a difficult lake to fish. But it does offer some fine fishing. The most popular area, although not the most productive, is on the north-east side where a minor road skirts the water. The fishing is better near Holme Wood on the opposite bank, but access to it is difficult, unless you enjoy a strenuous walk. The nearest car parking is at Waterend and from there it's a long way to the fishing. But it is worth it. Of course the easiest way to get there is by boat.

It's fly fishing only until June 16th and in the early season you'll need to get well down with one of the brighter lures. Any of the marabou flashers will take fish. From May onwards, when the weather has warmed up a bit, it's best to try sub-surface flies or buzzers. The native browns are prolific and fairly large and it is not unusual to take a couple of dozen in one session. Try for them in the evening - if the day has been warm there is almost certain to be a good rise. Beautifully marked full tailed fish over 3lb have been landed from here in the past and there is no reason why bigger browns should not be caught. After June 16th many of the bigger fish are taken on worm ledgered in the deeper water by Holme Wood and in the area of the outflow. Spinning is often productive. Try a Devon Quill, the mottled green variety seems to be best. The pike and perch fishing is equally as good in Loweswater as elsewhere in Lakeland but few anglers try their luck. Those that do report pike over 20lb and perch to nearly 3lb.

Fishery Rules
Fly only until June 16th then worm or spinning is allowed. No private boats to be launched.

Facilities on Site
Parking at Waterend and at a few places along the road from Loweswater to Mockerkin.

MEADLEY RESERVOIR

Location (OS89:050145)
About 2¹/₂ miles east of Cleator Moor in Western Cumbria. From Whitehaven take the road to Cleator Moor. Go through the village to Wath Brow and cross the River Ehen. Take the third road on the right and follow it up the hillside to the reservoir.

Fishery Controller
West Coast Trout Anglers on behalf of North West Water. *See Angling Clubs section.*

Water and Stock
A 1¹/₂ acre moorland reservoir with native brown trout and stocked rainbows.

Ticket Prices
Day ticket £12.00, for 3 fish, juniors (under 16) £7.00 for two fish, from Wath Brow Post Office, Ennerdale Road, Cleator Moor (Tel: 01946 810377). Six tickets only per day.

Opening Times
April 1st to October 31st from an hour after sunrise to one hour after dusk.

Description
This is yet another beautiful Lakeland reservoir. Set well away from the usual tourist routes and overlooking the lovely Ehen Valley, it's an ideal place for anglers wanting to get away from it all and catch

fish. Access is easy and it's possible to get a car to within a few yards of the dam wall. From the wall, the long distance views are quite spectacular as, on some days, is the fishing. It's stocked every two weeks with rainbows between $1^{1}/_{2}$lb and 4lb and, inevitably, there are heavier grown-on fish. Meadley also supports a good stock of native browns that spawn quite happily in the side streams. It's not known how big they are, but fish over the magical 4lb have been landed here. A popular fishing area is along the wall where it's possible to step down below the lip and get the inevitable wind at your back. Lures are good attractors. Early season black and green types when fished close to the stonework of the wall will usually take fish. In summer, when the fish come higher in the water Gold Ribbed Hares Ear, Montana nymphs and Parachute Suspenders are all killers. Try them in the shallower area to the left of the car parking space and on the right where the feeder stream enters. When the wind blows, a Jersey Herd or a Muddler will take fish from the wind lanes and a Daddy Long Legs or a sedge does well when skittered through the ripple.

Fishery Rules
No night fishing. Fly fishing only. No boats. No dogs. No catch and release permitted.

Facilities on Site
Car parking area.

MILL BECK FISHERY

Location (OS96:213688)
Situated in the heart of Barrow-in-Furness on Salthouse Road. Follow the A590 road into the centre of Barrow. Cross two roundabouts and continue until the road passes under the railway bridge. Turn right onto Salthouse Road. Continue to Salthouse Mill. The fishery entrance is alongside the mill.

Fishery Controller
Mr John Hutchinson, Millbeck Fishery, Salthouse Road, Barrow-in-Furness, Cumbria (Tel: 01229 837619).

Water and Stock
One lake of approximately 2 acres holding bream, common, crucian and mirror carp, rudd, tench and some trout.

Ticket Prices
Day tickets, adult £4.00, child £2.00 and father and son combined

£5.00.

Opening Times

All year from 0900 hrs to dark.

Description

Mill Beck is a mature lake of about 2 acres that will appeal to anglers searching for excellent quality coarse fishing. Situated on the outskirts of Barrow-in-Furness and easily accessible, it is good for those anglers who don't like long walks to the waterside. There is a solid path the whole way round and 26 pleasantly sited pegs. Entry from the car park is flat making access for wheelchair anglers relatively easy. The lake itself used to be fly fishing water, so there are some trout to be caught but they are now few and far between. It's clear and moderately deep with a good bottom for laying-on a bait. Most of the popular baits take fish. The dedicated carp anglers use home brewed concoctions based on bread and potato but the new baits are just as good. Maggots are always very popular as is luncheon meat and corn. The carp run to about 18lb, the tench to 6lb, and the bream to 5lb.

Fishery Rules

Barbless hooks only. Keepnets are allowed.

Facilities on Site

Car park. Toilets. Fishery holds a block EA rod licence. Horse riding, riding lessons and hacks available.

MOCKERKIN TARN

Location (OS89:083252) See map p97

From the centre of Cockermouth take the A5086 Cleator Moor road. Cross over the bypass. In approximately 5 miles, just after the turnoff for Mockerkin village, the tarn is on the lefthand side of the road.

Fishery Controller

Haig Anglers. Contact via The Compleat Angler, 4 King Street, Whitehaven CA28 7LA (Tel 01946 695322).

Water and Stock

A large tarn of about 6 acres holding mainly pike perch and a few eels.

Ticket Prices

Season tickets only.

Opening Times

Dawn to dusk during the coarse fishing season.

Description

Mockerkin is a pretty tarn often overlooked by serious coarse fishermen, which is a pity because it has a lot to offer. Although the fish are not very big, they are plentiful. The jack pike average about 4 to 5lb and live mainly in the area around the weedy margins away from the roadside. They will readily fall for a dead silver sprat laid on the muddy bottom or a flashy spoon pulled through the weed fringes. Take care when spinning as the lake is very shallow and there are underwater branches to trap your favourite spinner. It is no more than 3 feet deep near the reeds dropping to a maximum of about 8 feet at the centre. Without doubt, maggots are the best bait for the perch. Attract one of the big shoals and you will have a good day. Eels seem to like the habitat and grow well.

Fishery Rules

No night fishing.

Facilities on Site

Car park in the large lay-by alongside the tarn.

MOSS ECCLES TARN

Location (OS97:371969) See map p195

This remote tarn is best found from Hawkshead village. Take the B5285 south towards the ferry for Bowness-on-Windermere. In the village of Near Sawrey, facing the Tower Bank Arms, a small track leads to the fishery. No vehicles are permitted. Park in the village and walk to the tarn.

Fishery Controller

Windermere, Ambleside and District Angling Association on behalf of the National Trust. *See Angling Clubs section.*

Water and Stock

A very remote 5 acre Lakeland tarn stocked with brown trout only.

Ticket Prices

Weekly ticket £10.00, senior citizens and juniors £5.00. Day £3.50, seniors and juniors £2.00. Limit 2 fish per day. The closest ticket outlet is the Tower Bank Arms in Near Sawrey village (Tel: 015394 36334) who also have two free tickets for residents. Tickets can also be had from the Ings Service Station, on the A59 about 8 miles east of Windermere, Carlsons Fishing Tackle, Kendal (Tel: 01539 724867), Kendal Sports Shop (Tel: 01539 721554) and tourist information centres.

Opening Times

March 15th to September 30th from dawn to dusk.

Description

An unusual upland tarn situated well off the beaten track in a partly wooden area west of Windermere Lake, Moss Eccles is a delightful place to fish. It's a bit of a hike to get at it though. Leave your car in Sawrey village and follow the bridle track north for about 1 mile to the lake. It's uphill most of the way and only for the fit, but the trip is worth it because Moss Eccles is full of wild trout regularly supplemented with browns averaging 1lb. Some of the grown-on fish go over the 3lb mark and it is possible that the legendary 4lb barrier will be broken here. The area around the tarn is partly wooded and part open moorland and is designated as a Site of Special Scientific Interest. Wildlife breed in the undergrowth and aquatic insects thrive in the clear shallow water of the margins. It's also a cold place to fish in the early season but the temperature doesn't seem to bother the trout that will obligingly take the traditional north country patterns. The natural wets are best. Try a March Brown, a Mallard and Claret, a Grouse and Claret or an Invicta in the deeper water near the craggy overflow. As the season progresses most buzzers or nymphs will bring results. When it's hot and the sun is strong, try the area in the shade of the pine trees. A lot of the fish will have gone deep but there are sure to be a few in the shade. During the autumn, when there's a strong ripple on the water, try a dry fly. A big one to interest the big fish! Something like a Walker's Wake Fly or a Daddy Long Legs will bring a big brown from the bottom with a smash. Use a strong leader. If it's seclusion and great trout fishing that you're after, try Moss Eccles, you won't be disappointed.

Fishery Rules

Two fish limit. Catch and release encouraged using barbless hooks. No boats.

Facilities on Site

Car parking at Near Sawrey village.

NEW MILLS TROUT FISHERY

Location (OS86:549617)

From the centre of Carlisle, take the A69 Newcastle road and follow

*The big lake at **New Mills Trout Fishery**, Brampton*

the Brampton bypass to the end. Turn left as indicated by the signs showing New Mills Trout Farm. In about 500 yards turn right to the fishery.

Fishery Controller
Mr Bill Grey, New Mills Trout Farm, Brampton, Cumbria CA8 2QS (Tel: 016977 2384).

Water and Stock
There are three lakes, all holding rainbow trout. One, about 10 acres, is a fly fishing lake, another, called Ford Pool, is for 'duffers' and the smallest is for children.

Ticket Prices
Fly fishing lake day ticket £10.00 for 4 fish (two fish guaranteed), juniors £6.00 for 2 fish (one guaranteed). Rod hire £3.50. Ford Pool and Children's Pool, tickets £2.00 plus all fish killed at £1.70 per lb. Rod hire £1.50.

Opening Times
All year from dawn to dusk. Closed on Mondays.

Description
New Mills Fish Farm nestles alongside a tiny tributary of the River Irthing in a compact picturesque valley outside Brampton. The

man-made fly fishing lake of approximately 10 acres is situated some distance from the farm, down an unmade track. It lies in a pleasant wooded area, perfect for anglers who seek peace and solitude when fishing. The lake was re-excavated in 1997, the banks were flattened to give easy access and the area sensibly landscaped. Although the lake is set in a wooded area, there is plenty of back casting space. There is also an abundant supply of clean water keeping the water clear and making it easy to spot cruising trout in the lake margins. It's about 3 to 4 feet deep at the edge dropping away to around 18 feet near the long island. Only full tailed strong rainbow trout, averaging $1^{1/2}$lb with some fish to 3lb, are stocked and there are no doubt some bigger grown-on fish. In the early spring, lures are good. Try a Montana with a green beard. As the water warms up, large hatches of buzzers and caddis form most of the trout's diet. Goldheads are also good, as are the traditional dry patterns.

Ford Pool, about 2 acres, with a stream running through it, is close to the main car park. One end holds a complex of rearing cages so there's probably a fair number of escapees to supplement the already over-stocked water. It is essentially a 'duffer's' lake, as the literature states "for the impatient, the inexperienced and the hungry." To ensure that you catch a fish, it is any method water that is teeming with trout.

Behind the farm shop is a tiny junior pool, again with the stream running through it, where youngsters learning to fish can try their hand. It's also full of fish, so it should not be too long before a few plump trout are in the net.

Fishery Rules

Fly fishing only in the main lake.

Facilities on Site

Farm shop, toilets, car park, lunches and cream teas in the Old Granary.

OAKBANK LAKES COUNTRY PARK

Location (OS85:365700)

Situated just south of the Scottish Border at Longtown. From the A7 Carlisle to Canonbie road at Longtown, cross the River Esk. Follow the road for a further $1^{1/2}$ miles and turn left at a well-marked road leading to Oakbank Lakes Country Park.

Fishery Controller

Mr Mike Powell, Oakbank Lakes Country park, Longtown, Nr. Carlisle, Cumbria CA6 5NA (Tel: 01228 791108).

Water and Stock

Several lakes and pools holding a variety of coarse and game fish. Also stretches of game fishing on the Border Esk and the River Liddle.

Ticket Prices

Season, all lakes £80.00, disabled £50.00, junior £30.00 plus £20.00 joining fee. Visitor day tickets, £8.00, £5.00 and £3.00 respectively, plus entrance fee £1.50. Concessions for campsite residents and increased fees for 24 hour fishing. Trout day £13.00 for 3 fish, £10.00 disabled or student.

Border Esk fishing at Longtown Bridge. Day tickets, £5.00 (February-April), £20.00 (May), £30.00 (June-August) and £55.00 (September and October). Any method.

Opening Times

All year. Twenty four hours a day.

Description

Over the past decade, the 60 acre Oakbank Lakes Country Park has been nicely developed into a major recreational facility offering some superb fishing for both game and coarse anglers. There are three main lakes totally 25 acres plus the Monk's Pools, small waters for novices to catch their first fish. The over 3 miles of open bankspace have been sensibly landscaped to provide easy access whilst still maintaining the seclusion sought by many anglers. Disabled anglers are exceptionally well catered for. Paths, fishing stages and other special facilities have been specially constructed and The Oakbank Complex is the annual venue for the Jack Charlton Disabled Angling Trust national competition.

At 13 acres, Oakbank is the largest lake. It's a fine trout fishery holding both brown and rainbow trout, averaging approximately 6 to 7lb. This is a fly fishing only water where most of the popular flies attract trout. Lures cast into the deeper water in the spring will take fish. Try a Viva or similar patterns in black. Montanas are also good. In the early summer, a small Damsel nymph can be a killer. As the lake warms up, sub-surface flies and buzzers take their share of fish. There are also some big carp. Fish to 24lb have been taken on pork luncheon meat fished on a static rig. Barn Lake, 10 acres, is a mixed fishery well stocked with rainbow trout but also holding some big carp. Mirrors and commons in excess of 20lb are in here and it is not uncommon for several to be caught in one session. An angler recently had seven fish over 20lb, one tipping the scales at 21¾lb. Luncheon meat and sweetcorn are the favourite baits for carp and they have even been known to attract the rainbows. Both fly and bait fishing are allowed and boats are available by arrangement. Middle Lake, about 2 acres, and separated from Oakbank Lake by a narrow peninsula, is well stocked with trout, carp, tench and bream so it will suit most anglers. Both fly and bait fishing is allowed. Maggots, pinkies and worms are the best baits for the bigger bream. Sweetcorn is good for the tench - try the new flavoured varieties for a change. Monks' Pools have been developed and landscaped to provide sheltered pools that are intensively stocked with rainbow trout, carp and tench giving inexperienced anglers the opportunity to catch fish. The pools have very easy access, solid banks and are ideal for small children, with parental supervision, to try their hand.

Salmon fishing is also available on the famous Border Esk on the Longtown Bridge water. There are some excellent holding pools which, in the autumn, give up a number of large fresh run fish.

Fishery Rules
Use barbless hooks only. Keepnets prohibited. No tiger nuts or peanuts allowed.

Facilities on Site
Toilets. Disabled toilet and bath. Refreshments. Car park. Tuition. Tackle hire. Trophy
photo service. Holiday homes and static caravans for hire.

OVERWATER TROUT FISHERY

Location (OS90:250350)
From Keswick, take the A591 Carlisle road north to Kilnhill. Turn right towards Uldale. In about 3 miles turn right again to Overwater. The Lake is on the righthand side of this road.

Fishery Controller
Stan Edmonson, The Trout Farm, Seathwaite, Borrowdale, Keswick (Tel: 017687 77293).

Water and Stock
A moorland tarn extending to 35 acres fully stocked with quality brown trout in the range 1lb to 8lb.

Ticket Prices
Day ticket £18.00, including boat, for 3 fish; half day or evening
£15.00, including boat, for 2 fish. Three boats only per day. Tickets
from Field & Stream, Keswick (Tel: 017687 74396) and Mrs
Richardson, Fold Head Farm, Watendlath, Keswick (Tel: 017687
77255). Boats can be pre-booked (Tel: 017687 77293).

Opening Times
March 24th to September 30th from 0900 hrs until dusk.

Description
Situated in a flat fertile valley and surrounded by sheep grazed
rolling moorland, Overwater is a sun trap and a lovely water to fish.
It's full of high quality brown trout averaging between 1lb and 2lb
with some fish reaching 8lb. Fishing is only permitted from a boat
and as there are only 3 available, advanced booking is essential.
Boats hold two anglers and there is a 6 fish limit per boat. On a busy
day that means that six rods have over 35 acres of water to themselves!
The surrounding fells offer little protection from the wind and on
some days it can be wild. The best days are when a light breeze
blows insects onto the water from the prolific bracken bushes which
seem to be everywhere. When this happens, try a dry Greenwell's
Glory or an Olive. If they fail, a big bushy fly should take fish.
Depending upon the time of year, something in black or brown, like
a Black Palmer or Cinnamon Sedge will take fish. Later in the
season, an Iron Blue Dun is worth a try. During the evening rise, the
spent flies or parachute tied patterns can be killers. On the days
when there is a flat calm, fishing can be very difficult. When it's hot
and the water surface is as shiny as glass, sub-surface buzzers and
nymphs are worth trying, but you'll need to use a fine leader and be
very careful. If that fails, go deeper with one of the traditional wet
patterns, Mallard and Claret, Black Pennell or an Invicta. A floating
line with a long leader or a sink tip is best. No need for the fast
sinkers here.

Fishery Rules
Fly fishing from a boat only. Barbless hooks only.

Facilities on Site
The spectacular setting. Accommodation in Overwater Hall Hotel.

PENNINGTON RESERVOIR'
Location (OS96:258790)

From Barrow-in-Furness, take the A590 road towards Ulverston. After about 5 miles turn left to Loppergarth and Pennington. In Loppergarth take the second left to Castle Hill. Continue up Copse Hill and the reservoir is on the left.

Fishery Controller

Barrow Angling Association. *See Angling Clubs section.*

Water and Stock

A very large upland reservoir holding a good head of native and stocked brown trout.

Ticket Prices

Day ticket £12.00 for 3 fish. From Mr J. R. Jones, 69 Prince Street, Dalton-in-Furness (Tel: 01229 462955). Ticket also covers fishing on Harlock, Poaka Beck and Roosecote Reservoirs.

Opening Times

Dawn to dusk during the trout season, March 15th to September 30th.

Description

One of three reservoirs set high on the hillside overlooking Morecambe Bay, Pennington is a lovely place to fish. It's the lowest sited of the three and therefore enjoys more sheltered conditions. There are days when it's possible to fish here, but not at Harlock or Poaka Reservoirs a mere $^1/_4$ mile away. It's also easy to get at, the banks are solid and a reasonably good path follows the perimeter. At first sight these big reservoirs can appear to be daunting. It looks as if finding the fish will be a problem. Not so here. Pennington is stocked monthly with good quality brown trout and, because the insect life is prolific, they feed well and grow on quickly. When the wind blows from the south try a black lure, a Viva is the favourite, on a slow retrieve along the stony bottom. Black is also a good colour when there is a flat calm. A Black and Peacock Spider can be a killer as can a tiny Black Gnat. In the autumn try a big bushy dry fly, something like a Daddy Long Legs or Walker Sedge. Be prepared for violent takes. A Toby is the best spinner.

Fishery Rules

Fly fishing and spinning only. Barbless hooks only. No trebles. Catch and release operates but fishing must stop after killing three fish.

Facilities on Site

Car park.

PINE LAKE

Location (OS97:515725)

Situated between the M6 motorway and the A6 at Warton near Carnforth. The entrance to the Pine Lake Leisure Complex is from the slip road connecting the A6 to junction 35 of the M6.

Fishery Controller

Pine Lake Leisure Resort.

Water and Stock

One large gravel extraction lake supporting carp, eels, perch, pike and roach.

Ticket Prices

Day ticket £3.00, half day £2.00 from the Morecambe Angling Centre (Tel: 01524 832332). Fishing is free to chalet residents at the Pine Lake Resort.

Opening Times

All year from dawn to dusk.

Description

Pine Lake is the largest of a group of lakes formed by gravel extraction for the M6. The area around it has undergone extensive development to create, amongst other things, a leisure complex including lakeside chalets, swimming pool, night clubs, keep fit facilities and a sailing school. Consequently it's a busy place and not for an angler who values peace and quiet or one who wants to use a pole. Bankspace is restricted for visiting anglers but there is sufficient to get at the hot spots and there are some good coarse fish to be had. Pike are one of the targets. Fish can top 20lb and they have a liking for dead bait laid on the bottom. Carp anglers will be happy with the quality of the fish and, although they are not enormous, around 10 to 12lb, there are enough to keep most anglers busy. Boilies are the favourite bait, although a few fishermen wouldn't be without pork luncheon meat. Disabled access is fairly easy although no specific pegs have been allocated.

Fishery Rules

Fish in indicated areas only. No night fishing.

Facilities on Site

Car park.

PINFOLD LAKE

Location (OS91:646070)

Situated on the outskirts of the tiny village of Raisbeck. Leave the M6 at junction 38 and take the A685 towards Kirkby Stephen. The turn to Raisbeck is on the left in about 1¼ miles.

Fishery Controller

Mr John Pape, 12a High Wiend, Appleby-in-Westmoreland, Cumbria CA16 6RD (Tel: 017683 52148 or 0973 345342).

Water and Stock

One lake of approximately 3 acres holding rainbows averaging about 1lb with some fish up to 8lb.

Ticket Prices

Day £15.00 for 4 fish. Four rods only per day. Phone one of the numbers above to book. Tickets must be collected from Appleby before fishing.

Opening Times

Fishing from dawn to dusk during the trout season, March 15th to September 30th.

Description

This beautiful secluded lake is ideal for anglers who enjoy traditional fly fishing in uncrowded pleasant surroundings. It is spring fed and 'squarish' in shape with the deeper water, dropping to 18 feet, at the overflow end. Sensible landscaping has been undertaken to provide good seclusion and yet allow access for fishing, although there is no access for disabled anglers. The water is kept stocked with high quality rainbows and is operated as a traditional fishery. In the early season sunken small lures, anything in black, take fish as do the gold headed nymphs, but the fishing really comes into its own when the sun shines and there is a gentle breeze. That's when the fish come to the surface, or just below it, and take a variety of traditional offerings. Try a Gold Ribbed Hairs Ear or a Pheasant Tail, or if they fail, buzzers are always good. When a strong wind blows, try casting a bushy brown fly, a Walkers Sedge for instance, across the lanes and expect a vicious take. At tadpole time, a good imitation fished near the weeds at the top end of the lake will interest a fish. Also a corixa dropped on the nose of a cruising rainbow will generally induce a take. This quiet venue is ideal for a group of four anglers fishing together. They will have the entire lake to themselves.

Mr Pape also issues tickets to fish the River Eden at Appleby. *See River Eden entry.*

Fishery Rules

Fly fishing only.
Facilities on Site
None.

POAKA BECK RESERVOIR

Location (OS96:243784)
From Barrow-in-Furness, take the A590 road towards Ulverston. At Lindal-in-Furness, turn left to Marton. In the village turn right and follow the road uphill to Irelath. The reservoir is on the right in about 1 mile.

Fishery Controller
Barrow Angling Association. *See Angling Clubs section.*

Water and Stock
A very large upland reservoir holding a good head of native and stocked brown trout.

Ticket Prices
Day ticket £12.00 for 3 fish. From Mr J. R. Jones, 69 Prince Street, Dalton-in-Furness (Tel: 01229 462955). Ticket also covers fishing on Harlock, Roosecote and Pennington Reservoirs.

Opening Times
Dawn to dusk during the trout season, March 15th to September 30th.

Description
One of three reservoirs set high on a hillside overlooking Morecambe Bay, Poaka Beck is a pretty place to fish. It's lower down the valley than Harlock Reservoir and is easier to fish when the strong winds blow. Access is good, the banks are solid and a road follows the eastern bank. A good well-trodden path leads to the remaining bankside. Poaka Beck is stocked monthly with high quality brown trout and because the insect life is prolific they feed well and grow-on quickly. Fishing at Poaka Beck is much the same as it is at its two neighbours, Harlock and Pennington. When the wind blows from the south try a black lure, a Viva is the favourite, on a slow retrieve along the stony bottom near the dam wall. Black is also a good colour when there is a flat calm. A Black and Peacock Spider can be a killer as can a tiny Black Gnat. In the autumn try a big bushy dry fly, something like a Daddy Long Legs or Walker Sedge. Be prepared for violent takes.

Fishery Rules

Fly fishing and spinning only. Barbless hooks only. No trebles. Catch and release operates but fishing must stop after killing three fish.

Facilities on Site
Car park.

RATHERHEATH TARN

Location (OS97:485959)
From Windermere, take the A591 towards Kendal. After about 4 miles, the Plantation Bridge Filling Station, where tickets are sold, is on the left. Continue on the A591 until it becomes a dual-carriageway. After about 500 yards turn right into Ratherheath Lane. The tarn is about 500 yards further on the right.

Fishery Controller
Windermere, Ambleside and District Angling Association. *See Angling Clubs section.*

Water and Stock
A figure-of-eight shaped lake of about 5 acres holding a good head of coarse fish including bream, carp, chub, gudgeon, perch, roach

*Not a ripple disturbs the surface of the water at **Ratherheath Tarn,** a fine day ticket coarse fishery*

and tench.

Ticket Prices

Day £3.00, juniors £1.50 from the Plantation Bridge Filling Station near Staveley on the A591 (Tel: 01539 821753) and Carlsons Fishing Tackle 64-66 Kirkland, Kendal, Cumbria LA95AP (Tel: 01539 724867).

Opening Times

Open all year. Fishing is from dawn to dusk.

Description

Visiting coarse fishermen will like Ratherheath. It's bristling with good quality fish and all the bankspace is easy to get at. It is an unusual shape, almost figure-of-eight, and tree lined which means that it is possible to get out of the wind on most days. There are 43 easily accessed pegs. The water varies between clear and murky and the fishing is probably better on those days when it's coloured. It's a bream angler's delight with many fish over $6^{1}/_{2}$lb amongst the smaller fish in big shoals. Bread is always a good bait, as are pinkies and squats. Common and Crucian carp, to over 12lb, swim around the lily pads and will take bread, luncheon meat or the smaller boilies. In the summer try floating crust but use a strong leader and fish a long way off. Watch out for the lily pads - many a good fish has been lost in a tangle with these substantial weeds. Go deep for the tench. There are some really good fish in here, particularly in the back basin near the boathouse. They can be over 4lb and it's not uncommon to take a bag of over 60lb in one fishing session. It's a water worthy of attention and you are unlikely to find better coarse fishing water anywhere in Central Lakeland.

There is easy access to a disabled fishing platform only 30 metres from the car park.

Fishery Rules

No night fishing.

Facilities on Site

Car park. Disabled fishing platforms.

RED TARN

Location (OS90:348152)

Red Tarn sits in the shadow of Helvellyn about 2,000 feet above sea level.

Fishery Controller

Lake District National Park Authority.

Water and Stock
A medium sized tarn with an abundance of tiny trout.
Ticket Prices
Free fishing for holders of an Environment Agency rod licence.
Opening Times
April 1st to September 30th from dawn to dusk.
Description
There really is no easy way to get to Red Tarn. It sits below Striding Edge in the shadow of Helvellyn where only intrepid walkers and photographers dare to tread. If you have the stamina and are fit enough to brave the elements it's a delight to fish. You need to catch it on the right day, but because of its altitude, those days are few. The fishing is best when the sun is shining and there is a gentle breeze to ruffle the water. Red Tarn teems with small brown trout and they like worms, but they are just as happy to take flies or a flashy spinner. Go prepared for the weather. It can change very quickly in this part of the National Park.
Fishery Rules
None.
Facilities on Site
None.

REDWELL CARP & COARSE LAKE
Location (OS97:543699)
About 3 miles east of Carnforth and junction 35 on the M6. Take the B6254 towards Kirkby Lonsdale. Pass through Over Kellet village and in about 1¼ miles, the fishery is signposted on the right.
Fishery Controller
Diane & Ken Hall, Redwell Fishery, Kirkby Lonsdale Road, Arkholme, Carnforth, Lancs. LA6 1BQ (Tel: 015242 21979).
Water and Stock
One lake of about 3 acres subdivided into pools. Holding bream, carp, roach, rudd and tench.
Ticket Prices
Day ticket £5.00, evening £4.00. Redwell Fisheries Club members, day £3.50 and evening £2.50. *See Angling Clubs section.*
Opening Times
All year from 0700 hrs until dusk. Night fishing by appointment.
Description

This is a beautiful mature lake, cleverly designed with small bays and peninsulas to provide interesting fishing spots and seclusion. Most of the bankspace has been landscaped with shrubs and trees and access throughout is very easy. A few pegs close to the house are reserved for disabled anglers who may take a car close to the water. The lake is full of fine coarse fish. It has become very popular with bream anglers who enjoy sport with big numbers of fish to 7 or 8lb. They will take most of the popular baits plus the home produced favourites. It is also a popular lake for carp anglers. The fish are not very big, up to about 20lb, but they are plentiful and they are obliging. It is not unusual to catch half a dozen or more at one sitting. Small boilies in strawberry or chocolate flavour seem to do well. During the summer, when the carp are basking in one of the many weedy bays, try a floating bread crust. It's an exciting way to take a fish. Use a strong line though, the takes can be vicious. The tench run to about 5lb and are as mysterious as ever. Once you've found them, you should have a good day. This is a favourite venue with pole fishermen who manage to take heavy bags of roach and rudd with the odd big carp or tench making life challenging.

Fishery Rules

Two rods only per angler. No fish over 1lb to be kept in nets. Obtain a ticket from the office before starting to fish.

Facilities on Site

Car park. Self contained flats, one fitted for disabled persons. Disabled fishing pegs. Space for touring caravans.

ROANHEAD LAKES

Location (OS96:210755)

From Barrow-in-Furness, take the A590 towards Ulverston. Turn left just before Thwaite Flat roundabout and follow the road for about 1¹/2 miles. The lakes are on the right.

Fishery Controller

Furness Fishing Association. *See Angling Clubs section.*

Water and Stock

A group of flooded mines holding bream, carp, eels, perch, pike, roach, tench and trout.

Ticket prices

Day tickets: trout £8.00 and coarse £4.00. From Hools Fishing Tackle, Barrow (Tel: 01229 430425), Angling & Hiking, Barrow (Tel:

*After the carp at one of the smaller **Roanhead Lakes** near
Barrow-in-Furness*

01229 829661) and Coopers of Ulverston (Tel: 01229 580261).

Description

A very varied fishery, Roanhead is a string of flooded mine workings
stretching across flat countryside close to the seashore east of
Barrow-in-Furness. Some of the lakes, like Moorfoot and Burnhole,
are tiny, whereas Rita Pond, at 25 acres, is large and mostly they are
very deep. Nobody quite knows just how deep, but there is little
doubt that a few of them drop away sharply. Of course the fish don't
venture down into the murky depths. They are usually caught no
more than 10 feet down. The coarse lakes are very varied. Some of
them are better for bream, some for carp and some for pike. In
general most visitors stick to the lakes close to the road which offer
some fine fishing for carp, tench and roach. This is a good venue for
bream fishermen. The fish grow to about 6lb and are hard fighters.
Corn is the popular bait. Carp to over 20lb are not uncommon.
Luncheon meat is a good bait.

The trout lakes are well stocked with rainbows averaging about
$1^{1}/_{2}$lb with some fish going to over 4lb. Because the area is flat and
open to the estuary, winds can be a problem. Try not to pick a day

when a strong westerly blows. In the early season, lures are best fished well down. In the summer the fish come to the surface and then its buzzer time. Anything in dressed black will take fish.

Fishery rules

No night fishing. Barbless hooks only.

Facilities on Site

None.

ROOSECOTE RESERVOIR

Location (OS96:210680)

South of Barrow-in-Furness right on the estuary and sandwiched between the old docks and Roosecote Power Station.

Fishery Controller

Barrow Angling Association. *See Angling Clubs section.*

Water and Stock

A square man-made lake holding cooling water for Roosecote power station. It is stocked with brown trout.

Ticket Prices

Day ticket £12.00 for 3 fish. From Mr J. R. Jones, 69 Prince Street, Dalton-in-Furness (Tel: 01229 462955). Ticket also covers fishing on Harlock, Poaka Beck and Pennington Reservoirs.

Opening Times

Dawn to dusk from March 15th to September 30th.

Description

Situated right on the sea shore overlooking Roosecote Sands, this unusual fishery is actually a holding pond for cooling water for the power station alongside. Whilst it can't be described as a pretty lake, it is an interesting fishery and the views over Morecambe Bay can be spectacular, especially in the evening. Unfortunately it is bounded on two sides by a power station and a housing estate, neither of which add to its ambience. The water is brackish, warm and full of nutrients which make the stocked brown trout grow on quickly. Around 4,000 nine-inch trout are stocked at the beginning of each season and those that survive grow rapidly to $1^{1/2}$ or even 2 lb. It's best to visit in the early season because the survival rate is not high. Sadly, this water is continually poached. What humans leave behind the cormorants scavenge. However, it is well stocked and there seem to be plenty of fish for everyone. Try it if only for its uniqueness, but not when a strong southerly wind blows. Spinning, worm and fly are the methods permitted, with worm taking most of the fish. Best lure is a Viva or similar pattern. The evening dry fly rise can be particularly good.

Fishery Rules

Worm, spinning or fly fishing only. Barbless hooks only. No treble hooks. Spinner to have single hook. Catch and release fishing but when 3 fish killed, fishing must stop.

Facilities on Site

None.

RYDAL WATER

Location (OS90:355062)

Alongside the A591 Ambleside to Keswick road approximately 2½ miles north-west of Ambleside. Just before Rydal village turn left onto a small road over the River Rothay. Turn first right to find a car park.

Fishery Controller

Windermere, Ambleside and District Angling Association on behalf of The National Trust. *See Angling Clubs section.*

Water and Stock

Over a mile long and ¼ mile wide holding some good pike, perch, eels and roach. There are also some excellent brown trout and a few late sea trout and salmon.

Ticket Prices

Week £10.00, seniors and juniors £5.00. Day £3.50, seniors and juniors £2.00. From Go Fishing, Gilly's Landing, Glebe Road, Bowness-on-Windermere (Tel: 015394 47086), other fishing tackle shops in the area and tourist information centres.

Opening Times

Open all year, but from March 15th to June 15th inclusive the only permitted fishing methods are lures and fly, spinners or worms. Positively no fish baits during this period.

Description

About three-quarters of the bankside fishing on Rydal Water is controlled by the WADAA. That's all of the south side and the north side from the inlet down to the boathouse on the A591. Rydal Water is one of Central Lakeland's prettiest and most accessible lakes. Well-beaten public footpaths give easy access along the south side whilst the major road to Keswick gives access to part of the north

THE LAKE DISTRICT ANGLERS' GUIDE

shore. At times, the constant stream of visitors can be a nuisance but when fishing in the Lake District you have to get used to that. However, the fishing is brilliant and there are places to get away from the throng. Try the north-west shore where the WADAA has access to the private Rydal Estate waterside. There is plenty of bankspace, lots of fish and no hikers! Rydal Water is one of the places to go for pike. They grow big - fish over 25lb fall regularly to dead herring, sprat or mackerel baits ledgered in the lee of an island. One problem here though are the eels. They grow big, but they can cause a lot of false alarms when dead baiting. If this happens, try assembling a spinning rig with a flashy spoon and wandering round the lake fishing the weedy margins. It's surprising how many fish can be taken this way. The perch fishing is also excellent. Maggots on a floating rig is the most consistent method to take these, but perch will also readily take a spinner. Try one and you might even pick up one of the big brown trout. Get one over 4lb and you'll really feel that you've had a good day. Salmon and sea trout run into Rydal Water in the late season but they are few and far between. Very few have been recorded in the recent seasons. If you intend to try for a salmon do not forget that you will need a different EA rod licence and it is more expensive.

Fishery Rules
No night fishing or camping. No live bait fishing. No access to the islands. Carefully return all coarse fish to the water, alive - including pike.

Facilities on Site
Two boats for the use of members only. Car parking at Rydal village, Pelter Bridge, White Moss Common and in the two lay-bys alongside the A591.

SCHOOL KNOTT TARN

Location (OS97:428973)
School Knott Tarn, situated about 1½ miles south-east of Windermere railway station, is not easy to find. From Windermere, take the road towards Bowness-on-Windermere. In about ¾ mile, turn left to Heathwaite. Follow the road to the end of the built-up area and park near School Knott Stores. Follow the footpath up the hill to the tarn.

Fishery Controller
Windermere, Ambleside and District Angling Association. *See*

Angling Clubs section.

Water and Stock

A tiny man-made lake, a fraction under 1 acre, stocked annually with rainbow trout.

Ticket Prices

Week £10.00, seniors and juniors £5.00. Day £3.50, seniors and juniors £2.00. The closest outlet for tickets is the tourist information centre near Windermere railway station (Tel: 015394 46499). Other outlets are Go Fishing in Bowness-on-Windermere (Tel: 015394 47086), the fishing tackle dealers in Kendal and other tourist information offices.

Opening Times

March 15th to September 30th from dawn to dusk.

Description

Although this tiny man-made lake is close to both Windermere and Bowness, it is hard to find and rarely seen by visitors. It rests high on the fell-side, with magnificent views over Windermere Lake and it suffers badly when a westerly wind blows. But it's possible to use the wind to advantage and there are some good fish to be had. The native browns average about $3/4$lb but there are much bigger rainbows - the heaviest to date was a fine fish of $3^1/2$lb. Try a bushy fly on the surface and if nothing happens, jerk it through the ripple to induce a take. It's an exciting way to take rainbows on windy days, otherwise try lures. The ever popular Viva takes fish in the early season. Later in the year try a White Marabou lure or something similar. On the bright sunny days in summer, buzzers, goldheads and nymphs all come into their own. The best colours are green and brown. An artificial green shrimp is another good fly.

Fishery Rules

Fly fishing only. Two fish limit. Catch and release encouraged using barbless hooks. No boats.

Facilities on Site

None.

SILVER TARN

Location (OS89:985085)

On the coast, about 5 miles north of Sellafield. From Calder Bridge, near Sellafield, take the A595(T) north. In about 2 miles turn left towards Middletown. In the village, turn left to Nethertown. Turn right along the coast road and Silver Tarn is on the lefthand side of this road.

Fishery Controller

Not known.

Water and Stock

A very small pond teeming with tiny roach, perch, pike and eels.

Ticket Prices

Free fishing for holders of an Environment Agency rod licence. *See Legal section.*

Opening Times

All year.

Description

Silver Tarn is a small shallow lake sitting in a fold of rolling farmland immediately on the coast. There are plenty of fish, but they tend to be small. Maggots, casters and worms are the best baits. It is also worth trying bread, either as paste or flake. It's a comfortable place to fish, but there is only room for about 4 rods. All the banks are easily accessible and, although it sits near the sea it is sheltered from the worst of the winds. The road alongside the tarn is single track and parking space is very limited.

Fishery Rules

Park off the road.

Facilities on Site

None.

SKELSMERGH TARN

Location (OS97:534966)

From Kendal, take the A6 towards Penrith. In approximately 3 miles, turn right down a steep hill onto the Dales Way. The tarn is about 500 yards on the lefthand side of the road. A footpath from the road skirts the western edge of the water.

Fishery Controller

Not known.

Water and Stock

A very small tarn with thousands of tiny roach and rudd.

Ticket Prices

The fishing is free for holders of an Environment Agency rod licence.

Opening Times

All year from dawn to dusk. No night fishing.

Description

Not the typical Lakeland tarn that one would expect from its title, Skelsmergh is an unremarkable, almost circular pool. From an angler's point of view, the beauty of this water is that it positively teems with small roach and perch. There are thousands of them and, no doubt for this reason, food is in short supply. Consequently they are easy to catch. Maggots are by far the best choice of bait and big mixed bags have been taken of the white variety. It's a good venue for children, providing they are supervised, and for anyone just starting to pole fish. The banks are fairly flat, although they can be treacherous after heavy rain, so take care.

Fishery Rules

None.

Facilities on Site

None.

SMALL WATER

Location (OS90:455100)

Small Water feeds Haweswater Reservoir. Take the dead-end road alongside Haweswater right to the car park at the end. Then take the footpath to the feeder stream. Follow the lefthand branch up into the high fells and you will find Small Water.

Fishery Controller

Lake District National Park Authority.

Water and Stock

An 12 acre upland tarn holding small brown trout, perch and pike.

Ticket Prices

Free fishing for holders of an Environment Agency rod licence.

Opening Times

April 1st to September 30th from dawn to dusk.

Description

Small Water is a lovely fell lake nestling in a natural amphitheatre below High Street. Its crystal clear water is full of small trout and perch and they can be very greedy. They'll readily fall to bread, fly or spinning, but a float fished worm is usually the best option. Small Water is only for determined anglers. It is very remote, an hour of strenuous exercise is needed just to get to it and it is exposed to the vagaries of the weather which in Lakeland can close in very quickly.

Be prepared.
Fishery Rules
None.
Facilities on Site
None.

SOCKBRIDGE MILL TROUT FISHERY

Location (OS90:497277)
From Penrith, take the A6 south. After crossing the River Eamont,
take the B5320 towards Pooley Bridge and Ullswater. In the village
of Tirril, turn right to Sockbridge and follow the road-signs for Pony
Trekking. Continue past the trekking centre down a single track
road to the mill.
Fishery Controller
Mr Jolyon Claridge, Sockbridge Mill Trout Farm, Sockbridge,
Penrith, Cumbria CA10 2JT (Tel: 01768 865338).
Water and Stock
A very small 'Catch Your Own' pool holding lots of rainbow trout
and about $1/2$ mile of the River Eamont.
Ticket Prices
Session ticket £1.50 plus fish taken, £1.60 per lb. £1.00 for children
using any method of fishing. Day ticket, fly fishing only, for the
River Eamont, £2.50.
Opening Times
All year from 0830 to 1800 hrs or dusk.
Description
Sockbridge is a working trout farm with facilities for fun fishing in
a catch-your-own fish pool, but it's not the place for dedicated
anglers, unless you try the small stretch of the River Eamont. The
one tiny overstocked pool, set in an easily accessible wooded area
between the Eamont and its attendant streams, gives young and
inexperienced anglers a place to catch their first trout. The pond is
so small it's nearly possible to jump across it, but it is full of trout
averaging about 1lb with some better fish up to 2lb. Any method of
fishing is allowed for youngsters whilst older novices will get a
thrill from fly fishing. Almost any fly will take fish so there is no
need to worry about what to use.

For experienced fly fishermen, there is a pleasant $1/2$ mile stretch
of the small River Eamont to try. Access is difficult in places, but a

patient angler, one who is not afraid to lose a few flies, will have a good day. It's well stocked with native browns and some full tailed rainbows. The water is streamy, with good runs and plenty of shade from overhanging trees. For best results use a 7 foot nymph rod and travel light. Just a few traditional dry flies and nymphs will suffice. It's exciting fishing, especially when one of the better trout are hooked and they set off downstream.

Fishery Rules

For anglers fishing the Eamont. No wading. Fly fishing only. Traditional flies only. No lures.

Facilities on Site

Tackle hire, car park, toilet, fish sales and refreshments.

TALKIN' TARN

Location (OS86:545588)

Talkin' Tarn Country Park is about 4 miles south-east of Carlisle. Take the A69 east to Brampton and then the B6413 south towards Castle Carrock. In approximately 2 miles, just after the railway level crossing, turn left into the Country Park.

Fishery Controller

Cumbria County Council. Talkin' Tarn Country Park, near Brampton, Carlisle, Cumbria CA8 1XX (Tel: 016977 3129).

Water and Stock

A 65 acre lake holding mainly perch and pike with a few eels, chub and brown trout.

Ticket Prices

Day tickets: Adults £1.00 and children 50p. Obtainable on site.

Opening Times

Dawn to dusk during the coarse fishing season. June 16th to March 15th.

Description

Talkin' Tarn is a beautiful 65 acre mature lake set amid 120 acres of farmland and countryside. Its clear, clean water is fed by an underground spring which manages to hold the level constant even during the driest of summers. As you would expect in a country activities park there are other sports with a demand on the water. Sailing, windsurfing, rowing and canoeing all take place at some time but, because there are strict segregated areas, none of these interferes with angling. Fishing is only permitted in the areas shown on the map in the Tarn shop, but the lake is big, with lots and lots of accessible bankspace. A 1¹/₄ mile path, suitable for wheelchairs, has been laid around the entire water giving access to the best fishing areas. During the summer months, there are always plenty of quiet places to get away from the throng. The main targets are pike and perch. Big pike are known to be in here and there is a large stock of mid-range doubles. The best bait is undoubtedly a dead sprat or herring laid on the edge of the weed, although some anglers like to wobble a plug in the reeds near the woods. The shoals of good sized perch are almost always active and it's very rare to come away from Talkin' Tarn having had a blank day. Maggots and worm are best for the perch.

Fishery Rules

All fish to be carefully returned to the water. Ground baiting is prohibited. Fishing is only allowed in the areas marked on the map in the Tarn shop.

Facilities on site

Car park. Toilets with wheelchair access. Tea room with wheelchair access. Camping and caravaning. Lots of outdoor activities.

TARN HOWES

Location (OS97:330999) See map p195

From Hawkshead, take the B5285 towards Coniston. In about 1¹/₂ miles turn right to Tarn Howes.

Fishery Controller

The National Trust, North West Region, The Hollens, Grasmere, Ambleside, Cumbria LA22 9QZ (Tel: 015394 35599).

Water and Stock

Many would claim that Tarn Howes is Lakeland's most beautiful water. It is certainly visited by multitudes of walkers and bird watchers and although it holds a lot of small brown trout with a few perch, fishing is not permitted.

Ticket Prices

No fishing.

TARNSIDE CARAVAN SITE LAKE

Location (OS89:004057)

At the seaside on the coast about 3 miles north of Sellafield. From Calder Bridge, near Sellafield, take the A595(T) north. In about 1 mile turn left towards Beckermet. Go through the village to Braystones. Tarnside Caravan Park is just through the village.

Fishery Controller

Mr Lockhart, Tarnside Caravan Site, Braystones, Cumbria (Tel: 01946 841308).

Water and Stock

A fairly plain 2 acre lake supporting most coarse fish.

Ticket Prices

Day ticket £2.00 from the site reception office.

Opening Times

All year.

Description

An unremarkable lake set in a hollow, overlooked by caravans and, in the distance, Sellafield Nuclear Processing Plant, this lake is actually better than it sounds. Catch it on a good day when there is some sunshine and a slight breeze rippling the surface and it can be very productive. It holds a good stock of roach and perch, some of which top the 2lb mark, a few Jack pike and some good bream. It is mostly fished by visitors to the caravan site and it can get very busy in the summer months, but don't be put off as there is plenty of bankspace for all. Undoubtedly, maggots are the best bait although bread is very good, either in paste form or used as crust. Groundbait with hemp or similar, but don't overfeed.

Fishery Rules

None.

Facilities on Site

Car parking. Toilets. Refreshments.

THIRLMERE

Location (OS90:310160)

Thirlmere lies to the west of the A591 main road from Ambleside to Keswick. There is an information board in the car park at Wythburn on the right as you approach the lake.

Fishery Controller

Northern Estates Management Team, North West Water Ltd, The Old Sawmill, Thirlmere, Keswick, Cumbria (Tel: 01768 772334).

Water and Stock

A massive stretch of water holding a good stock of native brown trout and char. There are also pike and perch.

*Another of Lakeland's beautiful waters, the fishing on **Thirlmere** is free*

Ticket Prices
The fishing is free to holders of an Environment Agency rod licence.
Opening Times
March 15th to September 30th from dawn to dusk.
Description
Built in the 1930s, Thirlmere is a huge water supply reservoir for Manchester. It is big. At $3^1/2$ miles long, it is a daunting water which could be why so few people try it. It could also be the reason why few specimen fish are ever reported. It's actually a lovely water that no doubt holds some really big fish. But where to find them? That is the problem. The easiest access is at the northern end where a road crosses the dam wall. The water is very deep there, dropping away to about 150 feet. It's not the best place to try. It's better to follow the road along the west side to the car park at Armboth, or to Hause Point or Dob Gill. These are all favourite spots with local fishermen. The water is not stocked but the wild brown trout are plentiful and generally very greedy. They average about 1lb but there are some bigger fish if you can find them. You will also catch a lot of perch. Worm is probably the best bait. The southern end near the car park

at Wyth Burn is another popular spot. If it's the pike you're after, a dead bait laid on one of the shallower ridges along the west side should bring results. Don't expect fish bigger than 20lb. There are undoubtedly monsters in here but they have yet to show themselves.

Fishery Rules

Char must be returned to the water unharmed. No maggots, live bait or loose feed to be used. Fly, lures, worm and dead baits only permitted. No fishing from the dam, draw-off tower or slipway. No powered boats permitted. Buoyancy aids must be worn. No landing on the islands.

Facilities on Site

Car parks at various points along the eastern and western shore and at the southern end of the reservoir. Information board at Wythburn Car Park.

ULLSWATER LAKE

Location (OS9O:420200)

Situated about 8 miles north of Ambleside, Ullswater is easy to find.

Fishery Controller

Lake District National Park, The National Trust and private landowners.

Water and Stock

Over 8 miles long and up to 1/2 mile wide in places, Ullswater holds char, perch, pike, brown trout and schelley.

Ticket Prices

Free fishing for holders of an Environment Agency rod licence.

Boats

Boat hire at: Glenridding, Pooley Bridge and Watermillock.
Launch own boat at: Glenridding, Swarthbank and Waterside.

Opening Times

Open all year, but from March 15th to June 15th inclusive the only permitted fishing methods are lures and fly, worm, minnow, shrimp or prawns. The brown trout season is from March 15th to September 30th.

Description

Almost 8 miles long and over 1/2 mile wide in places, Ullswater is one of Lakeland's most beautiful and most dramatic fisheries. Place Fell, the 2,000 feet high backdrop, can appear calm and serene on a bright sunny morning, but by lunchtime, as the clouds roll in, it can

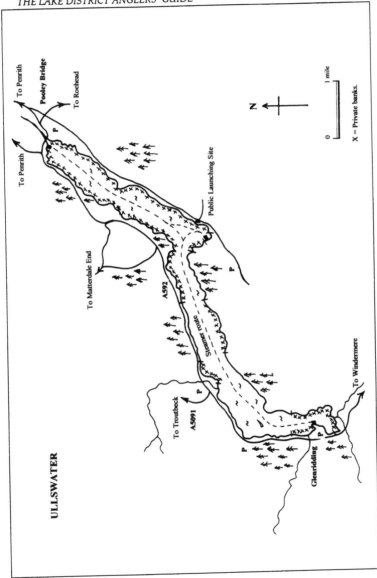

ULLSWATER

To Penrith
Pooley Bridge
To Rochead
To Penrith
To Matterdale End
A592
Steamer route
Public Launching Site
To Troutbeck
A5091
Glenridding
To Windermere

N

0 ___ 1 mile

X = Private banks.

be dark and menacing. Inevitably, the lake area at the foot of Place Fell follows its mood. One minute you may be fishing in warm sunshine and the next soaked to the skin with the misty rain that is so prevalent in the Lake District. The easiest waterside access is from the north-west bank where the A592 skirts the water, but when the sun does shine, it can get very busy. On hot days you will probably have to share the bankside with picnickers, swimmers, boaters and sunbathers. On those days it's better to travel a bit further and fish in the secluded bays of the, less accessible, south-east side. Hiring a boat gives the freedom to fish anywhere in the 2,200 acres of water, but don't bother with the deep water in the centre. There are undoubtedly large fish in the deeps, but they will be virtually impossible to catch and it can be very unpleasant in the waves caused by steamers and other powered craft. Stay in the quiet bays.

No one is certain just which species have found a home in the deep dark waters of Ullswater. Without doubt the best fishing is for brown trout, but the fish are not big. They tend to average about 8 ounces and there are plenty of them. Attract one of the big shoals and you will have a really good day. Worm is the best bait, either float fished or ledgered, but in the hot summer months it's worth trying fly. Mid April to August are the best months for brown trout. Try fly fishing in one of the quieter bays or in the shallow areas near the reefs between the sailing buoys and the shore. Any of the traditional north country wet flies or Scottish Loch flies will take fish. Be very careful, Ullswater is a deep lake. It drops to over 200 feet in places and in others, not very far out from the shore, the bottom quickly shelves to over 100 feet. The other big survivor in Ullswater it the perch. This game little fish is well worth any angler's attention. It's a hard fighter, very greedy and the lake is full of them. Drop a worm into the water anywhere and you'll pick up perch. There can be no doubt that Ullswater holds pike, but they seem very reluctant to show themselves. Perhaps this is because very few anglers bother to try for them. Whatever the reason, it would be very strange indeed if this predator were absent.

Despite the fact that there have been no recent reports of catches of either fish, it's accepted that both char and the schelley exist in Ullswater. You'll know if you catch one. They are easy to identify. A char is a bronze and dark green coloured cousin of our native brown trout, whilst the schelley is a slim silver scaled fish known colloquially as a freshwater herring. If you do get one of these rare fish, please return it carefully to the water. The River Eamont, flowing from Pooley Bridge to east of Penrith where it joins the River Eden, provides a route for salmon and sea trout to come into Ullswater. Despite a major reduction in numbers over the past decade, many fish do come into the lake, but they are unlikely to fall to any of the standard fishing methods. Occasionally one is caught by an angler fishing deep for big brown trout.

Fishery Rules
No night fishing or camping. Strictly no live bait fishing. Carefully return all coarse fish, to the water, alive - this includes pike.

Facilities on Site
Car parking at various points around the lake.

URSWICK TARN

Location (OS96:270745)
Urswick is about 2^1/$_2$ miles south-west of Ulverston. From the centre of Ulverston, take the A590(T) towards Barrow-in-Furness. In approximately 2^1/$_4$ miles, turn left for Great Urswick. In the middle of the village, at the Derby Arms, turn left. In about 500 yards turn right and follow the road to the car parking area near the lake.

Fishery Controller
Urswick Parish Council.

Water and Stock
One lake of about 6 acres holding carp, pike, tench and some bream and roach.

Ticket Prices
Day ticket £2.00 from the bailiff on the bank or the Derby Arms, Great Urswick, Cumbria LA12 OSP (Tel: 01229 586348).

Opening Times
All year.

Description
Urswick Tarn is a shallow mature lake surrounded on two sides by village housing. It's only a few inches deep at the edge and slowly shelves to 7 or 8 feet in the middle. Access is somewhat limited. A large section of the bankspace is private meadowland and more of it is someone's back garden! The easiest place to get to the water is to follow the road past the Derby Arms to the edge of the village.

Then turn right to the lake. Urswick is fished regularly by local youngsters, but visitors rarely find their way to the lakeside, which is a pity because it does offer some good fishing for bream and carp. The carp are not big, about 6lb, but they are plentiful and they do like boilies. Milk chocolate seems to be the favourite. The bream fishing is usually good. The tarn holds many medium sized fish of around 4lbs which are attracted to maggots. A dead silver sprat is a good bet for the pike which again are fairly small. They run to about 10lb but are usually nearer 4lb. There are also a few roach and tench.

Fishery Rules
None.
Facilities on Site
None.

WASTWATER

Location (OS89:160050)
Situated about 7 miles east of Sellafield in Western Cumbria.
Fishery Controller
The National Trust, North West Regional Office, The Hollens, Grasmere, Ambleside, Cumbria LA22 9QZ (Tel: 015394 35599).
Water and Stock
England's deepest lake, one of the most beautiful and almost certainly the most dramatic, is closed for fishing.
Tickets
No fishing.

WATENDLATH TROUT FISHERY

Location (OS90:275163)
From Keswick, take the B5289 road alongside Derwentwater into Borrowdale. After about 3 miles, turn left to Ashness Bridge and follow the beautiful valley to Watendlath.
Fishery Controller
Stan Edmonson, The Trout Farm, Seathwaite, Borrowdale, Keswick (Tel: 017687 77293).
Water and Stock
A beautiful Lakeland tarn of approximately $6^{1/2}$ acres well stocked with rainbow trout averaging 3lb with some into double figures and wild browns to about 3lb.

Ticket Prices

Day ticket (0800 to 1700 hrs) £15.00 for 4 fish, half day or evening £12.00 for 2 fish. Combined day and evening ticket £17.00 for 4 fish. Boat £10.00 (only two available, so book ahead on 017687 77293). Tickets from Mrs Richardson, Fold Head Farm, Watendlath, Keswick (Tel: 017687 77255).

Opening Times

March 28th to November 30th from 0730 hrs until dusk.

Description

Nestling in a fold in the hills at the head of one of Lakeland's most picturesque valleys, Watendlath is very popular and the bankside can get busy - not with anglers, but with sightseers and walkers passing along the lakeside on their way up the fells. Although this passing traffic doesn't seem to affect the fishing, on busy days it is wise to take out a boat or try the southern shoreline. Often the fishing is better there anyway, especially in the area where tiny streams wash insects into the water. The water bristles with top quality full-tailed rainbows some of which are over the magical ten pound mark. The fishery record is a lovely fish of 11lb. There are also some wild brown trout averaging between 2 and 3lb. Hook one of these and you'll be treated to a wonderful acrobatic display. Use a strong leader!

After a particularly cold winter and spring, the lake can be a late starter. In the early months it's always wise to start with a sunken line. Try a Viva, it's a consistent killer, as are Goldheads, Cat's Whisker and Montanas. When fishing sub-surface, try buzzers, Gold-Ribbed Hares Ear and Pheasant Tail Nymphs. Nymphing and dry fly fishing is better in the evening, especially after a warm sunny day. From June onwards there is usually an evening rise which includes some of the heavier trout.

Only two boats are available, each holding two people, so it's wise to book ahead if you want one. On a warm summer evening when the fish are showing and the sun dips behind the fells, there is no better place to fish in Lakeland.

Fishery Rules

No trolling. Catch and release operates after limit is reached. Fly only. Maximum of 12 rods.

Facilities on Site

Toilet. Rod hire and tuition. Bed and breakfast accommodation and the spectacular scenery.

WHINS TROUT FISHERY

Location (OS90:555310)

From Penrith, take the A686 towards Langwathby and Alston. In approximately 2¹/₂ miles just before the right turn to Eden Hall village, turn right onto a single track road to the pond. The turn is well signposted from the A686.

Fishery Controller

Mrs E. Siddle, Whins Fishery, Edenhall, Nr. Penrith, Cumbria (Tel: 01768 862671).

Water and Stock

About 20 acres of a 28 acre lake supporting rainbow trout to about 10lb.

Ticket Prices

Sporting ticket, day £10.00, half day £5.00, return all fish. Day £18.00 for 4 fish or £15.00 for 2 fish, half day £13.00 for 4 fish or £10.00 for 2 fish. Boats, day £8.00, half day £5.00. All tickets must be purchased before fishing, from the house about 100 yards up the track, or may be booked in advance. Bank permits may be purchased **in person** (no telephone calls) at the Tackle Counter, John Norris, 21 Victoria Road, Penrith. Bookings can also be made via Mr Julian Shaw, Penrith (Tel: 01768 865051 or mobile 0802 731789).

Opening Times

All year from 0700 until dusk.

Description

Whins Pond is a lovely 20 acre section of a large 200 year old lake set in rolling farmland east of Penrith. It is wooded on two sides but there is plenty of open bankspace available on the south bank and on the east side near the boat landing stage. Fishing is also permitted from sturdy boats, each of which comfortably holds two anglers. Whins is a fairly shallow lake with a maximum depth of about 10 feet and there are some reedy margins providing a fertile breeding ground for aquatic life. The fishery is regularly stocked with full tailed rainbows to about 10lb. It's best to use floating lines. On the rare occasions the fish are not showing, a lengthy leader will get your imitation down to the bottom. Most of the popular patterns do well. In the early season, mid size lures in orange or black will take fish. As the water warms up and they come to the surface, try buzzers, a Pheasant Tail Nymph or a Caddis. At sedge time, a

Daddy Long Legs, a Walker Sedge or a Brown Hopper fished in the area by the trees will induce a take and it will usually be vicious, so make sure you have a strong leader. All brown trout must be returned carefully to the water.

Fishery Rules

Fly fishing only. Barbless or debarbed hooks only. All brown trout must be released.

Facilities on Site

Car park. Light refreshments from the house. Tackle hire and tuition by advance booking.

WHINS POND COARSE FISHERY

Location (OS90:555310)

From Penrith, take the A686 towards Langwathby and Alston. In approximately 2¹/₂ miles just before the turn right to Eden Hall village, turn right onto a single track road to the pond. The turn is well signposted from the A686.

Fishery Controller

Mrs E. Siddle, Whins Fishery, Edenhall, Nr. Penrith, Cumbria (Tel: 01768 862671).

Water and Stock

About 8 acres of a 28 acre lake supporting a variety of specimen coarse fish.

Ticket Prices

Season, adult £50.00, senior or disabled £40.00 and child £30.00. Day, adult £5.00, senior or disabled £4.00 and child £3.00. Tickets on site from the house 100 yards up the track.

Opening Times

All year from 0700 until dusk.

Description

Good coarse fisheries are rare in Cumbria, but Whins Pond is one of them. It is a well-maintained, well-stocked fishery which should appeal to most visiting coarse anglers. The coarse fishing pond is actually part of a 28 acre, 200 year old lake set in rolling farmland and partially bordered by mature woodland. Originally a specimen pond, it was drained a few years ago, all the pike were removed, the banks were supported and fishing stages constructed before it was restocked with high quality fish. It's about 6 feet deep in the centre rising to 3 feet in the margins and now holds bream, carp, chub, perch, roach, rudd, tench and plenty of skimmers. Currently the carp run to about 18lb and of course they love luncheon meat. On its day it is probably the best bait around. Sweetcorn is also a winner. The tench, up to about $5^{1/2}$lb, love it. Try one of the new flavours, like strawberry. For the bream angler, expect fish around $7^{1/2}$lb. Red maggots fished close-in usually produces results. Whins Pond is also a good water for pole fishermen. Attract one of the large shoals of roach, rudd or skimmers and you'll have a good day. There are 27 fishing pegs with the highest number pegs in the wooded area offering the best fishing, particularly in the high summer. An open match is held here every Tuesday. It's very popular and has been won, in the past, with mixed bags of 70lb plus. The mid range pegs

*A course fisherman braves the cold wind at **Whins Pond** near Penrith*

alongside the car park are ideal for disabled anglers and wheelchair access has been provided.

Fishery Rules

No night fishing. Under 14 year old children must be supervised. No dogs. All nets to be dipped before fishing. Obtain a ticket before fishing.

Facilities on Site

Car park. Baits, maggots etc. for sale. Tackle for sale. Equipment hire. Light refreshments for sale.

WINDERMERE LAKE

Location (OS97:390950)

Lakeland's premier lake and very easy to find!

Fishery Controller

Lake District National Park, The National Trust and private landowners. Windermere, Ambleside and District Angling Association has access to some private shoreline. *See Angling Clubs section.*

Water and Stock

Over $10^1/_2$ miles long and $^1/_2$ mile wide holding some good pike, perch, eels and roach. There are also excellent brown trout, rainbow trout, char, sea trout and salmon.

Ticket Prices

Free fishing on some of the bankside. *See map.* Day tickets for the WADAA controlled water £3.50, seniors and juniors £2.00. Seven day permit £10.00, seniors and juniors £5.00. The nearest agent for permits is Go Fishing, Gilly's Landing, Glebe Road, Bowness-on-Windermere (Tel: 015394 43415). Tickets also sold at tourist information offices and other fishing tackle outlets.

Boats

Boat hire at: Bowness Bay (Tel: 015394 88510); Fell Foot Park (Tel: 015395 31273); Go Fishing, Bowness-on-Windermere (Tel: 015394 43415) and Waterhead (Tel: 015394 32225).

Launch your own boat at: Fell Foot Park; at Ferry Nab, off the B5285; and at Waterhead. All motorised craft must be registered. For a permit contact the Lake Wardens (Tel: 015394 42753).

Opening Times

Open all year, but from March 15th to June 15th inclusive the only permitted fishing methods are lures and fly, worm, minnow, shrimp

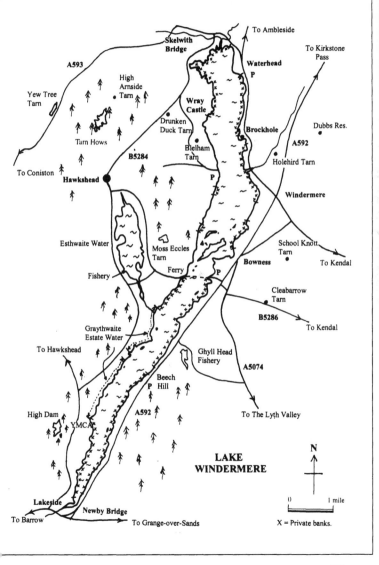

LAKE WINDERMERE

N

0   1 mile

X = Private banks.

or prawns. The brown trout season is from March 15th to Sept 30th.

Description

Windermere is a big lake and very daunting at first sight. The first question on a visiting angler's lips must be - where to fish? Well, to begin with, a lot of the bankside is private, with positively no access. If it's free fishing you're after, then there is limited easy access at Waterhead, Brockhole, Millerground, Bowness and Beech Hill, but you'll have to share with visitors who are there for boating, picnicing, swimming and walking. Quieter fishing and free access can be had on most of the western shore from the ferry northwards to Wray Castle, except for short lengths at Strawberry Fields and Belle Grange. Of course, the fishing is also free from a boat, but there is no landing on Belle Island. Alternatively, for the price of a day ticket, you can fish the Graythwaite Estate water controlled by the Windermere, Ambleside and District Angling Association. See map. It extends for about 4 miles of the western bank and is private land, free from sightseers.

Windermere holds many different species although a few of them have not been seen for some time. The char, the sea trout and the salmon are few and far between these days, but you may just be lucky and pick up a fish by accident. Deep trolling for brown trout around the islands is very productive. The wild brown average about 1lb but there are some real rod benders. Best months are from mid April to July when Mallard and Claret, Invicta or the Grouse Wing series will all catch fish. After that, fly fishing on or near the surface comes into its own. Buzzers are good and there is often a good rise for sedges, particularly in the evenings. Fishing maggots on a floating rig from the bankside anywhere around Windermere is another productive method. Big bags of roach, perch and eels are the order of the day. Some of the roach may tip the scales at $1^{1}/_{2}$lb, although they're more likely to be half that size. Many fishermen come to Windermere searching for some good pike. And they are in here. Fish over 20lb are fairly common, some even tip the scale at 25lb, but it's not likely that you'll see one over 30lb. There's no doubt that there are such monsters in Windermere, but they are difficult to find. To stand a chance of taking the biggest fish, hire a boat and fish a dead bait on the shelving area around the islands. Be patient though. Sit and wait for one to come to you.

Fishery Rules

No night fishing or camping. Strictly no live bait fishing. Carefully return all coarse fish to the water, alive - this includes pike.

Facilities on Site

Car parking at Waterhead, Brockhole, Millerground, Bowness, Beech Hill, Lakeside and Red Nab.

WITHERSLACK HALL TARN

Location (OS97:434863)

From Kendal, take the A591 south and then the A590(T) road towards Barrow-in-Furness. After about 8 miles, turn right at the Derby Arms, to Witherslack village. Continue through the village towards Witherslack Hall. Go past the entrance to the hall and park on the right near the reservoir.

Fishery Controller

Kendal and District Angling Club. *See Angling Clubs section.*

Water and Stock

A small mad-made reservoir with a good stock of eels, perch, pike and roach.

Ticket Prices

Day ticket £3.00, senior citizens and juniors £2.00. Weekly ticket £8.00, senior citizens and juniors £4.00 from Witherslack Post Office (Tel: 015395 52221) only a mile from the water. Also from Carlsons Fishing Tackle in Kendal (Tel: 01539 724867), The Fishing Hut in Grange-over-Sands (Tel: 015395 32854) and Go Fishing in Bowness-on-Windermere (Tel: 015394 47086).

Opening Times

All year from dawn to dusk.

Description

Witherslack Tarn is actually a small decorative pond nestling in the beautifully landscaped grounds of Witherslack Hall. It was created by damming a stream and consequently the water is deepest near the dam wall and progressively becomes shallow the closer you get to the feeder stream. The surrounding woodland is designated as a Site of Special Scientific Interest (an SSSI) so great care is needed not to damage the flora and fauna. It's a mixed fishery supporting eels, perch, pike and roach. None of them is particularly large but they are prolific. The bigger roach and rudd fall to maggot or caster fished near the lilies. Worm and sweetcorn are also good. A dead silver sprat or similar will attract one of the numerous small pike.

197

They rarely reach 10lb. It's a pleasant place to fish and one where you are virtually certain to catch a sizeable bag.

Fishery Rules

The boathouse area is out of bounds. No groundbait.

Facilities on Site

Car parking area near the lake.

WYCH ELM FISHERY

Location (OS97:518791)

From the M6 junction 36, take the A6070 southbound. Then take the second right and follow the road to a T junction on the B6384. Turn left towards Holme. Mr Gill's bungalow, with a sign indicating the fishing, is approximately ¹/₂ mile on the righthand side, on the outskirts of the village.

Fishery Controller

Mr Ken Gill, Wych Elm, Milnthorpe Road, Holme, Carnforth, Lancs LA6 1AX (Tel: 01524 781449).

Water and Stock

A pretty 2 acre lake stocked with brown, brook, golden and rainbow trout.

Ticket Prices

Day ticket £20.00 for 4 fish; £16.00 for 3 fish or £10.00 for a sporting permit. Half day (0800 to 1300 hrs or 1300 to 1800 hrs) £15.00 for 2 fish or £6.00 sporting. Evening (after 1800 hrs) £7.00 for 1 fish or £5.00 sporting. Any 3 hours £7.00 for 1 fish or £5.00 sporting.

Opening Times

All year from 0800 hrs until dusk.

Description

Wych Elm is a beautiful clear spring-fed lake with easy access to all the bankspace and full of hard fighting trout. There are 12 fishing platforms and a maximum of 11 anglers per day, so there's always space to move around and find the fish. Although the banks have been tastefully landscaped with trees and shrubs, back casting is not a problem. There are two small islands, one of which is linked to the bank by a walkway. It's a popular spot for fishing. Regulars often take several fish from the deeper water at the lake's centre when fishing from the island. Wych Elm is stocked daily with full tailed rainbows averaging about 2lb and, as is evident from the shadows lurking in the lake's margins, there are much bigger fish to be had.

The fishery record is 16lb. All brown, brook and golden trout must be returned.

To add interest to the fishing, a few tagged fish have been introduced. Catch one of these and you will be rewarded with a free half day fishing permit.

Sub-surface flies and nymphs always take fish here. Buzzers are also a good bet. Try them in green or black. Damsel nymphs are good early in the season. When there is a slight ripple on the water try a floating fry -- regulars swear by them on the right day.

Disabled anglers are allowed to take a car down to the water's edge and the well-constructed gravel path poses no problem for wheelchair users. There are special fishing stages, near the fishing hut, for the disabled.

Because there is a maximum of only 11 anglers, it is advisable to book before going especially at weekends and over holiday periods.

Fishery Rules

Fly fishing only. Only rainbow trout may be taken.

Facilities on Site

Disabled access. Free coffee and tea for anglers. Toilet. Tuition can be arranged. Fishing hut.

YEW TREE TARN

Location (OS90:331011) See map p195

This tiny tarn is easily found from Skelwith Bridge. Take the A593, over the River Brathay, towards Coniston. In approximately 3 miles, the road skirts Yew Tree Tarn.

Fishery Controller

Coniston & Torver Anglers' Association rents the rights from The National Trust. *See Angling Clubs section.*

Water and Stock

A small tarn of approximately $1^1/2$ acres supporting stocked brown and rainbow trout. Some native browns.

Ticket Prices

Day tickets £6.00 and £3.00 for juniors for 2 fish. From Nicholson's Sports, 3 Tiberthwaite Avenue, Coniston (Tel 015394 41639), the Sun Hotel, Coniston (Tel: 015394 41248) and Coniston tourist information office (Tel: 015394 41533).

Opening Times

Open all year at all times subject to permit and closed season restrictions.

Description

A beautiful clear-water tarn, sandwiched between steep fells, Yew Tree is a delight to fish. The hard fighting trout are usually in perfect condition and in common with many of the wild fish of Lakeland, they are greedy. They'll snap at almost any fly although the traditional patterns do best. Access to most of the water is easy. From the lay-by skirting one bank of the lake, a well-trodden path extends around the water. Only the most northerly part is difficult to get at, but as it is the most shallow, few anglers bother with it preferring instead the deeper water near the overflow. Reeds grow along the edge by the road which is a good place to try a corixa or even a small fry imitation. Be careful when back casting though. Casting is not easy from the opposite side which is thickly wooded, but with patience it is possible and long casts are not required. Because Yew Tree Tarn sits in a narrow valley the sun disappears quickly from the water, even in summer, so take something warm to wear.

Fishery Rules

Fly fishing only.

Facilities on Site

None.

Yew Tree Tarn near Coniston. Good trout fishing in lovely surroundings

Canals

LANCASTER CANAL

Location (OS97:520854 to 485638)

The Lancaster Canal starts on the outskirts of Preston and weaves its way north to Stainton, about 6 miles south of Kendal, its original destination. With considerable effort and expertise British Waterways lovingly tends to the needs of this fine waterway keeping it in tiptop condition to be used by anglers, boaters, walkers and cyclists, all of whom gain great pleasure from its presence. Throughout its length, the fishing is brilliant. Depending upon where you fish you may encounter bream, carp, chub, dace, eels, gudgeon, pike or roach. A flight of derelict locks at Tewitfield signals the northernmost point for navigation. The fish tend to be bigger in the un-navigated stretch, where the water is clear and weedy, but don't shy away from the water between Tewitfield and Lancaster. True, there are boats but they few and far between. Unlike the canals of the midlands, this is effectively a landlocked waterway. With the exception of a few visitors braving the difficult passage through tidal waters, the number of boats is quite small and they don't adversely affect the fishing.

A big advantage of canals is that they are easily accessible, particularly in urban areas where roads and canals run side-by-side competing for the level ground. Disabled anglers can often get a vehicle right to the water's edge making for easy wheelchair access.

A lot of the fishing rights are leased from British Waterways by angling clubs most of whom in turn permit fishing for the modest cost of a day ticket. Water that is not currently let to fishing clubs, or which cannot be made available for some other reason, may also be fished as part of a new scheme called 'Waterways Wanderers'. For a modest fee, a ticket holder in this scheme can fish hundreds of miles of canal bank on dozens of canals throughout the country. Some angling clubs have an agreement with British Waterways, which they call 'Waterways Anglers Together' whereby their fully paid-up members may fish BW Wanderers lengths free of charge.

Waterways Wanderers twelve month tickets cost just £15.00 for an adult and £7.50 for a junior, OAP or disabled person. Monthly tickets are £10.00 for an adult and £5.00 for a concession, and daily tickets cost £2.00 for an adult and £1.50 at the concession rate.

All permits for this area and further information can be obtained from Mr John Harding. 34 Nantwich Road, Tarporley CW6 9UW (Tel: 01829 732748).

Stainton to Tewitfield Locks

Approximately 9 miles of brilliant coarse fishing on the only boat-free stretch of canal is controlled as part of the Waterways Anglers Together scheme by the Kendal and District Angling Club. It's a lovely stretch of water ideally suited to casual angling or pole fishing. There are plenty of chub, perch and roach plus some good grass carp and tench. All the popular baits will take fish. Maggots, of course, casters, bread and sweetcorn are the best baits. There are a lot of smallish pike. It is a good water for roving anglers who enjoy spinning. Use a flashy spoon and walk the towpath looking for signs of moving fish.

Day tickets £3.00 for adults and £2.00 for senior citizens and juniors. From Carlsons Fishing Tackle in Kendal (Tel: 01539 724867). *For season tickets see British Waterways Anglers Together above.*

Tewitfield to Lancaster

Below Tewitfield the canal has been dredged for boats and consequently it is wider and deeper. The water is very clean and holds large fish stocks throughout the entire length. Inevitably certain species are more readily found in specific areas, but the roach and perch get everywhere and there are enough of them to keep anyone occupied. Maggots are undoubtedly the best bait and one of the best areas is around Hest Bank and Bolton-le-Sands. Carp and tench seem to like the rural area between Borwick and Holme. Try fishing sweetcorn or luncheon meat in the weedy areas on the offside opposite the towpath. Pike get everywhere and will readily take a small dead bait or a flashy spoon.

Day tickets. *See above under British Waterways.*

*Access is easy to the fishing pegs on the **Ulverston Canal***

ULVERSTON CANAL

Location (OS97:294786 to 312777)

In Ulverston, the canal meets the A590 road to Newby Bridge, at the Canal Tavern. It extends about 1¹/₄ miles south-east to the Bay Horse Inn at Canal Foot on Morecambe Bay.

Fishery Controller

Ulverston Angling Association. *See Angling Clubs section.*

Water and Stock

Most coarse fish including bream, carp, chub, eels, perch, pike, roach, rudd and tench.

Ticket Prices

Day ticket £2.50, senior citizen, disabled anglers, junior £1.25. Season £20.00, concessions £10.00. From the bailiff on the bank or

Coopers of Ulverston, Fishing Tackle, 1 White Hart Yard, Market Place, Ulverston LA12 7BB (Tel: 01229 580261)

Opening Times
Open all year

Description
Here is a water to make midland anglers feel at home. Although only 1¹/₄ miles long, a mere tiddler compared with the Grand Union Canal, for instance, it has the advantage of clear water and no boats. It's now simply a linear stretch of waterway holding some fine fish and offering excellent coarse fishing prospects. A tarmac road runs down the length of the waterway, on the towing path side, giving very easy access, but there is no parking permitted for most of its length. You'll need to drop off the tackle and then park near the end.

Thousands of roach, up to about 1¹/₂lb, rudd, perch, to 1lb, and bream to 4lb, are the majority of the stock, so it's a good water for a pole fisherman to get his teeth into. As always, maggots are the best bait with pinkies and squats doing well in ground baited areas. Fishing in the shade of the trees on the far bank is a good bet.

It's also a good water for pike anglers. Although they are not large, typically 4 or 5lb, the fish are here in big numbers and there are a few over 20lb. All the usual baits will take them, but as the canal is relatively shallow (about 6 or 7 feet at most) try a spinner or plug in the weedy areas under the trees or in one of the three wide basins. There's a basin at each end and one near the railway bridge.

Sweetcorn or boilies are the best baits for the carp, which can go over 20lb, and for the tench, up to 6lb. Use them singly as hook bait and try not to overfeed them as groundbait. Strawberry and chocolate flavours are good in 12 to 15mm sizes.

There are 180 pegs and the water is occasionally used for matches, but it is rarely, if ever, full. Phone ahead for details or check the noticeboard situated near the Canal Tavern on the A590.

Fishery Rules
No keepnets allowed.

Facilities on Site
None.

Angling Clubs

Angling clubs and societies are an essential part of the sport. If it was not for the hard work, often without reward, of club officials, many of the fishing waters listed in this guide would be the preserve of exclusive syndicates and not available to the casual angler. The listing below is the most comprehensive ever produced for Cumbria and The Lake District National Park. It is as complete as possible from the information provided. Some of the clubs catalogued are huge, holding the rights to fishing on dozens of waters throughout the area, like the Windermere, Ambleside and District Angling Association, temporary membership of which gives visitors access to some great sport on several tarns and lakes and two rivers in Southern Lakeland. The WADAA, as it is known locally, makes all this available on a daily, weekly or seasonal basis. Other clubs are tiny, having the rights to one water only. Visitors who like to fish the same water, getting to know it year by year, may wish to join one of the very small clubs, whilst roving anglers, wanting more of a challenge, will probably wish to join one of the big ones and try their skill on a variety of waters. Many clubs are dedicated to game fishing only, others are aimed at the coarse fishermen and some offer mixed fishing opportunities. There are clubs which favour river fishing and others fish still waters. Some are expensive and some are not. Many offer weekly and day tickets and some do not. However, in a number of cases the annual fee is so small that a visiting angler will often find it cheaper to take out a season ticket rather than buy a number of day tickets. This comprehensive listing has been produced to help you decide what is the best way for you to gain access to the waterside.

If you telephone any of the contacts listed, please remember that their official position is a labour of love. They have other things in their lives besides fishing. Try to phone outside busy times and please be patient. And, when writing for information always enclose a stamped self-addressed envelope for the reply.

APPLEBY ANGLING ASSOCIATION
Mr D. Noble, 33 Glebe Road, Appleby-in-Westmoreland CA16 6RT
(Tel: 017683 51966).
Rivers: Eden
Still waters: No.
Membership: Open. Currently no waiting list.
Season fees: Non resident £70.00. Joining fee £20.00.
Day tickets: £4.00.

BARROW ANGLING ASSOCIATION
Mr J. R. Jones, 69 Prince Street, Dalton-in-Furness, Cumbria LA15 8ET
 (Tel: 01229 462955).
Rivers: None.
Still waters: Harlock, Pennington, Poaka Beck and Roosecote Reservoirs.
Membership: Approximately 200 members. Closed. By invitation only.
Season Fees: £80.00 plus £35.00 joining fee. Seniors, ladies and juniors £56.00.
Day tickets: £12.00 from the Hon. Secretary above.

BOWLAND GAME FISHING ASSOCIATION
Mr J. D. Pilling, 20 Swinshaw Close, Badgercoat, Loveclough, Rossendale,
Lancs BB4 8RJ (Tel: 01706 215639).
Rivers: Lune and Rawthey.
Still waters: None in the area covered by this guide.
Membership: Open. Waiting list, about 12 months.
Season fees: £315.00 plus £500.00 entrance fee.
Day tickets: Members' guests only.

BRAMPTON ANGLING ASSOCIATION
Mr T. Donockley, 1 Denton Crescent, Low Row, Brampton, Cumbria
(Tel: 016977 46518).
Rivers: Gelt and Irthing.
Still waters: None.
Membership: Open. Applications for membership, proposed and seconded
by 2 committee members, to the address above.
Season fees: Full members, living within 4 miles of Association waters, adult
£20.00, junior £5.00. County members, living outside 4 mile zone (limit 50),
adult £22.00, junior £11.00. Concessions for others including retired members.
Day tickets: £4.00, junior £2.00, and weekly tickets £12.00, junior £6.00.

BRITISH WATERWAYS (Waterways Wanderers)
Mr S. Griffiths, Fisheries Manager, Regional Office, Navigation Road,
Northwich, Cheshire CW8 1BH (Tel: 01606 723800).
Still water: Lancaster Canal.
Season fee: Adult £15.00, senior, junior and disabled £7.50.
Day tickets: £2.00, concessions £1.50. Monthly tickets £10.00, concessions
£5.00.

BROUGHTON WORKING MEN'S ANGLING ASSOCIATION

Mr T. H. Large, 23 Knowefield Avenue, Stanwick, Carlisle, Cumbria.
Rivers: Derwent.
Still waters: None.
Membership: Restricted to local working men.
Season fees: Not known.
Day tickets: Restricted to local working men.

BURNESIDE ANGLING ASSOCIATION

Mrs C. G. Gregg, Jolly Anglers Inn, Burneside, Kendal, Cumbria LA9 6QS
(Tel: 01539 732552).
Rivers: Kent and Sprint.
Still waters: None.
Membership: Restricted.
Season fees: Not known.
Day tickets: Yes.

CALDER ANGLING ASSOCIATION

Mr A. W. Rigg, 'Allona' Calderbridge, Seascale, Cumbria CA20 1DN
(Tel: 01946 841674).
Rivers: Calder and Wormgill Beck.
Still waters: None.
Membership: Limited to 20 members.
Season fees: Not known.
Day tickets: No.

CARK ANGLING ASSOCIATION

Mr Ray Hadwin, 4 The Boulevard, Windermere Road, Grange-over-Sands,
Cumbria LA11 6EG (Tel: 015395 32854).
Rivers: Eea.
Still waters: None.
Membership: Closed. Usually about 1 year waiting list. Local members,
living within 4 miles of Cark Station, only. Limited to 60 members.
Season fees: £30.00.
Day tickets: No.

CARLISLE AND DISTRICT COARSE ANGLING CLUB

Mr R. Irving, 31 The Green, Houghton, Carlisle CA3 ONG
(Tel: 01228 592459).
Rivers: None.
Still waters: Crofton Lake and Talkin' Tarn joint permit.
Membership: Open. Normally prospective members must be proposed, but
currently anyone wishing to join should write to the Hon. Secretary.
Season fees: Adult £25.00, seniors and disabled £12.50, juniors £5.00. All plus
£5.00 joining fee.
Day tickets: For Talkin' Tarn.

CARLISLE ANGLING ASSOCIATION

Mr Graham Proud, 39 Borland Avenue, Carlisle, Cumbria CA1 2SY
(Tel: 01228 401151).
Rivers: Eden and Caldew.
Still waters: None.
Membership: There is a considerable waiting list for salmon season tickets.
Trout season membership open.
Season fees: Salmon, not known. Trout £15.00.
Day tickets: Weekly and day tickets available for salmon and trout fishing.

CARNFORTH ANGLING ASSOCIATION

Mr W. Lambert, 57 Kings Drive, Carnforth LA5 9AN (Tel: 01524 736428).
Rivers: None.
Still waters: Pine Lake.
Membership: Open.
Season fees: Not known.
Day tickets: Yes.

COCKERMOUTH & DISTRICT ANGLING ASSOCIATION

Mr K. Simpson, Tranby, Moore Road, Great Broughton, Cockermouth,
Cumbria CA13 0XB (Tel: 01900 815523).
Rivers: Cocker (all) and Derwent (2 1/2 miles above/below town).
Still waters: Cogra Moss Fishery.
Membership: Open.
Season fees: Not known.
Day tickets: Yes.

CONISTON AND TORVER ANGLERS' ASSOCIATION

Mr J. Carroll, 8 Old Furness Road, Coniston, Cumbria LA21 8HU
(Tel: 015394 41713).
Rivers: None.
Still waters: Yew Tree Tarn.
Membership: Open. Non-resident member numbers limited.
Season fees: £12.00, juniors £5.00. Non-residents pay double for first year.
Day tickets: Yes.

CUMBERLAND & WESTMORELAND ANGLING ALLIANCE

Mr T. Cousin, 28 Mayburgh Avenue, Penrith, Cumbria. (Tel: 01768 864590).
An advisory body only.

EDEN AND DISTRICT FISHERIES ASSOCIATION

Mr A. G. Britton, 24 Cammock Avenue, Upperby, Carlisle, Cumbria CA2
4PD (Tel: 01228 539752).
Fisheries consultants.

ENNERDALE ANGLING ASSOCIATION

Mr D. Crellin, 3 Parklands Drive, Egremont, Cumbria CA22 2JL

(Tel: 01946 823337).
Rivers: Ehen.
Still waters: Ennerdale Lake.
Membership: Open. No restrictions.
Season fees: £12.00.
Weekly tickets: £6.00 from Wath Brow Post Office.

EGREMONT ANGLING ASSOCIATION
Mr C. Fisher, 69 North Road, Egremont, Cumbria CA22 2PR
(Tel: 01946 820855).
Rivers: Ehen.
Still waters: Joint permits with Wath Brow & Ennerdale AA for Ennerdale.
Membership: Open.
Season fees: Adults £30.00, juveniles £7.50. Prospective members must be
proposed by an existing member.
Day tickets: Weekly tickets only.

FURNESS AND SOUTH CUMBRIA FISHING ASSOCIATION
Mr F. French, Sweden How, Sweden Bridge Lane, Ambleside, Cumbria
LA22 9EY (Tel: 015394 32463).
Fishery consultants.

FURNESS FISHING ASSOCIATION
Mr R. Henry, 23 Shakespeare Street, Barrow-in-Furness (Tel: 01229 826662).
Rivers: None.
Still waters: Roanhead Lakes.
Membership: Open.
Season fees: Not known.
Day tickets: Yes.

GOSFORTH ANGLERS' CLUB
Mr G. Thomas, 11 Fell View Caravan Site, Gosforth, Seascale, Cumbria CA20
1HY. (Tel: 019467 25367).
Rivers: Bleng and Irt.
Still waters: None.
Membership: Closed.
Season fees: Not known.
Day tickets: No.

HAWKSHEAD ANGLING CLUB
Mr J. L. Locke, Flat 1 The Croft, Victoria Street, Hawkshead, Ambleside,
Cumbria LA22 0NX (Tel: 015394 36724).
Rivers: No.
Still waters: Esthwaite Water.
Membership: Limited to 100. Long waiting list. Priority given to locals.
Season fees: £75.00.
Day tickets: No.

KENDAL AND DISTRICT ANGLING CLUB
Mr A. Ryan, 8 Hayfell Rise, Kendal, Cumbria LA59 7JP (Tel: 01539 735481).
Rivers: Winster.
Still waters: Banks Pond, Gatebeck Reservoir, Lancaster Canal and Witherslack Tarn.
Membership: Open. Restricted to 75 members, only 10 of which come from outside a 25 mile radius of Kendal Town Hall.
Season fees: £23.00; seniors, over 65, and juniors under 16 £10.00. Joining fee £6.00. Family ticket £30.00.
Day tickets: Adult £3.00, concessions £2.00 for all waters.

KENT, BELA, WINSTER, LEVEN AND DUDDON FISHERIES ASSOCIATION
Mr O. R. Bagot, Levens Hall, Nr. Kendal, Cumbria (Tel: 015395 60585).
An advisory body.

KENT (WESTMORELAND) ANGLING ASSOCIATION
Mr J. Atkinson, Town End, Natland, Kendal, Cumbria LA9 7QL
 (Tel: 015395 60962 or possibly - 01539 23223).
Rivers: Kent, Mint and Sprint.
Still waters: Killington Reservoir.
Membership: Open.
Season fees: £11.00.
Day tickets: Yes.

KESWICK ANGLING ASSOCIATION
Mark Cockburn, 55 Latrigg Close, Keswick CA12 4LF (Tel: 017687 72954).
Rivers: Derwent and Greta.
Still waters: Derwentwater.
Membership: Open.
Season fees: Salmon £110.00, trout £70.00, pike and coarse fish £40.00.
Day tickets: Yes.

KIRKBY LONSDALE ANGLING ASSOCIATION
Mr David Halton, The Bungalow, Birglands, Wennington Road, Wray, Lancaster LA2 8QH (Tel: 015242 21263).
Rivers: Lune.
Still waters: None.
Membership: Limited places for non residents. Waiting list typically 12 months.
Season fees: Local members, £100.00 plus £15.00 joining fee. Non residential members £250.00 plus £30.00 joining fee.
Day tickets: Only for residents, or visitors staying in local hotel accommodation.

KIRKBY STEPHEN AND DISTRICT ANGLING ASSOCIATION

Mr H. Kilvington, Solicitor, Market Square, Kirkby Stephen, Cumbria.
Rivers: Eden and the tributaries, Belah, Scandal and Swindale Becks.
Still waters: None.
Membership: Open.
Season Fees: Visitors £75.00 plus £20.00 joining fee. Local anglers £45.00 plus £20.00 joining fee.
Day tickets: £15.00, weekly tickets £30.00.

LAKELAND FLY DRESSERS GUILD

Hon. Secretary Mr F. French, Sweden How, Sweden Bridge Lane, Ambleside, Cumbria LA22 9EY (Tel: 015394 32463). Guild meets monthly in the Eagle and Child Hotel, Staveley.

LANCASHIRE FLY FISHING ASSOCIATION

Mr J. Winnard, Manor House, Grunsagill, Long Preston, North Yorks (Tel: 01729 840491).
Rivers: Lune.
Still waters: None.
Membership: Very short waiting list.
Season fees: £250.00, concession £125.00. Joining fee £250.00.
Day tickets: No.

LANCASTER AND DISTRICT ANGLING ASSOCIATION

Mr V. C. Price, 19 Church Brow, Halton, Lancs LA2 6LS (Tel: 01524 812141).
Rivers: Lune.
Still waters: None.
Membership: Long waiting list, approximately 15 years. All prospective new members are subject to approval by the committee.
Season fees: Local members (residing within 12 miles of Lancaster Town Hall) £160.00. Senior citizen (subject to 15 years membership) £125.00. Associate members £185.00 and seniors (subject to 15 years membership) £150.00.
Day tickets: Between £10.00 and £20.00 depending upon season.

LONSDALE ANGLING CLUB

Mr M. Cassidy, 33 Bridge Road, Lancaster (Tel: 01524 65199).
Rivers: None.
Still waters: Bellrig Lake and Overkellet Lake.
Membership: Open to local anglers only.
Season fees: Not known.
Day tickets: No.

MANCHESTER ANGLERS' ASSOCIATION

Mr F. Fletcher, 7 Alderbank Close, Kearsley, Bolton, Lancs BL4 8JQ
Rivers: Lune and Ribble.

Still waters: None in the area covered by this guide.
Membership: Short waiting list.
Season fees: £180.00 plus £100.00 entrance fee. Juniors half price.
Day tickets: Members' guest tickets only.

MILLOM AND DISTRICT ANGLING ASSOCIATION

Mr D. J. Dixon, 1 Churchill Drive, Millom, Cumbria LA18 5DD
(Tel: 01229 774241).
Rivers: Annas, Black Beck, Bleng, Duddon, Esk, Irt, Lazy and Lickle.
Still waters: Baystone Bank Reservoir and Devoke Water.
Membership: Open.
Season fees: £80.00, lady and senior £30.00, junior (under 17) £10.00. Entry fee £10.00.
Day tickets: £15.00, week £40 and two week £50.00.

MILNTHORPE ANGLING ASSOCIATION

Mr A. R. Park, Hawkshead House, Priest Hutton, Carnforth, Cumbria LA6 1JP
Rivers: Bela.
Still waters: No.
Membership: Closed.
Season fees: Not known.
Day tickets: No.

PENRITH ANGLING ASSOCIATION

Miss E. Lomas, 3 Newtown Cottages, Skirwith, Penrith, Cumbria CA10 1RJ
(Tel: 01768 88294).
Rivers: Eamont, Eden, Kirkby Thore Beck, Lowther and Petterill (Eden) .
Still waters: None.
Membership: Open. No waiting list. No restrictions.
Season fees: Local adult member £84.00. Associate members (outside a 10 mile radius) £135.00. Joining fee £10.00. Extensive range of concessions apply.
Day tickets: Yes.

PRINCE ALBERT ANGLING SOCIETY

Hon. Secretary, Mr J. A. Turner, 15 Peckshill Drive, Macclesfield, Cheshire SK10 3LP (Tel: 01625 422010).
Membership Secretary, Mr C. Swindells, 37 Sherwood Road, Macclesfield SK11 7RR (Tel: 01625 427078).
Rivers: Dee, Greta, Lune, Rawthey, Ribble and Wenning.
Still waters: None in the area.
Membership: Long waiting list. Typically two years.
Season fees: £60.00 plus £60.00 joining fee.
Day tickets: No.

REDWELL FISHERIES CLUB
Diane & Ken Hall, Redwell Fisheries, Kirkby Lonsdale Road, Arkholme, Carnforth, Lancs LA61BQ (Tel: 015242 21979).
Rivers: None.
Still water: Redwell Fishery Lake.
Membership: Open to everyone.
Season fees: £15.00.
Day tickets: £3.50, evening £2.50.

SALMON AND TROUT ASSOCIATION, SOUTH CUMBRIA BRANCH
Mr F. French, Sweden Howe, Sweden Bridge Lane, Ambleside, Cumbria LA22 9EY (Tel: 015394 32463).

SEDBERGH AND DISTRICT ANGLING ASSOCIATION
Mr Gilbert Bainbridge, El-Kantara, Frostrow, Sedbergh, Cumbria LA10 5JL (Tel: 015396 20044).
Rivers: Clough, Dee, Rawthey and Lune.
Still waters: None.
Membership: Waiting list. Currently 2 to 3 years.
Season fees: Adult £110.00 plus £50.00 joining fee. Concessions for local residents.
Day tickets: (March 15th to August 31st) £10.00. Weekly tickets; £50.00. Mid September to October 31st £100.00.

SOUTH CUMBERLAND FLY DRESSER'S GUILD
Hon. Secretary Mr David Nixon (Tel: 01229 467211).

SOUTH AND WEST CUMBERLAND FISHERIES ASSOCIATION
Hon. Secretary Mr W. M. Arnold, Knotts End Estate, Ravenglass, Cumbria CA18 1RT (Tel: 01229 717255).
Fishery consultants.

STAVELEY AND DISTRICT ANGLING ASSOCIATION
Hon. Secretary Mr David Andrews 17, Rawes Garth, Staveley, Kendal LA8 9QH (Tel: 01539 821673).
Permit Secretary Mr Robin Leck, 20, Rawes Garth, Staveley, Kendal LA8 9QH (Tel: 01539 821776).
Rivers: Gowan and Kent.
Still waters: None.
Membership: Open. No waiting list.
Season fees: £30.00. Concessions for juniors half price.
Day tickets: For all waters.

TEBAY AND DISTRICT ANGLING CLUB
Mr H. Riley, White Cross House, Tebay, Via Penrith, Cumbria CA10 3UY (Tel: 015396 24376).

Rivers: Lune. Also Birk, Borrow, Chapel and Raise Becks.
Still waters: None.
Membership: Open. Restricted to 130.
Season fees: £85.00, senior citizen £45.00 and juniors £15.00. Concessions for local residents.
Weekly tickets: £45.00 or £25.00.

ULVERSTON ANGLING ASSOCIATION

Mr H. B. Whittam, Tunstead, Lyndhurst Road, Ulverston, Cumbria (Tel: 01229 582322)
Rivers: Crake.
Still waters: Knottallow Tarn and Ulverston Canal.
Membership: Open.
Season fees: Not known.
Day tickets: For the Ulverston Canal only.

WATH BROW & ENNERDALE ANGLING ASSOCIATION

Mr J. McGlennon, 51 Mill Hill, Cleator Moor, Cumbria CA25 5SQ (Tel: 01946 812344).
Rivers: Ehen.
Still waters: Ennerdale (joint permits with Egremont Angling Association) and Longlands Lake.
Membership: Open to local residents living within a 10 mile radius of Cleator Moor.
Season fees: £30.00, junior £7.00.
Day tickets: Weekly and day permits for anglers living outside a 10 mile radius of Cleator Moor.

WEST COAST TROUT ANGLERS ASSOCIATION

Mr J. Kelley, Holly Croft, Braystones Road, Beckermet, Cumbria CA21 2XX (Tel: 01946 841677).
Rivers: None.
Still waters: Meadley Reservoir.
Membership: Closed. Waiting list of 20.
Season fees: Not known.
Day tickets: £12.00.

WINDERMERE, AMBLESIDE AND DISTRICT ANGLING ASSOCIATION

Hon. Secretary Mr John Newton, 3 Lumley Road, Kendal LA9 5HT (Tel: 01539 728341).
The largest angling club in Cumbria controlling many high quality fisheries in Southern Lakeland. The WADAA offers a range of permits for local and visiting anglers.

WADAA Visitors' Membership Permit

Rivers: Brathay and Rothay.

Still waters: Blelham Tarn, Grasmere Lake, Hayeswater, High Arnside Tarn, Moss Eccles Tarn, Rydal Water, School Knott Tarn and some areas of Windermere Lake.

Membership: Open.

Season fees: £30.00, half price for senior citizens and juniors; weekly fee £10.00, half price for senior citizens and juniors and daily permit £3.50, senior citizens and juniors £2.00 from tourist information centres. Also from Go Fishing, Tackle Shop, Gilly's Landing, Glebe Road, Bowness-on-Windermere (Tel: 015394 47086), Charlton & Bagnell Ltd. Fishing Tackle, 5 Damside Street, Lancaster (Tel: 01524 63043), Nicholson's Sports, 3 Tiberthwaite Avenue, Coniston (Tel: 015394 41639) and Coopers of Ulverston, Fishing Tackle, White Hart Yard, Market Place, Ulverston (Tel: 01229 580261).

WADAA Coarse Membership Permit

In advance from Mr Chris Sodo, Ecclerigg Court, Ecclerigg, Windermere, Cumbria LA23 1LQ (Tel: 015394 45083).

Available to those anglers who are not eligible for full membership.

Rivers: None.

Still Waters: Atkinsons Tarn, Blelham Tarn, Cleabarrow Tarn, Grasmere Lake, Holehird Tarn, Ratherheath Tarn, Rydal Water, Windermere Lake.

Membership: Open.

Season fees: £30.00, senior citizens and juniors half price.

WADAA Hotel Membership Permit

Hotel Membership Secretary Mr Fred French, Sweden Howe, Sweden Bridge Lane, Ambleside, Cumbria LA22 9EX (Tel: 015394 32463).

Free fishing on all WADAA waters for bona fide guests staying at certain hotels in the area. Enquire at reception.

WADAA Full Membership

Membership Secretary Mr Mike Smith (Tel: 015394 33012 after 1900 hrs).

Available only to permanent residents living within a 10 mile radius of St Mary's Church in Ambleside, or within a 3 mile radius of the weir at Newby Bridge.

Rivers: Brathay and Rothay.

Still waters: Blelham Tarn, Dubbs Trout Fishery, Cleabarrow Tarn, Ghyll Head Trout Fishery, Grasmere Lake, Hayeswater, High Arnside Tarn, High Newton Trout Fishery, Holehird Tarn, Moss Eccles Tarn, Ratherheath Tarn, Rydal Water, School Knott Tarn and Graythwaite Estate Shoreline on Windermere.

Membership. Open to local residents only.

Season fees: £20.00, senior citizens £10.50 and juniors £10.00. Joining fee £30.00.

No joining fee for juniors.

WADAA Associate Membership.

Apply to Membership Secretary.

Available to anglers not eligible for full membership.
All waters as listed above.
Membership: Limited to 100. Waiting list of over 3 years.
Season fees: £80.00 with a £30.00 joining fee.

WIGAN AND DISTRICT ANGLING ASSOCIATION

Mr G. Wilson, 11 Guildford Avenue, Chorley, Lancs (Tel: 01257 265905).
Rivers: Winster. Also Ribble and Wyre outside the area of this guide.
Still waters: None in the area covered by this guide.
Membership: Closed.
Season fees: Not known.
Day tickets: No.

YORKSHIRE FLY FISHERS' CLUB

Hon. Secretary, Margaret House, 2 Devonshire Crescent, Leeds LS8 1EP
(Tel: 0113 2370099).
Rivers: Eden. Also River Ribble and Ure. *See Yorkshire Dales Anglers' Guide.*
Still waters: None.
Membership: Waiting list.
Season fees: Not known.
Day tickets: No.

Fishing Tackle Outlets

Fishing tackle shops are the obvious place to go for the best baits and tackle for local waters, but they are not always easy to find. The list which follows has been compiled to help visitors to find these 'centres of knowledge.' Not surprisingly many of them are situated in the major towns because that's generally where people live and work, however they are fairly evenly spread throughout the whole area. Some of the shops are small whilst others are huge and stock a massive range of fishing tackle. Visitors to the area may know of two of the biggest, McHardy's in Carlisle and John Norris of Penrith, both of whom have for many years operated national mail order services. Not so well known are the smaller local shops which, for their size, offer a tremendous selection of tackle and bait. Some outlets specialise in game fishing, others in coarse fishing and some cater for sea anglers and in every case I have given an idea of the shop's specialism. A listing of fresh baits refers to a selection of maggots, casters, squats, pinkies, worms, cooked hemp amongst other things and preserved baits are usually boilies, canned sweetcorn or one of a multitude of modern delights. Some shops also stock frozen sprats for pike fishing and others sell prawns or shrimps for salmon fishing. Fishing tackle shops are also a good source for buying visitor's tickets. Many of them also hold season membership books for angling clubs so you can join on the spot and be at the water's edge in the shortest possible time.

Barrow-in-Furness
Angling & Hiking Centre, 275-277 Rawlinson Street, LA14 1DH (Tel: 01229 829661).
Open 0900 to 1730 hrs (1015 to 1300 hrs on Thursday). Closed Sunday. Comprehensive range of game, coarse and sea tackle. Flies and tying materials. Fresh baits, maggots, worms etc. Preserved baits, Frozen sea and pike baits. Club season books held: Ulverston Angling Association. Day tickets: Furness Fishing Association, game and coarse, waters; Furness Peninsula waters and Ulverston AA waters.

Hools Fishing Tackle, 185 Rawlinson Street (Tel: 01229 430425).
Open 0900 to 1600 hrs. Closes at 1200 hrs on Thursday. Closed Sunday. Game, coarse and sea tackle. Flies. Fresh baits, maggots etc. Frozen and

preserved baits. Club season books held: Ulverston Angling Association. Day tickets: Furness Fishing Association waters, Ulverston AA waters and Esthwaite Water.

Bowness-on-Windermere

Go Fishing, Gilly's Landing, Glebe Road (Tel: 015394 47086). Open in summer (March 1st to October 31st): 0900 to 1730 hrs seven days a week. Winter (November 1st to February 28th): 0900 to 1730 hrs, closed all day Wednesday. A huge selection of game, coarse and sea tackle. Clothing. Fresh, dead and preserved baits. Flies and tying materials. Club season books held: Wimbledon, Ambleside and District AA. Day tickets: For the above listed clubs' waters where applicable and Kendal and District AA waters. Also hires rowing boats on Windermere Lake. Full day, half day or 2 hours.

Brampton

B. Warwick, Sporting Guns & Fishing Tackle, 2 Market Place
 (Tel: 016977 2361).
Open 0930 to 1700 hrs. Closes 1300 hrs on Thursday. Closed on Sunday. Game, coarse and sea tackle sold. Fresh baits, maggots etc, and preserved baits. Flies and tying materials.

Carlisle

Eddie's Fishing Tackle, 70 Shaddon Gate (Tel: 01228 810744). Open 1000 to 1700 hrs Monday to Friday and 0900 to 1800 hrs on Saturday. Closed on Sunday. Game, coarse and sea tackle. Flies and tying materials. Fresh baits, maggots, worms and sea worms. Most frozen baits. Club season books held: Carlisle and District Coarse Angling Club. Day tickets for above club waters.

Geoff Wilson, 36 Portland Place (Tel: 01228 531542). Open 0915 to 1730 hrs Tuesday to Saturday. Specimen game, coarse and sea tackle. Fresh baits, maggots and worms etc. Preserved baits and frozen pike and sea baits. Club season books held: Carlisle and District Coarse Angling Club and Bigwater Angling Club for High Stand Lakes. Day tickets for Bassenthwaite Lake, Longtown Gravel Pit, Talkin' Tarn and Carlisle AA waters on the Eden etc.

McHardys, South Henry Street, CA1 1SF (Tel: 01228 523988). Open 0900 to 1730 hrs Monday to Saturday. Closes at 1630 on Thursday. Specimen game and some sea tackle. Flies and tying materials. Preserved baits, including shrimps and prawns. Day tickets for Carlisle AA waters on the River Eden. Operates an extensive mail order service. Phone for catalogue.

Murray's Fishing Tackle, 16 Fisher Street, CA3 8RN (Tel: 01228 523816). Open 0900 to 1730 hrs Monday to Saturday (closes at 1630 hrs on Thursday). Game fishing tackle and rod building service. Flies and tying materials. Spinning tackle. Preserved shrimps and sprats. Day tickets: Both day and weekly tickets for Carlisle Angling Association water on Rivers Eden and Caldew. Casting tuition available in the evenings.

Cleator Moor
Wath Brow Post Office, 121 Ennerdale Road, CA25 5LP (Tel: 01946 810377).
Open 0800 to 1730 hrs Monday to Friday, 0800 to 1930 hrs on Saturday.
Closed Sunday. Game, coarse and sea tackle. Flies and tying materials. Day
tickets: Wath Brow & Ennerdale AA waters on River Ehan, Ennerdale Water
and Longlands Lake. West Coast Trout Anglers water, Meadley Reservoir.

Coniston
Nicholson's Sports, 3 Tiberthwaite Avenue, LA12 8ED (Tel: 015394 41639).
Open 0930 to 1730 hrs Monday to Saturday. Game and coarse tackle. Flies.
Day tickets: Coniston & Trover AA waters, Coniston Lake and Yew Tree
Tarn.

Egremont
J. W. N. Holmes & Son, Fishing Tackle & Firearms, 45 Main Street, CA22 2AB
(Tel: 01946 820368).
Open normal shop hours. Closed Wednesday half day. Closed Sunday.
Game, coarse and sea tackle. Fly tying materials. Fresh and preserved baits
sold. Club season books held: Egremont AA and Wath Brow & Ennerdale
AA. Day tickets: Ennerdale Lake and Longlands Lake.

Grange-over-Sands
The Fishing Hut, 4 The Boulevard, Windermere Road, LA11 6EG
(Tel: 015395 32854).
Open 0930 to 1800 hrs Monday to Saturday. 1000 to 1600 hrs on Sunday.
Game, coarse and sea tackle. Flies and tying materials. Large range of fresh
and preserved baits. Day tickets for own private trout and coarse fishery and
Kendal and District AA waters. Tackle hire and casting tuition arranged.

Kendal
Carlsons Fishing Tackle, 64-66 Kirkland (Tel: 01539 724867).
Open 0900 to 1700 hrs. Closed all day Thursday and Sunday. A huge
selection of game and coarse tackle. Clothing. Flies and tying materials.
Fresh baits - in season. Preserved baits. Club season books held: Windermere,
Ambleside and District AA. Day tickets: WDAAA and Kendal and District
AA waters.

Kendal Sports Shop, 30 Stramongate (Tel: 01539 721554).
Open 0900 to 1700 hrs. Close at 1600 hrs on Thursday. Closed Sunday. Sells
game and coarse tackle. Clothing. Flies and tying materials. Day tickets:
Kent (Westmoreland) AA waters and Fisher Tarn.

Keswick
Peter Thorburn, Field and Stream, 79 Main Street (Tel: 017687 74396).
Open 0900 to 1730 hrs every day (close at 1700 hrs on Sunday). January 1st
to Easter, closed on Sunday. Game, coarse and some sea tackle. Most baits
sold. Season, weekly and day permits sold for Bassenthwaite Lake,
Derwentwater, Overwater Fishery and the River Greta.

Lancaster

Charlton & Bagnall Ltd. Fishing Tackle, 3-5 Damside Street, LA1 1PD
(Tel: 01524 63043).
Open 0900 to 1730 hrs Monday to Friday, closes at 1700 hrs on Saturday. 0930 to 1230 hrs on Sunday. Game, coarse and sea tackle. Fresh baits, maggots, pinkies etc. Club season books held: Castletown Angling Club and Lonsdale Angling Club.

Stephen F. Fawcett, 7 Great John Street (Tel: 01524 32033).
Open 0900 to 1700 hrs (closed all day on Wednesday and Sunday). Predominantly game but also some coarse and sea tackle. Flies and tying materials. Fresh and preserved baits, frozen sea baits and shrimps. Club season books held: Lonsdale Angling Club. Day tickets for British Waterways Northwest canals including Lancaster Canal.

Maryport

Solway Leisure, 66 Senhouse Street (Tel: 01900 815109).
Open 0900 to 1715 hrs. Closed Sunday. Predominantly game and sea fishing tackle. Flies and materials. Season and day tickets for River Ellen.

Morecambe

Gerry's of Morecambe, Fishing Tackle and Bait, 5-7 Parliament Street
(Tel: 01524 422146).
Open 0900 to 1700 hrs, Monday to Saturday. 0900 to 1200 hrs, Sunday. Game, coarse and sea tackle. Most coarse baits. Maggots, casters etc. Frozen pike baits. Sea baits. Club season books held: Lonsdale Angling Club. Day tickets: For Lonsdale AC waters and Windermere, Ambleside & DAA, Ratherheath Tarn. Also offers a specialist mail order service. Phone for details.

Morecambe Angling Centre, Grand Garage, Thornton Road, LA4 5PB
(Tel: 01524 832332).
Open 0900 to 1730 hrs Monday to Saturday. 0900 to 1200 hrs on Sunday. Game, coarse and sea tackle. Flies and tying materials sold. Most baits. Maggots, casters, squats, worms, etc. Sea baits. Preserved baits. Club season books held: Lonsdale Angling Club and British Waterways Wanderers. Day tickets: Lancaster Canal, Windermere, Ambleside and DAA waters, Carnforth Anglers, Pine Lake and Littledale Hall Coarse Fishery.

Penrith

J. Norris, 21 Victoria Road (Tel: 01768 864211).
Open 0900 to 1730 hrs Monday to Saturday. Sunday 1000 to 1600 hrs. Closed on bank holidays. Game and coarse tackle. Clothing. Extensive range of flies and tying materials sold. Preserved baits. Day tickets for Whinn's Pond and the Rivers Eden and Eamont. One of the country's biggest mail order outlets. Phone for a catalogue.

Charles R. Sykes, Tackle and Guns, 4 Great Dockray, CA11 7BL
(Tel: 01768 862418).
Open 0930 to 1730 hrs, 1700 on Saturdays. Closed on Wednesdays and

Sundays. Game, coarse and sea tackle. Specialist fly tying materials and flies. Fresh bait, maggots and worms sold seasonally. Day tickets: Both weekly and day tickets for Penrith AA waters on Rivers Eden, Eamont and Lowther.

Sedbergh
Lowis's Country Wear Ltd, 25 Main Street (Tel: 015396 20446).
Open 0930 to 1700 hrs. Closed Thursday and Sunday. Small range of tackle. Spinners. Flies. No baits. Day and weekly tickets for Sedbergh & District AA waters on the River Lune, Rawthey, Dee and Clough.

Ulverston
Coopers of Ulverston, 1 White Hart Yard, Market Place, LA12 7BB
(Tel: 01229 580261).
Open 0900 to 1800 hrs. Open Sunday during the summer. Coarse, game and sea fishing tackle. Maggots. Day tickets for Furness Fishing Association waters, Roanhead Lakes.

Whitehaven
The Compleat Angler, 4 King Street, CA28 7LA (Tel: 01946 695322).
Open 0830 to 1700 hrs Monday to Saturday. (Wednesday, closed 1430 hrs in summer and 1230 hrs in winter). Game, coarse and sea fishing tackle. Fly tying materials. Fresh bait, maggots, groundbait and sea baits. Day tickets: Bassenthwaite Lake.

The Tackle Shack, A9 Haig Enterprise Park, High Road, Kells
(Tel: 01946 693233).
Open 0900 to 1800 hrs Monday to Saturday (closes at 1700 hrs on Saturday). Open Sunday from 1000 to 1400 hrs. Game, coarse and sea tackle. Fresh baits, maggots and worms plus preserved and frozen baits. Day tickets for National Trust waters.

Wigton
Rod & Line, 19 High Street, CA7 9NJ (Tel: 016973 45744).
Open 0930 to 1700 hrs Monday, Tuesday and Saturday. 0930 to 1730 hrs, Thursday and Friday. Gale, coarse and sea tackle. Fly tying materials. Also offers fly tying help and advice including beginners free $^1/_2$ hour tuition. Fresh and preserved sea and pike baits. Club season books held: Keswick Angling Association. Day tickets: Keswick AA on River Derwent and Greta. Derwentwater.

Workington
Grahams Gun and Sport Services, 9-15 South William Street, CA14 2ED
(Tel: 01900 605093).
Open 0900 to 1730 hrs, Monday to Saturday. Game, coarse and sea fishing tackle. Fresh, frozen, preserved and groundbaits sold. Season ticket for River Ellen. Day tickets: Bassenthwaite Lake, Buttermere, Crummock Water and Loweswater.

Maps of Still Water Day Ticket Fisheries

NORTHWEST AREA

1. Oakbank Lakes, mixed fishery.
2. Longtown West Pond, coarse fishery.
3. Lough Lake, trout fishery.
4. Brayton Park Lake, coarse fishery.
5. Gilcrux Lakes, trout fishery.
6. Overwater Tarn, trout fishery.
7. Bassenthwaite Lake, mixed fishery.
8. Ellerbeck Lakes, coarse fishery.
9. Loweswater, mixed fishery
10. Crummock Water, mixed fishery.
11. Buttermere, mixed fishery.
12. Derwentwater, mixed fishery.
13. Watendlath Tarn, trout fishery.
14. Thirlmere Reservoir, mixed fishery.

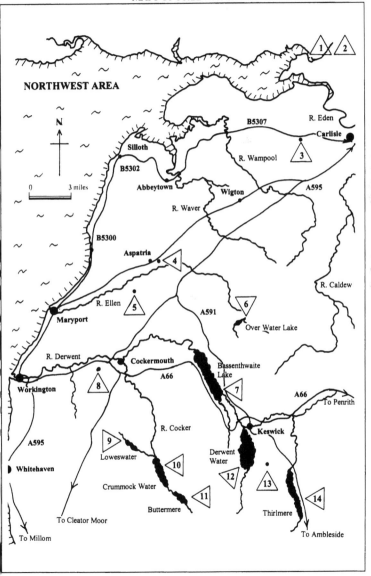

NORTHWEST AREA

NORTHEAST AREA MAP

1. New Mills, trout fishery.
2. Talkin' Tarn, coarse fishery.
3. Lonsdale Park Lakes, coarse fishery.
4. High Stand Lakes, coarse fishery.
5. East View Lake, coarse fishery.
6. Crossfield Lakes, coarse fishery.
7. Whins Pond, mixed fishery.
8. Blencarn Lake, trout fishery.
9. Sockbridge Mill, trout fishery.
10. Ullswater, mixed fishery.
11. Brotherswater, trout fishery.
12. Hayswater Reservoir, trout fishery.
13. Haweswater, mixed fishery.
14. Blea Water, trout fishery.
15. Small Water, trout fishery.
16. Eden Valley Lake, trout fishery.

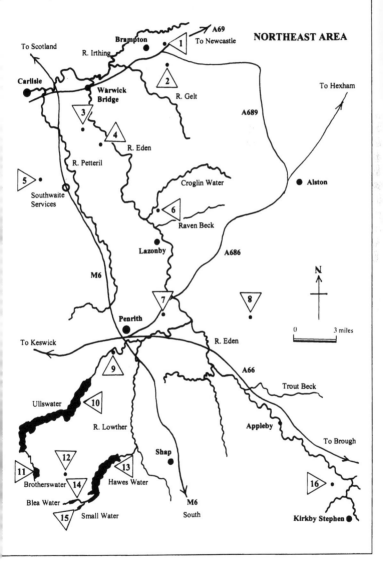

SOUTHWEST AREA MAP

1. Ennerdale Water, trout fishery.
2. Thirlmere Reservoir, mixed fishery.
3. Longlands Lake, trout fishery.
4. Meadley Reservoir, trout fishery.
5. Silver Tarn, coarse fishery.
6. Tarnside Lake, coarse fishery.
7. Burnmore Tarn, mixed fishery.
8. Knott End Tarn, trout fishery.
9. Devoke Water, trout fishery.
10. Coniston Water, mixed fishery
11. Esthwaite Water, trout fishery.
12. Moss Eccles Tarn, trout fishery.
13. Windermere, mixed fishery.
15. Beacon Tarn, mixed fishery.
16. High Dam, coarse fishery.
17. High Newton Reservoir, trout fishery.
17. Baystone Bank Reservoir, trout fishery.
18. Harlock Reservoir, trout fishery.
19. Poaka Reservoir, trout fishery.
20. Pennington Reservoir, trout fishery.
21. Bigland Hall, mixed fishery.
22. Ulverston Canal, coarse fishery.
23. Roanhead Lakes, mixed fishery.
24. Urswick Tarn, coarse fishery.
25. Mill Beck Lake, coarse fishery.
26. Roosecote Resevoir, trout fishery.

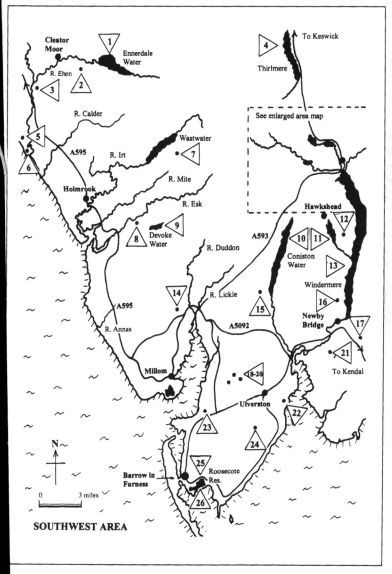

SOUTHWEST AREA

SOUTHWEST AREA MAP - Enlarged section

Blea Tarn, trout fishery.
Blelham Tarn, coarse fishery.
Codale Tarn, trout fishery.
Drunken Duck Tarn, trout fishery.
Dubbs Reservoir, trout fishery.
Easdale Tarn, mixed fishery.
Grasmere, mixed fishery.
High Arnside Tarn, trout fishery.
Holehird Tarn, coarse fishery.
Loughrigg Tarn, coarse fishery.
Rydal Water, mixed fishery.
Windermere, mixed fishery.
Fishing is prohibited in the following waters:
Elterwater.
Little Langdale Tarn.
Tarn Howes.

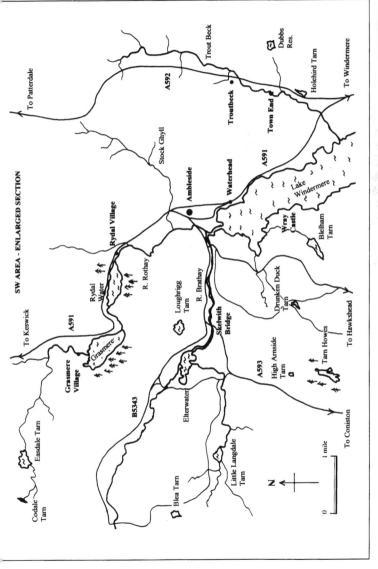

SW AREA - ENLARGED SECTION

SOUTHEAST AREA MAP

1. Pinfold Lake, trout fishery.
2. Bessy Beck Lakes, trout fishery.
3. Kentmere Lakes, trout fishery.
4. Skelsmergh Tarn, coarse fishery.
5. Ratherheath Tarn, coarse fishery.
6. Killington Reservoir, mixed fishery.
7. Banks Pond, coarse fishery.
8. Gatebeck Reservoir, mixed fishery.
9. Witherslack Hall Tarn, coarse fishery.
10. Wych Elm Lake, trout fishery.
11. Hallmore Lake, coarse fishery.
12. Pine Lake, coarse fishery.
13. Redwell Lake, coarse fishery.
14. Bank House Lake, trout fishery.
15. Littledale Hall Lake, coarse fishery.

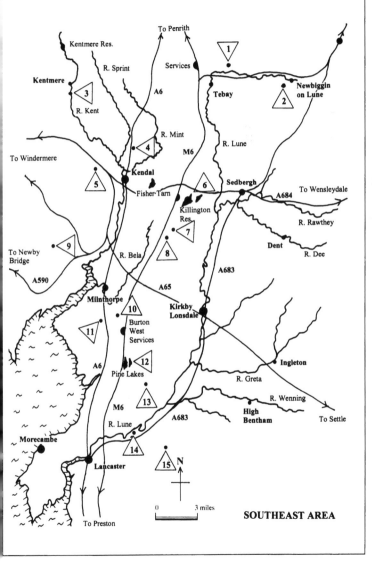

SOUTHEAST AREA

Index

NOTES

LISTING OF CICERONE GUIDES

**BACKPACKING AND
CHALLENGE WALKING**
Backpacker's Britain:
Vol 1 – Northern England
Vol 2 – Wales
Vol 3 – Northern Scotland
Vol 4 – Central & Southern
Scottish Highlands
Book of the Bivvy
End to End Trail
The National Trails
Three Peaks, Ten Tors

BRITISH CYCLING
Border Country Cycle Routes
Cumbria Cycle Way
Lancashire Cycle Way
Lands End to John O'Groats
Rural Rides:
No 1 – West Surrey
No 2 – East Surrey
South Lakeland Cycle Rides

PEAK DISTRICT AND DERBYSHIRE
High Peak Walks
Historic Walks in Derbyshire
The Star Family Walks – The Peak
District & South Yorkshire
White Peak Walks:
The Northern Dales
The Southern Dales
**MOUNTAINS OF ENGLAND
AND WALES**
FOR COLLECTORS OF SUMMITS
Mountains of England & Wales:
Vol 1 – Wales
Vol 2 – England
Relative Hills of Britain

IRELAND
Irish Coast to Coast Walk
Irish Coastal Walks
Mountains of Ireland

THE ISLE OF MAN
Isle of Man Coastal Path
Walking on the Isle of Man

**LAKE DISTRICT AND
MORECAMBE BAY**
Atlas of the English Lakes
Coniston Copper Mines
Cumbria Coastal Way
Cumbria Way and Allerdale Ramble
Great Mountain Days in the
Lake District
Lake District Anglers' Guide
Lake District Winter Climbs
Lakeland Fellranger:
The Central Fells
The Mid-Western Fells
The Near-Eastern Fells
The Southern Fells
Roads and Tracks of the Lake District
Rocky Rambler's Wild Walks
Scrambles in the Lake District:
North
South

Short Walks in Lakeland:
Book 1 – South Lakeland
Book 2 – North Lakeland
Book 3 – West Lakeland
Tarns of Lakeland:
Vol 1 – West
Vol 2 – East
Tour of the Lake District
Walks in Silverdale and Arnside
THE MIDLANDS
Cotswold Way
NORTHERN ENGLAND
LONG-DISTANCE TRAILS
Dales Way
Hadrian's Wall Path
Northern Coast to Coast Walk
Pennine Way
Teesdale Way
NORTH-WEST ENGLAND
OUTSIDE THE LAKE DISTRICT
Family Walks in the
Forest of Bowland
Historic Walks in Cheshire
Ribble Way
Walking in the Forest of Bowland
and Pendle
Walking in Lancashire
Walks in Lancashire Witch Country
Walks in Ribble Country
**PENNINES AND
NORTH-EAST ENGLAND**
Cleveland Way and Yorkshire
Wolds Way
Historic Walks in North Yorkshire
North York Moors
The Canoeist's Guide to the
North-East
The Spirit of Hadrian's Wall
Yorkshire Dales – South and West
Walking in County Durham
Walking in Northumberland
Walking in the South Pennines
Walks in Dales Country
Walks in the Yorkshire Dales
Walks on the North York Moors:
Books 1 and 2
Waterfall Walks – Teesdale and
High Pennines
Yorkshire Dales Angler's Guide
SCOTLAND
Ben Nevis and Glen Coe
Border Country
Border Pubs and Inns
Central Highlands
Great Glen Way
Isle of Skye
North to the Cape
Lowther Hills
Pentland Hills
Scotland's Far North
Scotland's Far West
Scotland's Mountain Ridges

Scottish Glens:
2 – Atholl Glens
3 – Glens of Rannoch
4 – Glens of Trossachs
5 – Glens of Argyll
6 – The Great Glen
Scrambles in Lochaber
Southern Upland Way
Walking in the Cairngorms
Walking in the Hebrides
Walking in the Ochils, Campsie Fells
and Lomond Hills
Walking on the Isle of Arran
Walking on the Orkney and
Shetland Isles
Walking the Galloway Hills
Walking the Munros:
Vol 1 – Southern, Central and
Western
Vol 2 – Northern and Cairngorms
West Highland Way
Winter Climbs – Ben Nevis and
Glencoe
Winter Climbs in the Cairngorms
SOUTHERN ENGLAND
Channel Island Walks
Exmoor and the Quantocks
Greater Ridgeway
Lea Valley Walk
London – The Definitive Walking
Guide
North Downs Way
South Downs Way
South West Coast Path
Thames Path
Walker's Guide to the Isle of Wight
Walking in Bedfordshire
Walking in Berkshire
Walking in Buckinghamshire
Walking in Kent
Walking in Somerset
Walking in Sussex
Walking in the Isles of Scilly
Walking in the Thames Valley
Walking on Dartmoor
**WALES AND THE
WELSH BORDERS**
Ascent of Snowdon
Glyndwr's Way
Hillwalking in Snowdonia
Hillwalking in Wales:
Vols 1 and 2
Lleyn Peninsula Coastal Path
Offa's Dyke Path
Pembrokeshire Coastal Path
Ridges of Snowdonia
Scrambles in Snowdonia
Shropshire Hills
Spirit Paths of Wales
Walking in Pembrokeshire
Welsh Winter Climbs

For full and up-to-date information
on our ever-expanding list of guides,
please visit our website:
www.cicerone.co.uk.

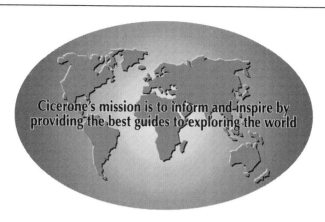

Cicerone's mission is to inform and inspire by providing the best guides to exploring the world

Since its foundation 40 years ago, Cicerone has specialised in publishing guidebooks and has built a reputation for quality and reliability. It now publishes nearly 300 guides to the major destinations for outdoor enthusiasts, including Europe, UK and the rest of the world.

Written by leading and committed specialists, Cicerone guides are recognised as the most authoritative. They are full of information, maps and illustrations so that the user can plan and complete a successful and safe trip or expedition – be it a long face climb, a walk over Lakeland fells, an alpine cycling tour, a Himalayan trek or a ramble in the countryside.

With a thorough introduction to assist planning, clear diagrams, maps and colour photographs to illustrate the terrain and route, and accurate and detailed text, Cicerone guides are designed for ease of use and access to the information.

If the facts on the ground change, or there is any aspect of a guide that you think we can improve, we are always delighted to hear from you.

Cicerone Press
2 Police Square Milnthorpe Cumbria LA7 7PY
Tel: 015395 62069 Fax: 015395 63417
info@cicerone.co.uk www.cicerone.co.uk